LIFE'S HEALING CHOICES

Foreword by Rick Warren
Author of #1 *New York Times* Bestseller *The Purpose Driven Life*

LIFE'S HEALING CHOICES

FREEDOM FROM YOUR HURTS, HANG-UPS, *and* HABITS

JOHN BAKER

HOWARD BOOKS®
A DIVISION OF SIMON & SCHUSTER, INC.

NEW YORK · NASHVILLE · LONDON · TORONTO · SYDNEY · NEW DELHI

Howard Books
Division of Simon & Schuster, Inc.
1230 Avenue of the Americas
New York, NY 10020

First Howard Books trade paperback edition April 2013

HOWARD and colophon are trademarks of Simon & Schuster, Inc.

For information about special discounts for bulk purchases, please contact Simon & Schuster Special Sales at 1-866-506-1949 or business@simonandschuster.com.

The Simon & Schuster Speakers Bureau can bring authors to your live event. For more information or to book an event, contact the Simon & Schuster Speakers Bureau at 1-866-248-3049 or visit our website at www.simonspeakers.com.

Edited by Philis Boultinghouse
Cover design by John Lucas
Interior design by John Mark Luke Designs

Manufactured in the United States of America

20 19 18 17 16 15 14 13

Library of Congress Cataloging-in-Publication Data is on file

ISBN 978-1-4165-4395-4
ISBN 978-1-4767-2658-8 (pbk)
ISBN 978-1-4165-6705-9 (ebook)

This book is dedicated to

My Lord and *Savior,* Jesus Christ

To my *family* for loving me, no matter what

To pastors *Rick Warren* and *Glen Kreun*
for trusting and believing in me.

To the thousands of *courageous* men and women
who have *celebrated* their recoveries
with me over the last sixteen years

Contents

Foreword by RICK WARREN

Do you ever eat or drink more calories than your body needs? Do you ever feel you ought to exercise but don't? Do you ever know the right thing to do but don't do it? Do you ever know something is wrong but do it anyway? If you answered yes to any of the questions above, you'll know without a doubt that you are a citizen of the human race. As fellow members of the human race, we all deal with life's hurts, hang-ups, and habits. And Jesus, who left heaven to become one of us so that He could minister to those needs, said, "It is not the healthy who need a doctor, but the sick. I have not come to call the righteous, but sinners" (Mark 2:17). At Saddleback Church, we take these words seriously. We've learned that every single person—as a member of the human race—deals with a hurt, a hang-up, or a habit at some level, in some form.

Of course, when you're serious about dealing with broken people, then those people are going to bring a lot of problems with them when they come to church. In 1991, to help deal with these problems, my good friend and the author of this book, John Baker, founded Celebrate Recovery—one of the most successful ministries in Saddleback's history. This ministry, which is a biblically balanced approach to repentance and recovery, is one of the secrets of Saddleback's amazing growth. Over 9,500 hurting people have participated in Celebrate Recovery at Saddleback, with most of them eventually joining our church and getting involved in ministry. Nearly one-third of the over 9,000 lay ministers at Saddleback have emerged from this single program.

Soon after the onset of Celebrate Recovery, I did an intense study of the Scriptures to discover what God had to say about bringing hope and healing into broken lives. To my amazement, I found the principles of healing—even their logical order—given by Christ in his most famous message: the Sermon on the Mount. My study resulted in a ten-week series of sermons called "The Road to Recovery." Using the principles of that series, John Baker developed the workbooks that became the heart of our Celebrate Recovery program and now has written this life-changing book. He has taken my sermon series and used it as the foundation of this book. In it you will read the eight principles from my study and how you can choose to make these teachings a part of your own "life's healing choices."

Now, you may be thinking that this book is only for people with serious addictions, for people whose lives seem out of control. Well, I believe the Bible teaches that all of us have some form of addiction. Sin is addicting and "all have sinned." That means we've all created ungodly and unhealthy methods for handling life. Not one of us is untainted, and because of sin, we've all hurt ourselves, we've all hurt other people, and others have hurt us.

The goal of Celebrate Recovery and this book is not simply to help hurting people recover from past sins and hurts. The goal is to teach them—and you—to make the healing choices that will help you become Christlike in character. We begin this journey to healing by admitting our need. In the very first beatitude, Jesus said, "God blesses those who realize their need for him" (Matthew 5:3 NLT). When we reach the end of our rope and give up our self-sufficiency, God can move into our lives with healing and growth.

In addition to these revolutionary, biblically based principles, you will also read real life stories of lives inspired and transformed by the life-changing power of Jesus Christ and the fellowship of other believers. You'll hear about hopeless marriages restored and people set free from all kinds of sinful hurts, hang-ups, and habits as they practice the Lordship of Jesus and live out the Beatitudes.

You will be inspired, and your life will be changed in dramatic ways as you read through the pages of this book.

Rick Warren

Pastor, Saddleback Church

Author, *The Purpose Driven Life*

Finding FREEDOM

from Your *Hurts*, *Hang-ups*, and *Habits*

One Sunday afternoon a father was trying to take a nap, but his little boy kept bugging him with "Daddy, I'm bored." So, trying to occupy him with a game, the dad found a picture of the world in the newspaper. He cut it up in about fifty pieces and said, "Son, see if you can put this puzzle back together." The dad lay back down to finish his nap, thinking the map would keep his son busy for at least an hour or so. But in about fifteen minutes the little guy woke him up: "Daddy, I've got it finished. It's all put together."

"You're kidding." He knew his son didn't know all the positions of the nations, so he asked him, "How did you do it?"

"It was easy. There was a picture of a person on the back of the map, so when I got my person put together, the world looked just fine."

How is your "person" doing? Are you all put together? The fact is that many of us are a mess. We're scattered all over the living-room floor, with no one to put us together and no idea where to begin the process of healing. Each of our lives is tangled up with *hurts* that haunt our hearts, *hang-ups* that cause us pain, and *habits* that mess up our lives.

Hurts, hang-ups, and habits. There's not a person in the world who doesn't deal with at least one of these on some level—and many of us struggle with all three.

The truth is, life is tough. We live in an imperfect world. We've been hurt by other people, we've hurt ourselves, and we've hurt other people. The Bible says it plainly: *"All have sinned."*[1] That means none of us is perfect; we've all blown it; we've all made mistakes. We hurt, and we hurt others.

It's amazing how much better the world looks when our person is put together. And that's what we're going to do in this book. With God's help in making eight healing choices, you are going to be able to put the pieces of your world back together.

We'll start with a promise straight from God. There are five ways He promises to help us find freedom from our hurts, hang-ups, and habits.

"I have seen how they acted, but I will heal them.
I will lead them and help them, and I will comfort those who mourn.
I offer peace to all, both near and far! I will heal my people."[2]

Notice the five promises God extends:

1. If you are *hurt*, God says, "I will *heal* you."

2. If you're *confused*, God says, "I will *lead* you."

3. If you feel *helpless*, God says, "I will *help* you."

4. If you feel *alone*, God says, "I will *comfort* you."

5. If you feel *anxious* and *afraid*, God says, "I will *offer peace* to you."

Trusting in His promises, we find hope for a better future—a life of freedom, peace, and happiness.

HAPPINESS IS POSSIBLE—BUT YOU'VE GOT TO *CHOOSE* IT

Since the beginning of time, men and women have searched for happiness—usually in all the wrong places, trying all the wrong things. But there's only one place where we can find tested-and-proven, absolutely-gonna-work principles that will lead to healing and happiness. These principles come in the form of eight statements from the truest of all books—the Bible—and from the most revered Teacher of all time—Jesus Christ. Jesus laid out these principles for happiness in the Sermon on the Mount in the Gospel of Matthew, chapter 5. Today we call them "the Beatitudes."

Happiness, Jesus says, can be ours, but the pathway to happiness may not be exactly what we're expecting. From a conventional viewpoint, most of the following eight statements don't make sense. At first they even sound like contradictions. But when you fully understand what Jesus is saying, you'll realize these eight statements are God's pathway to wholeness, growth, and spiritual maturity.

"Happy are those who know they are spiritually poor."

"Happy are those who mourn, for they shall be comforted."

"Happy are the meek."

"Happy are the pure in heart."

"Happy are those whose greatest desire is to do what God requires."

"Happy are those who are merciful."

"Happy are those who work for peace."

"Happy are those who are persecuted because they do what God requires."[3]

MY OWN PERSONAL CHOICE

I know that the eight healing choices work. Why? Because they worked in my life. I have not always been a pastor. Prior to being called into the ministry, I was a successful businessman. I was also a "functional alcoholic." I struggled with my sin addiction to alcohol for nineteen years. Eventually I came to a point where I was losing everything. I cried out to God for help, and He led me to Alcoholics Anonymous. Even then I knew that my higher power had a name—Jesus Christ!—and I started attending Saddleback Church in Lake Forest, California. After a year of sobriety, I answered God's call to start a Christ-centered recovery program called Celebrate Recovery. Since 1991, hundreds of thousands of courageous individuals have found the same freedom from their life's hurts, hang-ups, and habits that I did. If these eight choices worked for someone like me, I promise they can work for you too!

MY PARTNERSHIP WITH PASTOR RICK

After Celebrate Recovery had been going for a year, Pastor Rick Warren, my senior pastor, saw how Celebrate Recovery was helping people in our church family find God's healing from their hurts, hang-ups, and habits. He decided to take the entire church family through a sermon series called the "Road to Recovery." I want to thank Pastor Rick for allowing me to use his "Road to Recovery" series as the foundation of this book.

Pastor Rick's R-E-C-O-V-E-R-Y acrostic identifies eight principles. As you read the eight principles and the corresponding beatitudes, you'll begin to understand the choices before you.

CHOICES THAT WILL CHANGE YOUR LIFE

1. **R**ealize I'm not God. I admit that I am powerless to control my tendency to do the wrong thing and that my life is unmanageable.

   "Happy are those who know they are spiritually poor."[4]
   We finally understand that we do not have the power to control

our hurts, hang-ups, and habits on our own. When we admit this, God can begin His healing work in our lives.

2. **E**arnestly believe that God exists, that I matter to Him, and that He has the power to help me recover.

"*Happy are those who mourn, for they shall be comforted.*"[5] As we begin to believe that we are important to God, we find great comfort in knowing that He has the power to change us and our situation.

3. **C**onsciously choose to commit all my life and will to Christ's care and control.

"*Happy are the meek.*"[6] When we commit our lives to Christ, we become a new person. We can finally give up trying to control ourselves and others. We replace our willpower with our willingness to accept God's power.

4. **O**penly examine and confess my faults to myself, to God, and to someone I trust.

"*Happy are the pure in heart.*"[7] In order to have a clear conscience, in order to deal with our guilt and have a pure heart, we need to admit all the wrongs of our past and present. We do this by writing it all down and sharing it with another person.

5. **V**oluntarily submit to every change God wants to make in my life and humbly ask Him to remove my character defects.

"*Happy are those whose greatest desire is to do what God requires.*"[8] We submit to all the changes God wants to make in our lives, and we humbly ask Him to work in our lives to bring about the needed changes.

6. **E**valuate all my relationships. Offer forgiveness to those who have hurt me and make amends for harm I've done to others, except when to do so would harm them or others.

> *"Happy are those who are merciful."*[9]
> *"Happy are those who work for peace."*[10]

We do our best to restore our relationships. We offer forgiveness to the people who have hurt us, and make amends to the people we have hurt.

7. **R**eserve a daily time with God for self-examination, Bible reading, and prayer in order to know God and His will for my life and to gain the power to follow His will.

We maintain these daily habits of spending time with God in order to keep our recovery on track.

8. **Y**ield myself to God to be used to bring this Good News to others, both by my example and by my words.

> *"Happy are those who are persecuted*
> *because they do what God requires."*[11]

Through God's grace and living these eight principles, we have found freedom from our hurts, hang-ups, and habits. Now that we have been changed by God, we yield ourselves to be used by Him as we share our story and serve others.

Jesus's eight principles for healing and happiness are the basis for the eight choices outlined in the chapters of this book. With the exception of choice 7, each choice has a corresponding beatitude; choice 6 actually has two. Regardless of the problem you are struggling with—whether it's emotional, financial, relational, spiritual, sexual, or whatever—regardless of what you need recovery from, the principles that lead to happiness and recovery are always the same, and the choice is always yours.

After reading this book and applying its principles, you will be able to join the many others who can say . .

+ "I've been living with shame or guilt from my past, and *now I don't have to live with that pain anymore!*"

+ "I've been trapped in a habit or hang-up that is messing up my life, and *now I can be free from its hold on me!*"

+ "I've always been afraid and worried of what may happen tomorrow, and I *now can face my future with peace and confidence."*

That's the freedom I hope and pray you will find by making the eight choices offered in this book: freedom to know peace, freedom to live without guilt, and freedom to be happy—the choice is yours.

OUR JOURNEY TOGETHER

As we take this amazing journey to freedom together, I will lead you, principle by principle, choice by choice, into the healing you desire.

WE'LL SHARE STORIES OF HOPE

In the pages of this book, you will find sixteen life-changing stories of people who have completed the eight biblical choices found in this book. The men and women who so honestly tell their stories want to share with you how, with God's power, they found freedom from their hurts, hang-ups, and habits. They'll tell you how they overcame their struggles. Some will share how they were trying to control themselves as well as friends, relatives, and coworkers. Others will share how they struggled with workaholism, overeating, sexual and physical abuse, addiction to drugs and alcohol, sexual addiction, perfectionism, legalism, abortion, loss of loved ones or a job, and much more.

WE'LL FOCUS ON THE FUTURE

This book is forward looking. We will spend some time looking at the good and bad things that happened in our past. But rather than wallowing in the past or dredging up and reliving painful memories over and over, we will focus on the future. Regardless of what has already happened, due to either your poor choices or the hurtful choices made by others, you and your situation can change. The solution is to start making these healing choices now and depend on Christ's power to help you.

WE'LL ACCEPT PERSONAL RESPONSIBILITY

This book emphasizes taking personal responsibility. Instead of playing the "accuse and excuse" game of victimization, it will help you face up to your own poor choices and deal with things you can do something about. We cannot control all that happens to us, but we can control how we choose to respond to what happens to us. That is a secret of happiness. When we stop wasting time fixing the blame, we have more energy to fix the problem. When we stop hiding our own faults and stop hurling accusations at others, the healing power of Christ can begin working in our hearts, our minds, our wills, and our emotions.

WE'LL MAKE A SPIRITUAL COMMITMENT

We'll also emphasize spiritual commitment to Jesus Christ. Lasting recovery cannot happen without total surrender to Him. Everybody needs Jesus.

WE'LL SAY "YES" TO A CALL TO ACTION

At the end of each chapter, you will be asked to complete three action steps. Completing these actions will help you apply the choice you have just read about to your own life. I want to encourage you to take your time and complete each action step honestly and to the best of your ability. Through completing each of the steps, true and lasting healing will occur. The three action steps included in each chapter are "Pray about It," "Write about It," and "Share about It."

1. Pray about It

In this action step, you will be prompted to pray for specific things regarding each choice. If you are not used to praying, don't worry; I have written prayers to help you get started! As you move through this book, you will see how important prayer is in helping you make the changes and healing choices you desire in your life.

2. Write about It

This action will ask you to put your thoughts and insights down in black and white. When a thought passes from the lips to the fingertips, it becomes specific. This is also called journaling. As you progress through each of the choices, you will learn to rely on your writings. We've created a *Life's Healing Choices Journal*, available in bookstores specifically to help you journal your way through these choices. What you write in your journal will help you see your areas of growth and the areas you still need further work on.

3. Share about It

This book is built on the New Testament principle that we don't change or get well by ourselves. We need each other. Fellowship and accountability are two important components of spiritual growth. In this action step, you will be asked to find a safe person—an "accountability partner"—to share your journey with as you go through these eight choices. You will also find some suggestions and guidelines to help you make your selection of this safe person. You will be guided on what to share and how.

As you start reading, I suggest that you take your time. The hurts, hang-ups, and habits that have been interfering with your happiness did not happen or develop overnight. It makes sense that they are not going to simply disappear from your life or be changed by the snap of your fingers. You will discover that you must rely on God's power to help you take the actions necessary to complete the eight choices. Only by God's power will lasting life-changes occur.

I invite you to travel with me on this amazing journey!

Realize I'm not God.

R

I *admit* that I am powerless to control my tendency to do the wrong thing and that my life is unmanageable.

E

C

O

V

E

R

Y

"Happy are those who know they are spiritually poor."[1]

Admitting NEED

The REALITY Choice

Part of our human nature is to refuse change until our pain exceeds our fear—fear of change, that is. We simply deny the pain until it gets so bad that we are crushed and finally realize we need some help. Why don't we save ourselves a bit of misery and admit *now* what we're inevitably going to have to admit later? *We are not God,* and we desperately need God because our lives are unmanageable without Him. We'll be forced to learn that lesson someday. We may as well admit it now.

If you answer yes to any of the questions below, you'll know without a doubt that you are a citizen of the human race.

+ Do you ever stay up late when you know you need sleep?
+ Do you ever eat or drink more calories than your body needs?
+ Do you ever feel you ought to exercise but don't?
+ Do you ever know the right thing to do but don't do it?
+ Do you ever know something is wrong but do it anyway?
+ Have you ever known you should be unselfish but were selfish instead?

+ Have you ever tried to control somebody or something and found them or it uncontrollable?

As fellow members of the human race, we all deal with life's hurts, hang-ups, and habits. In the next pages, we'll look at the *cause* of these hurts, hang-ups, and habits, their *consequences*, and their *cure*.

As we look at the causes and consequences of our pain, our spiritual poverty will become obvious. How can we be happy about being spiritually poor, as the beatitude for this chapter tells us we will be? Admitting the truth that we are spiritually poor—or powerless to control our tendency to do wrong—leads us to this happiness and to the cure we so desperately need.

THE CAUSE OF OUR PROBLEMS

The cause of our problems is our nature! No, not the trees, rocks, and lakes kind of nature, but our human nature—that is, our sin nature. The Bible tells us that this sin nature gets us into all kinds of problems. We choose to do things that aren't good for us, even when we know better. We respond in hurtful ways when we are hurt. We try to fix problems, and often in our attempts to fix them, we only make them worse. The Bible says it this way: *"There is a way that seems right to a man, but in the end it leads to death."*[2] This verse lets us know we can't trust our human nature to lead us out of our problems. Left on its own, our sin nature will *tend to do wrong, desire to be God,* and *try to play God.*

1. OUR TENDENCY TO DO WRONG

We will always have this sin nature—this tendency to do the wrong thing. In fact, we will wrestle with it as long as we are on this earth. Even if you have already asked Christ into your life, even after you become a Christian, you still have desires that pull you in the wrong direction. We find in the Bible that Paul understood this, for he struggled with his sin nature just as we do: *"I don't understand myself at all, for I really want to do what is right, but I don't do it. Instead, I do the very thing I hate. I know perfectly well that what I am doing is wrong . . . but I can't help myself, because it is sin inside me that makes me do these evil things."*[3]

Do Paul's words sound vaguely familiar to you? Sure they do. We end up doing what we *don't* want to do and not doing what we *do* want to do. For years I thought I could control my drinking. I

> We try to fix problems, and often in OUR attempts to fix them, we only make them worse.

believed the lie that I could stop whenever I wanted. It really wasn't that bad. My choices were not hurting anybody. I was deep into my denial. As the pain of my sin addiction got worse, I would try to stop on my own power. I was able to stop for a day, a week, or even a few months, but I would always start drinking again. I wanted to do what was right, but on my own I was powerless to change.

2. OUR DESIRE TO BE GOD

Why do we continue making poor choices? Why do we repeat the same mistakes? At the root of our human tendency to do wrong is our desire to be in control. We want to decide for ourselves what is right and what is wrong. We want to make our own choices, call our own shots, make our own rules. We don't want anybody telling us what to do. In essence, we want to be God. But this is nothing new. Trying to be God is humankind's oldest problem. In Genesis 3, even Adam and Eve tried to be in control. God put them in Paradise, and they tried to control Paradise. God told them, "You can do anything you want in Paradise except one thing: Don't eat from this one tree." What did they do? You got it; they made a beeline for the forbidden tree—the only thing in Paradise God said was off-limits. Satan said, "If you eat this fruit, you will be like God."[4] And they wanted to be God. That's been our problem from the very start of humanity. Today, we still want to be God.

3. OUR ATTEMPTS TO PLAY GOD

We play God by denying our humanity and by trying to control everything for our own selfish reasons. We attempt to be the center of our own universe. We play God by trying to control our *image*, *other people*, our *problems*, and our *pain*.

We Try to Control Our Image

We care so much about what other people think of us. We don't want them to know what we're really like. We play games; we wear masks; we pretend; we fake it. We want people to see certain sides of us while we hide others. We deny our weaknesses, and we deny our feelings. "I'm not angry." "I'm not upset." "I'm not worried." "I'm not afraid." We don't want people to see the real us. Why are we afraid to tell people who we are? The answer is, "If I tell you who I really am and you don't like me, I'm in trouble—because then I'm all I've got."

We Try to Control Other People

Parents try to control kids; kids try to control parents. Wives try to control husbands; husbands try to control wives. Coworkers vie for office control. People try to control other people. And along the way we develop a lot of tools to manipulate each other. Everyone has his or her preferred methods: Some use guilt and shame; some use praise and affirmation. Others use anger, fear, or an old favorite—the silent treatment. All in efforts to gain control.

We Try to Control Our Problems

"I can handle it," we say. "It's not really a problem." "I'm okay, really. I'm fine." Those are the words of somebody trying to play God. When we try to control our problems, we say, "I don't need any help, and I certainly don't need counseling or recovery." "I can quit anytime. I'll work it out on my own power." When a TV repairman was asked about the worst kind of damage he'd ever seen to a television set, he said, "The kind that results from people trying to fix their TVs on their own." The more we try to fix our problems by ourselves, the worse our problems get.

We Try to Control Our Pain

Have you ever thought about how much time and effort you spend running from pain? Trying to avoid it, deny it, escape it, reduce it, or postpone it? Some of us try to avoid pain by eating or not eating. Others try to postpone it by getting drunk, smoking, taking drugs, or abusing prescription medications. Some try to escape through sports, traveling, or jumping in and out of relationships. Others withdraw into a hole and build a protective wall of depression around themselves. Still others become angry, abusive, critical, and judgmental. We'll try almost anything to control our pain.

But the real pain comes when we realize, in our quieter moments, that no matter how hard we try, we're not in control. That realization can be very scary.

You may remember on *Saturday Night Live* when Chevy Chase would come on and say, "Hi, I'm Chevy Chase, and you're not." Can you imagine God saying, "Hi, I'm God, and you're not"? Agreeing with God that He's God and we're not leads us into our first healing choice:

Admitting NEED

Realize I'm not God.

I admit that I am powerless to control my tendency to do the wrong thing and that my life is unmanageable.

CHOICE 1

The first step is always the hardest, and this first choice is no exception. Until you are willing to admit your need and recognize that you are not God, you will continue to suffer the consequences of your poor choices. As the beatitude says, *"Happy are those who know they are spiritually poor."*[5] Admitting your need is what being "spiritually poor" is all about.

THE CONSEQUENCES OF OUR PROBLEMS

If the cause of most of our problems is our efforts to control everything, then what are the *consequences* of playing God? There are four:

1. FEAR

When we try to control everything, we become afraid. Adam said, *"I was afraid because I was naked; so I hid."*[6] We are afraid somebody will find out who we really are—that we're fakes and phonies, that we really don't have it all together, that we're not perfect. We don't let anybody get close to us because they'll find out that we're scared inside, and so we fake it. We live in fear, afraid someone will reject us, not love us, or not like us when they know what we are really like. We believe they will only like the image we work to present. So we are afraid.

2. FRUSTRATION

Trying to be the general manager of the universe is frustrating. Have you ever been to Chuck E. Cheese's? They have this game called Wacka Wacka. You use a big mallet to beat down these little moles that keep popping up. But when you whack one, three more pop up. You whack those, and five more pop up. That machine is a parable of life. We whack down one relational conflict and another pops up. We whack down one addiction or compulsion and another one pops up. It's frustrating because we can't get them all knocked down at the same time. We walk around pretending we're God: "I'm powerful; I can handle it." But if we're really in control, why don't we just unplug the machine?

The apostle Paul felt this same frustration: *"It seems to be a fact of life that when I want to do what is right, I inevitably do what is wrong. . . . There is something else deep within me . . . that is at war with my mind and wins the fight and makes me a slave to the sin."*[7] David felt it too: *"My dishonesty made me miserable and filled my days with frustration."*[8]

Frustration is a symptom of a much deeper issue: a failure to acknowledge that we are not God.

3. FATIGUE

Playing God makes us tired. Pretending we've got it all together is hard work. David experienced the fatigue of pretending: *"My strength evaporated like water on a sunny day until I finally admitted all my sins to you and stopped trying to hide them."*[9] Denial requires enormous amounts of emotional energy—energy that could be used in problem solving is actually diverted into problem denying, problem hiding, and problem avoiding.

Most of us try to run from the pain by keeping busy. We think, "I don't like the way I feel when I slow down. I don't like the sounds that go through my mind when I lay my head back on the pillow. If I just keep busy, maybe I can block out those feelings and drown out the sounds."

You must admit that you're POWERLESS *to do it on your own—that you need other people, and you need God.*

We run from pain by constantly being on the go. We work ourselves to death, or we get involved in some hobby or sport until it becomes a compulsion. We're on the golf course or tennis court or somewhere all the time. Even overinvolvement in religious activities can be an attempt to hide our pain. We say, "Look at me, look at all the ways I'm serving God." God does want you to serve Him out of love and purpose. He does not want you to use serving Him or the church to escape your pain.

If you're in a constant state of fatigue, always worn out, ask yourself, "What pain am I running from? What problem am I afraid to face? What motivates and drives me to work and work so that I'm in a constant state of fatigue?"

4. FAILURE

Playing God is one job where failure is guaranteed. You're not big enough. The wisdom of Proverbs tells us, *"You will never succeed in life if you try to hide your sins. Confess them and give them up; then God will show mercy to you."*[10] We need to be honest and open about our weaknesses, faults, and failures.

THE CURE FOR OUR PROBLEMS

The cure for our problems comes in a strange form: it comes through *admitting weakness* and through *a humble heart.*

ADMITTING WEAKNESS

The Bible says that in admitting my weakness, I actually find strength. *"I just let Christ take over! And so the weaker I get, the stronger I become."*[11] This is not a popular idea in our self-sufficient American culture that says, "Raise yourself up by your own bootstraps; don't depend on anybody else; do the Lone Ranger thing, be the strong, silent type." The Bible also says that knowing we are "spiritually poor" will make us happy.[12] This is the first step to getting your act together. You must admit that you're powerless to do it on your own—that you are spiritually poor—that you need other people, and you need God.

Making the first choice to healing means acknowledging that you are not God. Doing so means recognizing and admitting three important facts of life:

1. *"I admit that I am powerless to change my past."*

"It hurt. I still remember the pain, but all the resentment and shame in the world isn't going to change what happened. I'm powerless to change my past."

2. *"I admit that I am powerless to control other people."*

"I try to control others. I actually like manipulating them. I use all kinds of little gimmicks, but it doesn't work. I am responsible for my actions, not theirs. I can't control other people."

3. *"I admit that I am powerless to cope with my harmful habits, behaviors, and actions."*

"Good intentions don't cut it. Willpower is not enough. I need something more. I need a source of power beyond myself. I need God, because He made me to need Him."

21

CHOICE 1

A HUMBLE HEART

A second portion of our cure is having a humble heart. God cannot work His change if our hearts are filled with pride. The Bible tells us that *"God opposes the proud but gives grace to the humble."*[13] God's grace has the power to heal us, enabling us to *change*. Even after all we've talked about in this chapter, it's still difficult for us to admit our need. Our pride continues to insist that we can go it alone. Some of us may still be thinking, "I can do this on my own. I can solve my own problems." No. You can't. If you could, you would have already done so, but since you can't, you won't.

What needs changing in your life? What hurt or hang-up or habit have you been trying to ignore? Choosing to admit that you can't do it alone and that you need God is the first and hardest choice. It's hard to admit, "I have a problem, and I need help." Admitting we have a problem and giving it a name is humbling. Doing it says, "I'm not God, and I don't have it as together as I'd like everybody to think." If you admit that truth to someone else, he or she will not be surprised. Others know it, God knows it, and you know it. You just need to admit it. Stop right now and name the hurt, hang-up, or habit you've been trying to ignore. Then admit to God that you are powerless to manage your life on your own.

Congratulations! You've made the first choice on the road to healing!

Admitting that you have a hurt, hang-up, or habit is just the beginning. To implement this first choice, as well as the seven choices to come, you need to take three actions: (1) pray about it, (2) write about it, and (3) share about it. Working through these action steps is where the real work gets done. This is where the change happens. Some of you may be tempted to skip this part and just move on to the next chapter. *Don't do it!* These three interactive steps, found at the end of every chapter, are your pathway to healing. Make the choice.

MAKE THE *Choice*

ACTION 1: *Pray about It*

Ask God to give you the courage to admit your inability to control yourself or your world. Pray that you will begin to depend on His power to help you make positive changes. Ask God to take control of your life and help you stop trying to control your image, other people, your problems, and your pain. Let Him know you are weary of carrying the fear, the frustration, the fatigue, and the failures of trying to be the general manager of the universe.

If you do not know all the words to pray and say to God right now, don't worry. You can pray as David did, "*God! Please hurry to my rescue! God, come quickly to my side!*"[14] Or you can pray with me:

Dear God, I want to take the first choice to healing and spiritual health today. I realize I am not You, God. I've often tried to control my problems, my pain, my image, and even other people—as if I were You. I'm sorry. I've tried to deny my problems by staying busy and keeping myself distracted. But I'm not running anymore. I admit that I am helpless to control this tendency to do things I know are unhealthy for me. Today I am asking for Your help. I humbly ask You to take all the pieces of my unmanageable life and begin the process of healing. Please heal me. Please give me the strength to choose health. Help me stick with this process for the next seven choices. In Your name, I pray. Amen.

God will hear your cry for help and is ready to provide you with His strength, power, perfect love, and complete forgiveness as you choose to take your first step to healing!

ACTION 2: *Write about It*

As you begin your journey through the eight healing choices, it is important to write down your thoughts and insights. As God frees you from your hurts, hang-ups, and habits, He will reveal significant insights about yourself and others. Keep a daily journal of what God shows you and the progress and growth you are making day by day. Use the *Life's Healing Choices Journal*, a spiral notebook, or whatever works for you. Just a word of caution: *Keep your journal in a safe place!* What you write in your journal are your private thoughts. As we continue through the eight choices, you will learn when and with whom to share your journal notes.

The following questions will help you get started writing:

1. What people, places, or things do you have the power to control?

2. What people, places, or things have you been attempting to control? (Be specific.)

3. Describe how you try to control your image, other people, your problems, and your pain.

4. Write down how the fear, frustration, fatigue, and failures of trying to be the general manager of the universe has affected your relationships with God and others.

5. What specific hurts, hang-ups, or habits have you been denying?

You made it! Writing down the answers to these five questions was not easy, but it was a major beginning in your healing process. Now let's look at the third action.

ACTION 3: *Share about It*

As you move through the eight healing choices, you will discover that you need to share the life-changing truths God is showing you with someone you trust. The wise writer of Ecclesiastes said, *"Two are better than one, because they have a good return for their work: If one falls down, his friend can help him up. But pity the man who falls and has no one to help him up! . . . Though one may be overpowered, two can defend themselves. A cord of three strands is not quickly broken."*[15]

The next few chapters will guide you in choosing this person. You'll be looking for someone you can honestly and openly talk to. This person needs to be nonjudgmental and someone with whom you can safely share your personal journal notes. This person should be willing to share his or her life and struggles with you as well. Once God shows you that safe person, set up a meeting time and ask him or her to join with you in this recovery journey toward healing by being your accountability partner. This person may be a relative, a friend, a neighbor, a coworker, or someone in your church family.

Be sure the person you choose is of the same sex. You will be sharing very personal details of your life as you go through each of the healing choices. Some of the issues will be inappropriate to share with someone of the opposite sex.

As you work through the next few chapters, if you cannot find a safe person to share with, visit www.celebraterecovery.com to locate a Celebrate Recovery group near you. There you will find people who have worked through the eight choices and who will be glad to help and support you as you begin your healing journey. Just remember, this journey should not be traveled alone. You need others to listen to you, encourage you, support you, and demonstrate God's love to you.

If you choose to begin this journey, God will be faithful in giving you spiritual health and freedom from your life's hurts, hang-ups, and habits

STORIES OF *Changed Lives*

A little background: At Saddleback Church we're committed to being a "safe place"—a place where people can talk about and deal with real problems—real hurts, real hang-ups, and real habits—without being blown away by judgmental opinions. We are a family of fellow strugglers. There is not a person in our church who has it all together. We're all weak in different areas, and we all need each other.

One of our most effective ministries at Saddleback meets on Friday nights and is called Celebrate Recovery. This group is made up of hundreds of men and women dealing with all kinds of hurts, hang-ups, and habits. They all work together on the eight Christ-centered healing choices described in this book. At Celebrate Recovery they are called the Eight Principles.

At the conclusion of each chapter, you'll find two personal stories—testimonies from real people in our church family and Celebrate Recovery who have chosen to overcome their hurts, hang-ups, and habits.

These courageous individuals come from very different backgrounds with a variety of problems and issues. As you read their stories, please keep your heart and mind open. You will see how their journey relates to your own life or to someone's close to you.

Elaine's STORY

My name is Elaine and I am a believer who struggles with codependency. I am a mother and a grandmother, and I have seen God change what I thought was impossible to change—the lives of my husband, my children, and myself. I discovered that God has the power to make changes that I tried to make for years but couldn't.

I grew up in a home that was very loving. We did things as a family, like vacations, and we always went to visit grandparents for all the holidays. At a very young age I started going to church and had God in my life. I was involved in youth groups all through my young adult life. I thought all families were like that.

I met my husband in the summer of 1966. We started dating in the fall, and he asked me to marry him just before Christmas. We were married February 10, 1967. I should have known it wasn't going to be an easy life when Howard got to the church two minutes before we were to walk down the aisle. Howard was not used to being involved with family gatherings, so being the codependent, I thought I could fix him. I never thought his drinking was a problem—or at least that's what I kept telling myself.

Nine months and twelve days after we were married, our older son, Jim, was born. I was so happy. I was in love and a new mother. Two and a half years later, our younger son, Troy, was born. I attended church sporadically, going a couple of times a year. I was one of the "Poinsettia and Lily" people: in church on Christmas and Easter. Both of my boys were baptized, but I thought my life was complete without being involved in a church family.

My family never knew the anguish I was really going through with Howard's drinking and unfaithfulness. It was always easier to close my eyes and look the other way and pretend I wasn't hurting. I was deep into my denial. I was determined to keep our family together. I thought I could fix things eventually; my codependent traits were always at work. I put my hope in Howard's repeated promises to change. Every time I reached my

27

limit and thought that I couldn't go on living the way we were any longer, Howard would promise to clean up his life and change his ways.

Things would get better for a short while, but inevitably he would revert back to his old patterns and I would be hurt again and again. It was a vicious cycle. The most ridiculous hope I held on to for all those years was the false confidence that I could personally fix everything—eventually. I figured I could control the situation and fix Howard on my own if I just kept at it! I guess I was stubborn, because after twenty-eight years, I still held on to this false hope. I was determined I wasn't going to be another statistic; I was going to keep our family intact, no matter what.

We moved several times over the years, but of course, it didn't change anything. I naively hoped that each time we moved things would get better. I hoped that a change in location would produce a change in my husband and in our marriage. But we were still the same people. We moved to California in 1982. I now know that God was drawing us out there for a reason.

Howard and I both started new jobs. Several years after our move, he started using drugs along with the alcohol. He hit bottom in 1994, and our sons and I helped get him checked into rehab. I thought everything was going to be okay.

He wasn't drinking or using drugs anymore, so what else could go wrong? But one day Howard made an inappropriate comment to our younger son's wife. Of course, she was really offended. Howard tried to apologize, but the damage was done. It tore our family apart and caused great bitterness. That was the final straw. I just couldn't take anymore, and I was ready to give up on my marriage. We were living in the same house, but there was no love on my part. I didn't think I could forgive him this time.

On Easter in 1995, our older son, Jim, asked us if we wanted to go to church with him and his wife, Gail. We agreed to go, and that was our first weekend at Saddleback Church. Walking up the hill, I saw so many people and wondered what I was getting myself into. I didn't know what to expect. We saw everyone enjoying themselves in the service, and even

Howard wanted to come back the next week. God began softening our hearts.

Then in July, Jim asked us if we wanted to go to a crusade. When the pastor gave the altar call, Howard looked at me and asked me to go with him. I knew then my prayers had been answered. Howard committed his life to Christ, and I recommitted mine. Jim and Gail also committed their lives that night. Now I began to have real hope that things would change because Jesus Christ was included in the equation and because we had God's power to help us. In September, all four of us were baptized.

We started going to Celebrate Recovery in February of 1996. After being in the program several months, I began a step study with Cheryl, and we worked through the Christ-centered eight choices. This was a life-changing experience for me. I don't think I could have found healing without it.

I remember the first night and the very first question in choice 1. The question was, "What areas of your life do you have control over?" I sat there in a panic. I couldn't think of one thing I had control of. I thought there was something wrong with me. This was the first time I admitted to myself that I was powerless and could not change on my own. I finally understood that by my own power, I can't change my life; I have to depend on God to restore me.

CHOICE 1

Admitting NEED
Realize I'm not God.
I admit that I am powerless to control my tendency to do the wrong thing and that my life is unmanageable.

I was blessed to be able to work with a very special group of ladies that I still have a close bond with today. Working through the choices helped me grow in my walk with Christ. I can definitely see changes in me. I led my first step-study group, and because of that experience, I made a lifelong friend whom I can share anything with, and she can share with me. We hold each other accountable in all we do. Diane and I have been serving at Celebrate Recovery every Friday night at Solid Rock Café for the last seven years. We are lovingly known as the "cake whackers." Today I truly understand that God never wastes a hurt. Because of what I've gone through and the way God has worked in my life, I have been able to give back to others.

I've seen a miracle in my husband. Howard's whole family saw the change in him when he went back East a few years ago, when his mother was in the hospital. Howard was their rock and kept the family together. He told them how God had changed his life, and they definitely saw the change in him.

In May 1996, Howard and I renewed our wedding vows at the church. The last eleven years have been God's gift. I could say that I wish the first twenty-eight years would have been like the last few, but I know God was preparing me for the present. In February of 2007 we celebrated our fortieth wedding anniversary!

Because our family was torn apart, I hadn't seen my younger son, Troy, in several years. I had never even seen my grandson, Jordan. I prayed for reconciliation every day. Two years ago, I started getting Mother's Day cards with pictures, and finally Troy called to talk. I then found out that they were going to have another child. On the one hand I was happy for them, but I was also devastated, knowing I wouldn't see that child either. Troy called me after the baby was born to let me know that it was a boy and his name was Jacob. I continued to pray for God to soften the hearts of Troy and his family. That same year, just before Christmas, I was hospitalized with pneumonia, and Troy called me to see how I was doing. He told me that they were coming to California in March on vacation.

March came, but I hadn't heard from him. Then one afternoon my son Jim called and said someone wanted to see me. Troy came over to Jim's house and brought both of the boys. I knew God had finally answered my prayers and in His timing. He knew when we were all ready for that first meeting. It was very emotional, but good. This was just the first step in the healing process, and I know God will continue to help us every step of the way.

My son Jim and his wife, Gail, have adopted three children. Andrew is twelve, Carly is eleven, and Jeff is seven. They have brought so much joy into our lives, and I know they are truly gifts from God. I know God has been working through Jim and Gail. They have been a big part of our walk with Christ. They've been with us when things were really bad, and they've seen the change in both of us.

Sometimes I am asked, "How were you able to forgive twenty-eight years of shame, grief, and pain?" My answer is, "It's hard not to forgive when I know what Jesus sacrificed so I could be forgiven." Anyway, I have chosen to no longer live in the past but look to the future, and I am excited to experience what God has in store for me. It's true, I don't forget what's happened; but by following the choices to getting healthy again, I've learned to let go and let God.

If you've been living with false hopes—thinking that you or your situation will change simply out of your own persistence or your own willpower—I urge you not to waste another second with that dead end. I couldn't change myself or others by forcing the change through willpower. That kind of change never lasts. Instead, I encourage you to open the door of your heart and allow God's life-changing power to enter in—choice by choice, moment by moment. His power can do the impossible.

In closing, I would like to share my life verse with you:

"What a wonderful God we have—he is the Father of our Lord Jesus Christ, the source of every mercy, and the one who so wonderfully comforts and strengthens us in our hardships and trials.
And why does he do this? So that when others are troubled, needing our sympathy and encouragement, we can pass on to them this same help and comfort God has given us."[16]

Joe's STORY

My name is Joe, and I am a believer, an adult child of an alcoholic and also someone who also struggles with drugs. I grew up in a classic dysfunctional family. I have three older brothers and an older sister, all by different fathers. My younger sister, Jody, and I have the same father. My mom was married five times and had numerous boyfriends. When I was in kindergarten, my dad hooked up his boat, the Dreamer, and never came home. Shortly after that, my mom went into a mental hospital in Spokane, Washington. She suffered from manic depression, or bipolar disorder.

I had gone to seventeen different schools by the time I graduated high school, and we lived in twenty-eight different places, sometimes with Mom, sometimes not. During these years I learned to run away from my emotional problems.

When I was twelve, Mom lost her battle with depression again. Mom told us kids, "You're going to live with the Underwoods for a while." The Underwood family was very active in our church and gave us lots of love, discipline, order—and did I say love! Although this was the first stability I had ever known, I still cried myself to sleep at night, as I continued to deal with my dad's abandonment and wondered what I'd done this time to cause Mom to lose it.

Almost two years later Mom came home, and we moved again. Mom was so depressed, I rarely saw her out of her room. We were on welfare, and I did the grocery shopping with food stamps. I thought this was a normal activity for thirteen-year-olds. We were very active in our church, and I soon accepted Jesus Christ as my personal Lord and Savior. I learned all about hellfire and damnation. What I didn't learn was that God loved me.

In the summer of 1976 my little sister, Jody, drowned in the Chena River. She was on shore and some friends and I had canoed over to a little island. As a joke, one of the kids pushed the canoe off the island. Jody waded in after it and got caught in the current and was swept downstream. The river was high and muddy. I knew she was in trouble, so I swam after her. I was afraid of swimming directly toward her because of the strong current, so I swam straight across the main branch of the river. I still remember the look on her face and in her eyes. She was totally panicked and at the mercy of the river. When I reached the other side, I ran downstream as she was approaching a bend in the river. There was an eddy in that bend. I was twenty-five feet from her when I dove in. The eddy pulled me upstream and her downstream. That was the last I saw of her.

I remember walking, running, stumbling home, crying and screaming in rage and anger. As I stood in the shower, watching the muddy water flow down the drain, I blamed God, wondering how a loving God could let something like that happen, wondering why He didn't take me instead of her.

That day my life took a turn for the worse. I went down by the river and smoked my first joint and drank my first beer, trying to deal with the pain. I made the decision to quit going to church. By the time I was a senior in high school, pot was a daily habit. It was a self-medication that dulled the pain and emotional turmoil so I didn't have to deal with life on life's terms. I thought I was in control. I continued the pattern I learned as a child: run from responsibility and don't deal with emotional pain.

After high school I joined the navy as a nuclear-machinist mate. I wanted to be on a submarine. I lost my nuke rating because I was constantly late to class from staying up and partying all night. I went AWOL for six months, turned myself in, and received an "other than honorable" discharge. I remembered back to my days in my youth group and realized that everything I said I wouldn't do when I grew up, I was now doing. I was involved with drugs, sex, lying, cheating, and stealing. I continued running from city to city.

While in Anchorage, Alaska, I bartended. It was there that I developed cocaine and sex habits in efforts to fill the hole in my soul. Nothing worked. I went to bed with so many different women; I can see their faces but can't remember all their names. As a result of my poor choices I now have herpes. Sin is fun for a season, but the consequences are devastating. Many of my

33

poor choices have affected me for years; some will affect me for the rest of my life. I had attempted to control my life with sex, drugs, and geographic relocations, but they all left me empty and broken. In addition to all this, I learned that Mom's depression was hereditary. I found my depression seemed to get a little worse every year.

On Christmas of 1994, my mom and I visited my sister in Lake Forest, California. That's when I attended Celebrate Recovery for the first time. I went to an Adult Child of a Chemically Dependent Parent group. I was in denial that I had a severe problem with drugs. After all, my dad was the alcoholic. After Christmas I moved to Lake Forest and began attending Saddleback Church and sporadically attended Celebrate Recovery. I'd go to church, listen to the wonderful music, feel as though the pastors were talking right to me, and then go home and get high. Once I even got high before going to a Wednesday-night service. I felt so guilty that I got up and left. I was unconnected, uninvolved. I don't know how many times I'd start to go to Celebrate Recovery, then go somewhere else. Or I'd come to the meeting, hear the music and the testimony or lesson, and leave before the small groups started.

In 1996 I had a lump on the right side of my neck. By the time I went to the doctor, it was half the size of a baseball. I had Hodgkin's disease, a type of cancer. After treatment, I went into remission for a while, but the cancer came back. During my last cancer bout, I finally hit my bottom. I got serious about working on my life's hurts, hang-ups, and habits. I was ready to start working the first choice:

Admitting NEED

CHOICE 1

Realize I'm not God.

I admit that I am powerless to control
my tendency to do the wrong thing
and that my life is unmanageable.

Today, God has brought many of my hurts, hang-ups, and habits into the light and healed them. God wastes nothing. The pain I experienced in the past now helps me relate to others in pain. My head knowledge of salvation, as a youth, has become heart knowledge. God is now helping me control my thought life, because that is where my spiritual battle takes place. God always does His part, and to have peace, I must do my part every single day. If I don't, I struggle. God has also helped me get involved with others. Looking outside myself and reaching out to help others is what God designed me for. I serve others out of a grateful heart for all the miracles God has given me through my relationship with Him.

God is in the business of miracles. Look at me; God has healed me of cancer twice. On April 1, 2001, I married Gabby, a truly godly woman. Pastor John officiated the service attended by so many wonderful friends. I have been blessed with a new family and a wonderful wife who can live with and love a wacky individual like me. Praise God!

It is my prayer that the honesty and openness of Elaine and Joe help you to consider the hurts, hang-ups, or habits in your own life and how you can make choice 1: "Realize I'm not God. I admit that I am powerless to control my tendency to do the wrong thing and that my life is unmanageable." Once you make this choice, your life's healing journey can begin!

R
E
C
O
V
E
R
Y

Earnestly believe that God exists,

that I *matter* to Him, and that He has the power to help me recover.

"Happy are those who mourn, for they shall be comforted." [1]

Getting HELP

The HOPE Choice

It doesn't rain much in Southern California. And it rarely rains enough to cause any flooding. But several years ago it rained so hard that a portion of Lake Forest actually flooded! Glen lives in a low area. The flooding was so bad that the *Orange County Register* sent a reporter, in a boat, out to Glen's neighborhood. The reporter found Glen's wife, Jo Ann, sitting on their roof watching large objects floating by, so he climbed up on the roof to interview her.

As the reporter questioned Jo Ann, he saw a Weber barbecue float by, and then he saw a large golden retriever pass by on top of his doghouse, and finally, a sports utility vehicle! A few minutes later, he saw a hat float by; but after it floated about twenty feet past the house, it started floating back upstream. When it got about twenty feet on the other side of the house, it started floating back down again. The reporter watched the hat go by seven or eight times, and finally he asked Jo Ann, "Do you have any idea how that hat is floating up and down stream?"

"Oh, that's just my crazy husband, Glen. He said he was going to mow the lawn today, come hell or high water."

37

The problem with many of us is that we are still focusing on the lawn while our home is floating away. We have the crazy notion that we are in control.

In the first chapter, we learned that no matter how hard we try to keep everything under control, we are powerless to control our tendency to do wrong and that our lives are unmanageable. In this chapter we'll begin moving out of the role of playing God and into the role of receiving God's power. We will also gain a vision of the hope and help God offers us. But first, we'll look at two of God's blessings in disguise: grief and pain—and when we do, we'll learn how to tap into God's power.

GRIEF: GOD'S PATHWAY TO COMFORT

All of us have broken areas in our lives—things that bring us deep grief and pain. In fact, the things we carry around can be downright devastating. When we carry a hurt for a long time, we eventually find our identity in that hurt and become a victim. We may try to escape our pain by using drugs or alcohol. Or we may try to control all those around us with anger. The list goes on and on.

As we work through the eight choices of this book, we will come face-to-face with truths about ourselves and our lives that we have tried to hide—and hide from—our whole lives. We begin to experience hurt and a sense of loss. This is the process of "mourning," and it brings a whole new kind of pain. We mourn over our past mistakes, and we even mourn over our loss of control. In the end, God leads us to His comfort, if we will just trust in Him. As the beatitude for this choice says, *"Happy are those who mourn, for they shall be comforted."*[2]

WE MOURN OUR PAST MISTAKES

As you do the work of the eight choices in this book, you may begin to grieve over your past and find yourself filled with regret: "I wish I hadn't made those dumb decisions . . . I wish I hadn't responded as I did . . . I wish I hadn't done what I did . . . I wish . . ." It starts to dawn on us that we have hurt people and we have been hurt by others.

WE MOURN OUR LOSS OF CONTROL

Even though we never were really in control, we thought we were. Facing up to that fact brings a sense of real loss. Mourning is what happens when we finally face the truth of choice 1: admitting that we are powerless to control our tendency to do wrong and that our lives are unmanageable.

> *Just as grief is God's pathway to comfort, PAIN is God's antidote for denial.*

WE DISCOVER GOD'S PATHWAY TO COMFORT

As long as we don't get stuck in the mourning process, mourning can serve as the pathway to comfort and to the help and hope God has ready for us. The same promise God gave His people of old, He gives us today: *"To all who mourn in Israel, he will give beauty for ashes, joy instead of mourning, praise instead of despair. For the LORD has planted them like strong and graceful oaks for his own glory."*[3]

PAIN: GOD'S ANTIDOTE FOR DENIAL

Just as grief is God's pathway to comfort, pain is God's antidote for denial. In reality, denial is a kind of sickness and needs a powerful antidote. As strange as it may sound, *pain* is God's antidote for denial. C. S. Lewis helps us understand: "God whispers to us in our pleasures, speaks in our conscience, but shouts in our pain. Pain is God's megaphone to rouse a deaf world."[4] Pain is God's way of letting us know something is seriously wrong and needs our attention. If your appendix bursts, and you felt no pain, you wouldn't know your body needed help. The toxins from your appendix would infect your abdominal cavity and could eventually kill you. Pain alerts us to our need for help.

Pain is also God's fire alarm. If a fire alarm went off in your house, I don't think you'd say, "Oh, there goes that stupid fire alarm again! Somebody throw a rock at it and make it stop." Hopefully, you would do something about it. You would call the fire department and get some help. But when our "pain alarm" goes off, instead of dealing with the source of the pain, we often try to cover up the sound. We try to mute the noise with people, work, food, alcohol, sex, and many, many different things. If you ignore the alarm, your house could burn down.

An important point needs to be made here. Just because God *allows* pain to enter your life does not mean that He *causes* the pain, and it certainly doesn't mean that He enjoys seeing you in pain. Pain is often a consequence of our poor choices or the poor choices of others. God allows the natural consequences of these poor choices to play out. This is not the same thing as Him causing our pain. God loves us and wants to lead us out of our pain and into His healing. The miracle is that he brings *good* out of our pain by using it to lead us to His comfort and away from our denial.

With that said, take a look at yourself: How's your pain level? Is God using your pain to get your attention?

DENIAL—REFUSING GOD'S POWER TO HELP

To deny your pain is to refuse God's power to help you recover. You will never find healing from your hurts, hang-ups, and habits until you confront your pain. Unless you've lived a perfect life, it's a sure thing that you struggle with some kind of issue. How bad does the hurt, relationship, pain, or memory have to get before you are ready to face your denial and admit you cannot handle it by yourself?

Remember, if you could have handled that problem on your own, it wouldn't still be a problem. If you could handle it, you would have; but you can't, so you don't.

Sometimes in our denial, we excuse ourselves and we accuse others: "If my wife would just get her act together, then our marriage would be just fine." We play the blame game. Do you know how you spell blame? B- LAME! When we blame others for something we did, we are being lame!

Other forms of denial are just as strange. When someone asks us how we're doing, we often say "I'm fine" or "So far, so good." Who are we kidding? We could say the same thing if we'd just jumped off a building and were halfway down. We haven't hit bottom yet, so we say we're "fine . . . so far, so good."

Instead of denying your pain, allow it to motivate you to get help, to start making healing choices, to face the issue that you've been ignoring for ten, twenty, maybe thirty years. *Don't refuse God's power to help.*

GOD'S DENIAL BUSTERS

We rarely change when life is cool and comfortable. We change when we feel the heat. We start to change after our marriage falls apart or after our kids go off in the wrong direction. One man said, "The acid of my pain finally ate through the wall of my denial." Unfortunately, we usually don't change until our fear of change is exceeded by our pain. Most people never choose to move toward healing until there is no other option.

God uses three denial busters to get our attention, to force us to move into recovery and away from the choices and circumstances that have messed up our lives:

1. *Crisis:* God uses the pain of an unexpected crisis to shatter our denial: illness caused by years of substance abuse, stress brought on by workaholism, job loss due to inappropriate actions, or a divorce due to infidelity.

2. *Confrontation:* God can also use the people in our lives who care for us—people who care enough to say, "You're blowing it." He uses people who love us enough to confront us in truth and love and say, "You're about to lose your health." "You're about to lose your job." "You're about to lose your family."

There is an old saying in Texas: "If one person calls you a horse's rear, ignore it. If two people call you a horse's rear, look in the mirror. If three people call you a horse's rear, buy a saddle." If three people say you need to get some help with a hurt, hang-up, or habit—get some help!

3. *Catastrophe:* When the bottom falls out—physically, emotionally, spiritually, financially, relationally—God sometimes just steps back and lets us feel the full impact of our own poor choices. "You want to be God? Okay, have it your way."

Don't ignore your pain. Recognize it as God's denial buster and open yourself up to the hope and power He offers.

Choice 1 says, "I admit it. I'm helpless. I'm powerless." Choice 2 says, "There is a power greater than me, and there is hope. There is a power I can plug into that will help me handle things I can't handle on my own. That is the good news!

CHOICE 2

Getting HELP

Earnestly believe that God exists,

that I matter to Him, and that He has the power to help me recover.

As we'll see in the remainder of this chapter, choice 2 is made up of three magnificent truths about God: (1) *He exists,* (2) *I matter to Him,* and (3) *He has the power to help me.* As we begin to understand each truth, we'll see that each one involves a choice on our part—a choice to believe and a choice to receive. Unless we make this choice, His power cannot become real in our lives.

THE TRUTH ABOUT GOD

1. GOD EXISTS

The Bible makes it clear that belief in God is essential: *"Anyone who comes to him must believe that he exists and that he rewards those who earnestly seek him."*[5]

Most people do acknowledge that God exists. Why? Because it takes more faith not to believe in a creator than it does to believe in one. If you took your watch completely apart, put the pieces in a paper bag, shook it up, and dumped the bag out on a table, the odds of the pieces coming together randomly as a complete watch would be pretty incredible. And the world is much more complex than your watch. Where there is an effect, there must be a cause. Where there is design, there must be a designer. Where there is a creation, there must be a Creator. *"Since the* creation of the world God's invisible qualities—his eternal power and divine nature—have been clearly seen."[6]

2. YOU MATTER TO HIM

Since most people believe God exists, the real issue becomes, "What kind of God is He? Do I really matter to Him?"

The reason a lot of us don't know we matter to God is that we don't really know what God is like. And sometimes, when we don't have adequate information, we just make up our own. We say, "God as I understand Him or, "My idea about God is . . ." Just because we have a certain idea about God doesn't mean it's right. Our personal conception of God is not what matters. What matters is the *truth* of who He is. And sometimes we just don't have the correct information.

Until we UNDERSTAND *God's true character, we can't completely trust Him.*

Two young boys in a Catholic school had been continually misbehaving and were sent to the principal's office on several occasions. The principal knew what they really needed was to have God in their lives, so she brought the first boy in and set him down. "I want to ask you a question, son. Where is God?"

The young boy was scared to death by the question. He didn't know how to answer. He just sat there. She asked him three or four times, "Where is God?" Still, the young boy didn't answer. She told him that she wanted him to think about that question. So she sent him out of her office. As he was leaving, the second boy, whose turn it was to see the principal, asked the first, "What's going on?"

The first boy said, "I don't know, but evidently God is missing, and they're trying to pin it on us."

Sometimes our misconceptions about God confuse our picture of Him. Unfortunately, a lot of people think God is like one of their parents. People who had abusive fathers tend to think God, the Father, is abusive. Those whose mothers were aloof and unloving may think God is aloof and unloving. Those who had reason to fear their parents tend to be afraid of God.

Until we understand God's true character, we can't completely trust Him. It's hard to trust something or someone we do not know about or understand. Fortunately, we have a God who *cares* about us. We matter to Him.

Understanding the following truths about God's character gives us hope when we're in pain:

God Knows about Your Situation

God knows your hurts, hang-ups, and habits. He knows the good and bad. When we have had a tough week or month or life, we may think that no one really cares: "Nobody knows the pain I'm going through in this marriage." We're wrong; God knows. Or maybe we think, "Nobody knows how I'm struggling to break this habit." God knows. Perhaps we think, "Nobody knows the depression and fear I'm going through." God knows. He knows it all. And He cares. Nothing escapes His notice. King David had plenty of sorrow in his life, and he said of God, *"You have listened to my troubles and have seen the crisis in my soul."*[7] God sees the crisis you may be going through right now. *Your father knows what you need before you ask him.*[8] *"The LORD is close to the brokenhearted and saves those who are crushed in spirit."*[9] God is with you in your pain, and He is able to help you overcome your hurts, hang-ups, and habits.

Did you know that God keeps a record of every tear that has fallen down your cheek? *"You know how troubled I am. You have kept a record of my tears."*[10] Isn't that incredible? You have never, ever shed a tear that God missed. Nothing is beyond His love; nothing is beyond His compassionate gaze. He is with you, and He is aware of everything you've gone through, are going through, and will go through.

Job said of God, *"You keep close watch on all my paths."*[11] God is watching over you; nothing escapes His eye. Sometimes we wish God didn't have to see all the poor choices we make. The fact is, nothing is off the record with God: *"You know how foolish I am."*[12] God is not shocked by your sin. He knew it was coming long before you did. He knows why you did it, even when you don't. He knows your good days, your bad days, your foolish decisions, and all your secrets. Amazingly, He still loves you!

God Cares about Your Situation

Not only does God know about your situation, He cares all about it and you: *"As a father has compassion on his children, so the LORD has compassion on those who fear him; for he knows how we are formed, he remembers that we are dust."*[13] God made us, so He knows what we're made of—mere molecules—and He knows that we're frail creatures. God wants to be the Father that many of us never had. He is tender and sympathetic toward us. He says to us, *"I have loved you with an everlasting love."*[14] He cares about us when we serve Him and when we don't, when we're right and when we're wrong. How can God love and care about us when our lives are so messed up? Because His love for us is unconditional. It is not based on our performance. It is based on His character. This is how much God cares about us: *"God showed his great love for us by sending Christ to die for* us."[15] There is no greater love than this: that a man *"lay down his life for his friends."*[16] And this is exactly what Jesus did for you.

3. GOD HAS THE POWER TO CHANGE YOU AND YOUR SITUATION

Sometimes God changes you; sometimes He changes your situation. Sometimes He changes both. He's got the power. The magnitude of this power is hard to comprehend, so the apostle Paul prayed for our understanding: *"I pray that you will begin to understand the incredible greatness of his power for us who believe him. This is the same mighty power that raised Christ from the dead."*[17]

If God can raise Jesus Christ from the dead, He can certainly raise a dead relationship. He can set us free from an addiction. He can take away our guilt and shame. He can help us close the door on the past so those memories stop haunting us. God has the power to change us and our situation.

The Bible goes on to say that *nothing* is too hard for God: *"What is impossible with men is possible with God."*[18] The situation you are in right now may seem hopeless. But it's not.

In fact, in our Celebrate Recovery family, we have had thousands and thousands of people who were in impossible situations. They could not change these situations on their own power. They never thought in a million years that they or their circumstances could ever change. But they did! At the end of this chapter you'll find the stories of Mary and Tim—stories that show how God's power helped them change as they completed this second choice.

Now, we'll look at what you can do to make God's power a reality in your own life.

PLUGGING IN TO GOD'S POWER

Believe it or not, *things work better when they're plugged in.* This applies to toasters, vacuum cleaners, coffeemakers—and to us as well. In order to get rid of the pain, we must choose to plug in to God's power, and that means more than just believing. If simply believing in God were enough, most of us wouldn't need this book or these eight healing choices. Belief alone cannot wipe away the pain and devastation of the hurts, hang-ups, and habits in your life. In order to get rid of the pain, you've got to make a choice: you've got to choose to *plug in to* God's power. His power is where your *help* lies.

GOD'S TRIPLE POWER SURGE

A lot of Christians have no power in their lives because they're not plugged in. When we're plugged in to His power, God supplies us with all we need: *"The Spirit that God has given us . . . fills with power, love, and self-control."*[19] Power, love, and self-control—God's triple power surge, the very three things we need in order to be healthy, happy, and whole.

1. *Power.* We need power to break habits we can't break on our own. We need power to do what we know is right but can't seem to do by ourselves. We need power to break free from the past and let those memories go. We need power to get on with the kind of life God wants us to live. But we have found that we cannot change on our own power. We need a power much greater than ourselves—we need to plug in to God's power.

2. *Love.* We need real love. We want to be able to love people and have them love us back. We need to let go of the fear of getting hurt by the ones we love. We want the ability to establish deep, meaningful, authentic relationships rather than superficial, hurtful, selfish relationships.

3. *Self-control.* We also need self-control, but we can't have self-control until Christ is in control of us. When Christ is in control, we understand, perhaps for the first time, what it means to get it all together. When we're not trying to pull ourselves up by our own bootstraps, we'll find that Christ will stand us on our feet.

You can have access to God's triple power surge if you will just stay connected to the power source.

MAKING THE POWER CONNECTION—*BELIEVE* AND *RECEIVE*

How do I plug in to God's power?

Simple: *Believe* and *receive.*

First, believe the three truths about God that we shared earlier:

1. Believe that God exists.

2. Believe that you matter to Him.

3. Believe that He has the power to help.

Then receive Him into your life. Simply say, "Jesus Christ, put Your Spirit in me." You do that by using a four-letter word—HELP! It takes courage to say this word, but it is your connection to power: "HELP. God, I need Your help in my life."

Receiving God's help can be frightening because we know it means *change.* "I don't know if I *want* help to change," you may say. "I'm scared to death of change." You may not want to change until your pain exceeds your fear of change. But when you are ready to receive God's power, all you have to say is, "God, make me willing to be willing to change." Then He will give you the will and the power to plug in to Him. *"It is God who is at work within you, giving you the will and the power to achieve his purpose."*[20]

When you do call for help, God has promised to respond: *"When you go through deep waters and great trouble, I will be with you. When you go through rivers of difficulty, you will not drown! When you walk through the fire of oppression, you will not be burned up; the flames will not consume you."*[21] Where are you hurting today? Are you going through some deep waters? Do you feel like you're going under for the last time? Are you going through the fire? Is the heat on in your life? Do you feel like you're stuck in a rut and just can't find the power to change? Do you feel powerless?

God's power is available to you right now—it's just a choice away. All you have to do is *believe* and *receive*.

When I ran out of myself and had nowhere else to turn, I finally hit my bottom. I found God patiently waiting there for me. He gave me His power to make the changes that on my own I was powerless to make. Stepping out of my denial into God's grace was not easy. Admitting that I was an alcoholic and that my life was out of control was the hardest thing I ever had to do. But when I made this second choice, a huge weight was lifted off my shoulders. The hope and freedom that I began to experience was indescribable! All I had to do was believe and receive while God did the rest.

As you work through the "Make the Choice" section of this chapter, you may end up face-to-face with some real problems—maybe some you haven't wanted to deal with. It might mean taking some risks. It will most definitely mean being honest and trusting God.

MAKE THE *Choice*

ACTION 1: *Pray about It*

Laying down your denial and trusting that God will give you the *power* may be a daily exercise for some time. But God's power is real and amazing. And day by day as we plug in to that power, we will learn to trust Him more and more. Our job is to cry out for help and know He will keep His promise to hear our cries and help us.

Pray on your own, or read this prayer and pray these words in your heart:

> *Dear God, please help me not to ignore this pain You are using to alert me to my need for help. In the past, as I've ignored the denial busters You've allowed in my life, I have actually refused Your help. I am so sorry for this and ask Your help in facing the truth and trusting You to care for me. You know and care about all the pain and hurt I have in my life. Today I need Your help. I can't do it on my own. I have tried, and I keep coming up empty.*
>
> *First, I pray for Your power in my life. I need Your power to break habits I can't break. I need Your power to help me do the things that I know are right but can't seem to do on my own. I need Your power to break free from my past. I ask for Your power to get on with the plans You have for my life.*
>
> *Next, I pray for love. I want real love. I want to be able to love people and have them love me. I pray that with Your love I can let go*

of past hurts and failures so I can tear down the walls of fake intimacy. God, I ask You to help me have genuine intimacy with You and others. Help me not be afraid of really loving and of really being loved.

I also pray for real self-control. I realize that I'm really not in control until I allow Christ to be in control of my life and circumstances.

God, please grant me Your power, love, and self-control. Help me to continue making healing choices. Amen.

If you prayed that prayer, you just took a very significant step! Don't worry about understanding the how-to's right now; we will look at those in chapter 3. Just know that you are on your way to getting help for when you hurt!

ACTION 2: *Write about It*

Before you begin, take a minute and reread what you wrote in chapter 1. Sometimes we are in such a hurry to grow, to progress, that we do not take time to reflect on what God has already taught us about Himself or ourselves. Your journal will give you an encouraging picture of your growth as you move through these eight choices.

With that said, let's review the following scripture and see what principles we can draw from it: "*When you go through deep waters and great trouble, I will be with you When you go through rivers of difficulty, you will not drown! When you walk through the fire of oppression, you will not be burned up; the flames will not consume you.*" [22]

God promises to be with you today, tomorrow, next week, next month, next year as you face those issues you've been afraid to change all your life. Write out the answers to the following questions:

1. What pain has God been using as a megaphone in your life to alert you to your need for help?

2. Who or what have you blamed for your problems—either partially or completely?

3. What pain have you been denying?

4. What denial busters (crisis, confrontation, catastrophe) has God used to try to get your attention?

5. In what areas do you feel stuck in the pain of your past— powerless to change?

6. What area(s) of your life are you now ready to allow God to start helping you?

7. What are you still afraid to turn over to God?

8. How are your feelings for your earthly father and heavenly Father alike? How do they differ?

ACTION 3: *Share about It*

This may be the most difficult of the three actions for you to take. But the good news is that it gets easier as you continue to go through each of the eight choices. God's Word says, *"As iron sharpens iron, so people can improve each other."*[23]

If you are still looking for a safe person to share your healing journey with, here are some guidelines that will help you in your search:

1. *Does he or she have a growing relationship with Jesus Christ?* Do you see the character of Christ developing in this person?

2. *Does this person's walk and talk match?* Some Christians can quote the Bible, chapter and verse, but their lifestyle does not match their talk. Be certain that the person you choose to share your journey with is someone whose life is worthy of imitation.

3. *Is he or she a good listener?* Do you sense that this person honestly cares about what you have to say?

4. *Does he or she show compassion, concern, and hope but not pity?* You don't need someone to feel sorry for you, but you do need someone who can be sensitive to your pain.

5. *Is this person strong enough to confront your denial or procrastination?* Does he or she care enough about you and your progress to challenge you? There is a difference between helping others and trying to fix others. You need to be careful to guard the relationship from becoming unhealthy or codependent.

6. *Does he or she offer suggestions?* Sometimes we need help in seeing options or alternatives that we are unable to find on our own.

7. *Can this person share his or her own past and current struggles with you?* Is this person willing to open up and be vulnerable and transparent with you?

The journey to a happy, healthy, whole life is not easy. Along the way, you will have to face some problems you have not wanted to deal with. You'll have to take some risks. This journey is not one to be traveled alone. You need someone of the same sex, a trusted friend with whom you can share what God is doing in your life. As you complete this chapter, focus on the hope found in God's love for you and His ability to help you heal.

Mary's STORY

My name is Mary, and I am a believer who struggles with abuse, anger, eating disorders, and codependency. Growing up, I felt I stood out in a bad way and felt different from everyone else. I was born three months premature. My left hip, shoulder, and jaw were deformed. I felt like a burden to my family. My mom tried to make me feel special, but her actions made me feel inferior. Because I was allergic to milk, flour, and sugar, I had to eat special foods. My teacher kept them in the same drawer as another child's hearing-aid batteries. I truly believed the two of us were the only "special needs" kids at school.

My father was a pastor at our church, but I was not taught that I could have a personal relationship with a loving God. My brother and I were simply told to be on our best behavior and not to embarrass our parents at church. I learned it was normal to have two completely opposite sets of rules—one for home and one for church. Before I began kindergarten, my brother and I started looking at my dad's pornographic magazines. I decided at this young age that women were supposed to look like the women in the magazines. Since I thought my mom was the most beautiful woman I'd ever seen, I could not understand why my dad continued to look at the strangers in his magazines.

My mom was always on a diet and continually took appetite suppressants. Since I believed dieting was what kept her beautiful, at the age of five I also started trying to control my food intake. I would take the meat on my dinner plate and put it under my booster seat because it had "fat" on it. The family cat would eat it after dinner, so no one ever knew.

About this same time, my grandfather taught me a secret game of "different kisses." He taught me our eyelashes made a butterfly kiss, our noses made an Eskimo kiss, and he also taught me how to French kiss. I felt confused as to why this seemingly innocent game had to be our secret.

When I started losing my baby teeth, my dad did not like that they did not fall out in order. He would hold down my head and pull out my teeth that weren't even loose, with pliers. My dad justified it by saying, "They're going to come out sometime; they may as well come out now, and then you will look better." I lived in complete fear of my dad. I always wanted to please him and be on his good side. One day I was learning about gravity by throwing my brother's toys out of his bedroom window and watching them smash onto the cement below. My dad's punishment for me was to shoot the family cat and place him in the trash can. I felt the cat's death was my fault. To cope in life, I learned to mentally escape by going into a fantasyland I had created. I called it my safe place.

My parents soon started arguing a lot, and Mom became very depressed. One night Dad told us he hated our mom and was in love with someone else. When he left, he took almost all of the furniture, including our beds. I'll never forget my mom, brother, and me sitting on the bathroom floor sobbing. I felt helpless and abandoned, and I believed we had not been a good enough family for my dad to stay and work it out. Soon after, Mom started drinking. My brother and I had learned in school to stop, drop, and roll during a fire drill at school, so we used that technique to protect ourselves from our mother's blows.

I eventually decided I needed to take control of our family. I would sneak money out of my mom's wallet, ride my bike to the corner store, buy dinner, and then sneak the change back into her wallet before she woke up. One day when my mom was particularly violent, I begged a neighbor to let me come in. The neighbor said she wanted no part of the situation and for me to go home. I felt alone and petrified. That night my mom beat my back with a scorching frying pan. She then threw a gallon of milk at my head, and I fell to the floor, unconscious. I loved my mom so much, but I thought one day she was going to kill me.

My brother and I soon went to live with my dad, stepmom, and three stepbrothers. My stepbrothers were much older than me. Among many things, they taught me all about marijuana. But smoking my first joint made me hungry, and I knew it was not for me. I had been anorexic for years and wasn't about to get fat now. I became the object of my stepbrothers' abuse as well. They flushed my hamster down the toilet and put my cat in the freezer, alive. My feelings of violation and anger continued and became more permanent. I was a prisoner in my own home. When I got home from school, I would run as fast as I could to my bedroom and only came out for dinner.

I started having a recurring dream that I would die at the age of thirty-two. I planned my whole life according to this continual dream so I would be able to achieve everything I wanted to by that age. When my mom remarried, my brother and I asked to move back with her. She let us move in, and I had a good relationship with my new stepdad. I liked having chores and structure. I liked knowing that he was in charge, and I liked being a kid again. During this time my mom also became sober. I was so happy. But I continued to want to be in control by starving myself and using diet and caffeine pills all through high school. I only dated boys I thought were cute, and it didn't matter if they were into drugs, alcohol, or only wanted sex. My brother was very good-looking, and when the girls at school found out that I was his sister, they immediately befriended me. I felt used and that people did not like me for me.

I met my husband not long after graduating high school. He was tall, gorgeous, athletic, and quiet. I was very hyper, so I thought he could quiet me down and I could pep him up. A perfect match. Slowly, but constantly, he began making derogatory comments about me. I took all of his remarks to heart. They reconfirmed my low self-image and feelings of being different, deformed, and ugly. I thought if I could show him how fun, hilarious, and wonderful I was, then he would surely love me. But three months after he and I moved in together, I caught him in a lie. He admitted he had cheated on me. I was heartbroken and furious. I moved out for a while and told him to date as many women as he wanted. He promised me that if he ever found someone he liked better, he would leave me before starting a relationship with her. Because of my past, that actually sounded reasonable to me at the time.

Eventually, however, we decided to get married. I controlled everything. I planned our entire wedding, his bachelor party, even the strip clubs his friends could take him to. I renewed his subscriptions to a pornographic magazine. I decorated our home the way I wanted. My husband's taste simply did not matter to me. I chose to display all of his hard-earned athletic trophies in his closet on his shoe shelf.

Since I was just a few years away from thirty-two, the age I was supposed to die according to my recurring dream, I told my husband it was time to have children. I thought having a child would strengthen our relationship. After years of being anorexic, I lost four teeth while pregnant and five teeth afterward, but I loved the freedom of having an excuse to eat whatever and whenever I wanted. Eating food gave me a full feeling and dulled the pain. I had felt empty for so many years; it felt good to feel full. My husband, however, was disgusted with me. He said I was too hot to be next to, so I started putting ice packs under my clothes.

I didn't go on a diet after my daughter was born; I felt protected in my cushion of fat. My husband now turned to pornographic videos. I went along with it so he would accept me, but again it only made me feel inferior, ugly, and unacceptable.

Soon my husband told me how unhappy he was and that it was all my fault. I agreed and felt he was right. He did, however, agree to go to marriage counseling. But during that first session, my husband told me he had been having another affair. This was when I hit bottom. This was too much for me, and I lost all sense of reality. I could see no reason why he should keep on living. When we got home, he went right to bed. I was hysterical, crying. When I knew he was asleep, I took the biggest knife we had, braced myself against the wall, and held it up above his neck. For some reason I thought, "Maybe God doesn't want him dead." I had not thought about God in years. So I asked God aloud, "God, it's Mary here. You know all about my situation and that I am about to kill my husband. If You don't want me to do this, then You have to give me the power to put this knife back." The next thing I remember is feeling as if a person were hugging me from behind. I cried all night on the bedroom floor. That night I was completely emptied of myself. I asked God to fill my empty body with Himself and to show me where I could learn more about Jesus. I didn't know it then, but I was making the second choice in my journey toward healing.

CHOICE 2

Getting HELP
Earnestly believe that God exists,
that I matter to Him, and that He
has the power to help me recover.

The following Sunday I went to find Jesus with my two-year-old daughter in tow. Right down the street from our home was a large church. As I made my way up the long driveway, I kept yelling to God, "Are You sure this is where You want me to go?" As I entered the Saddleback worship center, I could hear beautiful music. Pastor Rick's message was on building better relationships and sex in marriage. I tried to write down everything he said, but there wasn't enough room on the bulletin. I saw a tape table and got that day's message. My husband listened to it at home but said it was too late. He said if only I had found out about this church sooner, things might have been different. I didn't agree. I finally understood that he would have to make his own choices and that I could not attempt to control him any longer.

My husband and I did try counseling once more through a lay counselor at Saddleback, but my husband said there was no hope of keeping our marriage together. He was in love with his girlfriend. He said he had *actually been with her for four of the six years we had been married. I knew I was home at Saddleback and that God cared about me, but I wondered if I could ever trust another man.*

A few days after my husband's revelation, I began taking Saddleback's membership class. During the class I kept thinking to myself, I hate men— all men—and I am never going to make myself vulnerable to another man. I am never going to trust another man as long as I live. Before I could finish my thought, Pastor Brett said, "Everybody, look up here. I have something to tell you: Your Father in heaven loves you. He wants you to put all your trust in one man, Jesus Christ, who died on the cross so you could live forever with Him in paradise." I felt God had spoken to me. I was baptized the following weekend. My stepdad and daughter watched me be baptized. It meant a lot for my stepdad to come. Pastor John, of the Celebrate Recovery ministry, baptized me. The whole time I was being baptized, I was thinking, I can't imagine ever being in recovery, let alone being able to celebrate it! The picture the church gave me of Pastor John baptizing me is a very special gift from God. Ironically, I was thirty-two years old!

The joy of my baptism didn't last long. I still had to allow God's power to change me. I soon found myself in a very deep depression. I now could relate to my mother's soul-wrenching grief when my dad left us. I felt helpless and completely rejected as a friend, wife, mother, and person. The betrayal and years of lies were more than I could take. I bought two bottles of sleeping pills and decided I would bury myself at a nearby construction site. In the middle of my catastrophe, the phone rang. It was the lay counselor I had seen a month before. He said he was following up on our last visit. I told him I had been baptized and that my husband had moved out. I did not tell him about my plans to kill myself right then. He said he was so sorry about what happened and that he had been praying for us. I could not believe that this person, whom we hardly knew, had been praying for us. God showed me that I do matter to Him and that He loves me.

The next day was my first day at Celebrate Recovery. I cried that first night, but one lady, Debbie, gave me a big hug and told me she was in the same situation just two years prior. Debbie will always be my soul sister. Lisa also gave me a hug and a phone list. She said I could call her any time. I was no longer alone. I taped my small recovery group's phone list on my kitchen cabinet and thanked God for twenty women who knew exactly what I was feeling. I took to heart everything taught at Celebrate Recovery. My mom and stepdad agreed to watch my daughter on Monday nights so I could meet with my step study group. My first night in the step study, I was amazed to hear the pain and struggles of the women in the group. As time passed, I began to see how my codependency and enabling had affected others and my marriage.

I learned to replace the unhealthy beliefs and reactions to the impersonal God of my youth. I began to understand God's true character. He is loving and forgiving. He can change my situation and me. Even though I thought I was getting into recovery to heal my broken heart over the loss of my marriage, I found that I had more than thirty years worth of hurts, hang-ups, and habits to reveal and allow God's power to heal. Although working through the eight recovery choices was the most heart-wrenching, soul-searching year of my life, I thank God for carrying me through with my safety net of friends. It was very hard for me to admit my part in the breakup of my marriage. I had to admit I was controlling, manipulative, prideful, selfish, unrealistic, blaming, and shaming. I also avoided confrontation and was a doormat. I remember thinking to myself, Even I wouldn't have wanted to be married to me.

I have learned to have boundaries with friends and relatives. God showed me that becoming a whole person meant apologizing from my heart to all those I had hurt and forgiving all who have hurt me. I learned that every day I need to put all my anxieties, frustrations, and hurt in God's capable hands.

Overcoming being painfully shy was a long and personally stretching experience. I attribute this victory to becoming a Celebrate Recovery greeter. As I came out of myself more, I felt the Holy Spirit pushing me to share

Christ and what He has done in my life with my unbelieving family. I prayed about the right timing. Then my stepdad had a massive heart attack and was paralyzed from the waist down. As he lay on the hospital bed, he looked up at me and said, "Mary, I have gone for a ride in a beautiful boat this morning on a smooth and clear lake. I see your Jesus at the end of the dock, but I cannot step out of the boat to go to Him. Do you know how I can step out of the boat and go to Him?" I was able to lead him in praying the sinner's prayer before he went home to be with the Lord.

My life took another huge turn when I opened my home to an out-of-state female Celebrate Recovery leader during the Celebrate Recovery Summit. Since I couldn't help at the summit, this was my way of serving. Two men traveled with her, and one of them, Jeff, said my house had "nice gutters." Only the Lord knew that one conversation would soon turn into a romance. After a year of phone calls and telephone Bible studies, we were married. Jeff is truly my soul mate and I am blessed to be best friends with and married to such a wonderful, kind, thoughtful, and godly man. Jeff has a son, Dustin, and is so excited to see the Lord work in him and through him. My daughter is being raised in a Christian home, learning values and morals and about a relationship with God—things that I did not have while growing up. God has restored my relationship with my mom. Today, she is a wonderful mom and grandmother. God has also restored my relationship with my dad and stepmom, one of my stepbrothers, and my own brother and sister-in-law.

It is an incredible honor to co-lead the junior-high Life Hurts, God Heals class with my husband, Jeff, Nicole, Laurel, and Sharon. It is hard for me to find the right words to express what a privilege it is to stand in the gap for these children. When I was their age, I had nobody. I want to be there for them and let them know, "I know what you are going through; I went through it too. We can do this together, and in the end, we'll be stronger and happier for it with Christ as our brother, friend, and guide!"

God fully accepts me as I am. I know Jesus will never leave me or make fun of me. I no longer run from my feelings. I feel them and turn to God *when I need support. He has also placed several caring and supportive women in my life to help hold me accountable. I now look to the Bible for direction and not my own thinking.*

I am by no means perfect. I still struggle daily with food and a low self-image. But I know that I have been given a second chance. I want to live my life for Jesus. I want to help others who are hurting find the strength, confidence, and healing power that comes from living life not for ourselves, but for God. I would like to end my story with one of my favorite scriptures:

"I am convinced that neither death nor life,
neither angels nor demons, neither the present nor the future,
nor any powers, neither height nor depth,
nor anything else in all creation,
will be able to separate us from the love of God
that is in Christ Jesus our Lord."[24]

My name is Tim, and I am a grateful believer who is a survivor of sexual abuse and in recovery from codependency and anger. I was born in Elyria, Ohio, the only son of an automotive service manager and a homemaker. Dad had a passion for racing stock cars. When I was four years old, I went to see Dad race for the first time. It was the only race I ever saw, because it was his last. During that short race, my dad's throttle stuck, and he crashed into the wall at the end of the track, where the car exploded. My mom screamed hysterically, but I didn't understand at that moment just what had happened.

During the six years that followed, I found solace for my pain in food. Captain Crunch and I became good friends. In the fourth grade, I weighed 142 pounds and had a waist of thirty-two inches—"husky," as we used to say. Being a fat kid was miserable because the other kids were brutal. I still hear their comments, still bear the scars, and I am still conscious of my weight and appearance. I learned to be an angry kid, and I expressed my anger often. It helped me to cope, giving me the false illusion of control.

My friend lived a few streets over from me. One day when I was nine years old, I went into the woods behind my house. My friend's older brother was waiting for me, and he sexually abused me. When he told me that he would kill my mother and me if I told anyone, I believed him. I carried the guilt and shame of his actions for years. I didn't realize that it was not my fault.

My mom found her solace for the loss of my dad in alcohol. Within six years, she managed to drink herself to death. She died of cirrhosis of the liver in December of 1966. I was ten years old and all alone. All I had left of my family was my dog, Molly. My aunt on my mother's side took me in. I changed schools and didn't do very well that year. I remember going into the bathroom to cry so nobody would see me. I felt so alone. My aunt and uncle cleaned out my house and either sold or gave away almost everything to their friends. Then they sold my dog, Molly. I think that hurt the most. That summer they left on vacation, leaving me with one of my uncles on my father's side of the family. After that they would never answer my phone calls or answer the door. It was their way of saying, "We don't want you anymore."

During that summer, I bounced from one uncle's house to the next. During my brief stay with one uncle, a family member threatened me with a knife and sexually abused me. Now I would no longer allow myself to trust anyone. Everyone I had ever cared about either left me, didn't want me, or abused me. I knew I was completely alone, and that to survive I would have to take care of myself. I was only eleven years old.

In August of 1967 I landed at my Uncle Walt and Aunt Agnes's home, and they already had four kids. As a child I thought that my uncle wanted me there more than my aunt did. Today I understand that my perception was wrong and that my aunt really did love me. I stayed there, and they eventually adopted me shortly after my fourteenth birthday. Life was not easy for an angry, suspicious fat kid who was used to being an only child. I didn't know what it was like to interact with siblings. I was selfish, untrusting, and had a pretty foul mouth. I had a new home and a new family but still lived in fear and loneliness. I was sure the relative stability of my new home wouldn't last. Nothing ever had. I had no sense of security.

It seemed that my new mom applied a different standard to me than to her own kids, which made me very resentful. So I was always in trouble. Not serious trouble, but in trouble nevertheless. Two weeks before my nineteenth birthday, I moved out. It was ugly; I hurt my adoptive parents. I falsely blamed them and others for my mother's death and used this as my excuse to move out to be free. Today I know that I was terribly wrong.

But my newfound "freedom" eventually brought me into bondage. My behavior turned dark, and I attempted to numb my pain with drinking, drugs, and whatever sexual encounters I could muster. I chose to marry a girl I knew while I was in high school. I was unfaithful and justified my actions because of her behavior. We moved to Columbus and attended Ohio State University. While there, I met another girl and was unfaithful once again. My wife never even knew of either affair. When I told her I wanted a divorce, she was shocked. The marriage lasted less than two years, and I was only twenty-two years old.

For the next six months, I bounced from one relationship to another, taking and discarding women, trying to fill my own loneliness. But no one ever really knew who I was on the inside because I never let anyone get that close. I created my own mental and emotional fortress. I had a false sense of security, and I was lonely and miserable.

I moved to California in 1978. The scenery and names changed, but my life didn't. I continued to drink and use drugs and women. I left these women when I was tired of them or when I felt they had gotten a little too close. I also left a lot of wreckage in the wake of my pursuit for some sense of peace and happiness. Drugs, alcohol, and sex never brought me any lasting relief from the intense isolation I felt.

I knew my second wife for only a month before I married her. Does this sound compulsive? Three months later I came to know Jesus Christ as my Lord and Savior. I'd like to say that at this point my inability to trust suddenly disappeared. But it didn't. It spilled right over into my relationship with God. I found it hard to trust Him because I didn't want to give up trying to control my life.

I found confidence in theology. I amassed quite a lot of Bible knowledge and felt as though I had the answers for everything and everyone— except me, of course. Without knowing it, I had become a Pharisee. I didn't understand just how much God cared about me. I became harsh, opinionated, and felt that everyone else was wrong except those in my own little group. My own little group was me.

During the next twenty-one years, my second wife and I had three kids. I went back to school, got two more degrees, ran a prison ministry for seven years, became an ordained pastor, planted a church, and established a sports ministry. The drugs had long since disappeared, and I chose not to drink to avoid putting a stumbling block in front of others. I was still motivated by fear and distrust. I was constantly driven to achieve and be recognized in order to find some shred of self-acceptance. The education and accomplishments couldn't do it. My life was a hopeless contradiction. As a pastor, who was I going to tell? Where was I going to go for help for my hurts?

Fifteen years into our marriage, my wife confessed to having had an affair. She confessed right after I had finished teaching about forgiveness. She sought it from me, and I felt obligated to give it. I was hurt and felt violated. I thought that granting forgiveness would take away the pain, but it didn't. I never processed the pain; I only stuffed it. Although I was always physically faithful to my wife, I had a number of mental affairs. I left the ministry.

I got into Christian therapy. I was willing to accept all the responsibility for my failed marriage and felt that everything was completely my fault. God brought a lot of healing this time and prepared me for His next step. When a friend suggested Celebrate Recovery to me, I thought he was mistaking me as one of "those people." I chose not to go. One day I was in a coffee shop reading my Bible, trying to deal with my anger on my own. A guy walked in wearing a Celebrate Recovery hat, and his name was Joe. I began to share my struggles with him, and he invited me to Celebrate Recovery. I agreed to attend that Friday.

When Joe was the first person I saw, I knew God had me there for a reason. Though I intended to go to the Men's Anger group, an old friend, Darrel, grabbed me and dragged me into the Friday night Men's Codependency group. A guy sitting across from me in the group looked familiar. When we introduced ourselves, he said, "I'm Jerry, a believer who struggles with codependency." I couldn't believe it was him. Nine years earlier, when I bought my house, I had my yard landscaped by this gifted and cocky guy. That night, after our small group ended, he invited me to join his new step study group. I got the Celebrate Recovery Workbooks and started working through the eight choices.

Celebrate Recovery and God's grace saved my sanity and my life. For the first time, I was able to tell everything about myself—who I was and what I felt—without any fear. My group listened to me, did not judge me, did not give me advice, and did not try to control me. They simply *loved and accepted me. For the first time in forty years, for the very first time, I saw God's unconditional love in action! I finally was able to make the second choice on the road to recovery:*

Getting HELP

CHOICE 2

Earnestly believe that God exists,

that I matter to Him, and that He
has the power to help me recover.

My story would be incomplete if I didn't share a very important breakthrough. God didn't just care about my situation, He wanted to change it! As I mentioned, I was sexually abused as a child. In my heart I had always hated the individuals who had done that to me. Yet God continued to show me that through His power, I could forgive them and be free of the hold they'd had on my life. I wrote both of these men letters I knew I couldn't send. I had no way of finding the first man. Regarding my family member, it was one of those issues that could seriously hurt the family. As I wrote the letters, I began to detail all the years of wreckage and pain that resulted from what they had done to me. I explained that I was extending forgiveness to them, that it wasn't about them but about me and God. Then I realized I didn't want them to suffer God's wrath for what they had done to me—the very thing I had hoped for my entire life. I began to weep. My anger melted away, and I felt only compassion. I began to pray for them, asking God to forgive them of their sins against me. How amazing, that in an instant, God changed my heart toward those I had hated for more than thirty-five years. I found myself weeping for their salvation.

During the past year of recovery, I have experienced more pain and shed more tears than I ever had before. I've revisited and reopened wounds that I had once hoped to bury. As I began to accept what I had done, what had been done to me, and to grieve openly, I found healing. My life has undergone a transformation, and God has given me miraculous hope. After my divorce from my second wife, I thought I could never open my heart to a woman again. Thankfully, I was wrong. God has brought into my life the most precious and wonderful woman I've ever known, my new bride, Lori. Through her I've come to understand God's love and grace as never before.

Today I accept that I am a person of value. I matter to God and to others. God loves me, others love me, and I love others. My value comes not from my achievements or education but from the simple fact that I am created in the image of God. Because of the infinite love and grace of God through Jesus, I am the object of His love.

I've learned that recovery is a journey, a process of continual growth rather than a destination. I've learned that to struggle is normal and a pathway to peace. I've also learned that to be reasonably happy in this life is as good as it gets.

Finally, I've learned I can trust God and others. My friends in recovery are the most real, accepting, and precious people I know. They struggle, but aren't in denial about it. They are just like me. And I was wrong; I am "one of those people," and thankfully so. My life verse is:

> "Christ died for all so that those who live
> would not continue to live for themselves.
> He died for them and was raised from the dead
> so that they would live for him."[25]

Mary and Tim are two courageous individuals with two life-changing stories! The longer they chose to postpone their pain, the further they moved from God's healing and recovery. The longer they denied and postponed dealing with their pain, the fewer days they had being all God meant for them to be. And the same goes for you. The longer you try to flee from your pain, your hurts, hang-ups, and habits, the fewer days you have being all God meant for you to be. Today can be a new beginning for you.

R
E

Consciously choose

to *commit* all my life and will
to Christ's care and control.

"*Happy are the meek.*" [1]

O
V
E
R
Y

Letting GO

The COMMITMENT Choice

A pet-store delivery-truck driver was traveling down the road. Every time he came to a stoplight, he would get out of the truck and grab a two-by-four. Then he'd run to the back and start beating on the truck's back doors. This went on for several miles, and nobody could figure out what he was doing. Finally the guy who had been behind him pulled alongside and just had to ask, "What are you doing?"

"This is only a two-ton truck," the truck driver said, "and I'm carrying four tons of canaries. I've got to keep two tons of them up in the air all the time."

That's how some of us try to live our lives. We take desperate measures, trying to keep our life's hurts, hang-ups, and habits up in the air so they don't come crashing down around us. We try so hard to keep up a good front—pretending that everything is okay—when in reality, we're struggling with real pain and real issues that we desperately try to ignore.

Then we get stuck. We get stuck trying to keep it all together while our world is falling apart. We get stuck in unhealthy relationships and in addictive habits. We get stuck in grief or sexual relationships. We get stuck, and we cannot get unstuck on our own power—and so despair sets in.

71

We start feeling *guilty* about our behavior. We wish we could get out of our mess, but we can't. After a lot of failed attempts, we get *angry* with ourselves and others: "I should be able to change. I ought to be able to get out of this." But we can't, and our anger grows. Over time, our anger turns to the *fear* that things are never going to change. We begin to realize that our hurts, hang-ups, and habits are controlling us, and our fear eventually turns to *depression*. We start feeling sorry for ourselves, and we become filled with yet more guilt.

Finally, we give up and say, "I can't change. I quit." The cycle of despair starts all over again!

CYCLE OF DESPAIR

How do you break out of the cycle of despair? If you've followed through on the choices in the first two chapters of this book, you're already moving out of this vicious cycle: you've made the "reality choice," where you admitted your need. You've also taken the "hope choice," believing that you matter to God and that He has the power to help you.

Now you are ready for the "commitment choice" where you make the decision to walk across the line. You take a step across that line of decision—a step *toward* God that says you are giving it all to Him and a step *away* from the old way of doing it all yourself. If you haven't made this choice as yet, it will be the most important choice in your life—the choice to accept Christ. For others, who have already chosen Christ, this choice will mean a renewed commitment to let go of their lives and give them over to Christ's care and control.

Letting GO

CHOICE 3

Consciously choose to commit all my life and will to Christ's care and control.

Right now, Jesus is reaching out to you, waiting for you to step across that line and into His open arms: *"Come to me, all of you who are weary and overburdened, and I will give you rest! Put on my yoke and learn from me. For I am gentle and humble in heart and you will find rest for your souls. For my yoke is easy and my burden is light."*[2]

"Come to me," Jesus says. "Your life will be easier, your load lighter. You will have relief, release, and rest. You will be rejuvenated. Give Me the control and care of your life, and watch what I do for you."

What an amazing deal! Why would anybody turn Him down? Yet many have heard this invitation before but never walked across that line. Choosing to step across that line into Christ's care and control is the most important decision you will ever make.

WHAT'S HOLDING YOU BACK?

What's holding you back? What is delaying your decision to surrender your problems and your life to the care and control of Christ? It has been said that our choices determine our circumstances and our decisions determine our destiny. There are five things that keep us from making this third choice: *pride, guilt, fear, worry*, and *doubt*.

1. PRIDE

Pride often keeps us from admitting we need God's help. *"No one is respected unless he is humble, arrogant people are on the way to ruin."*[3] This proverb presents a pretty clear picture of those of us who think we can do it on our own: *"A self-sufficient fool falls flat on his face."*[4]

> *God doesn't ask you to be weak, but he does ask you to* LAY DOWN *your pride and be meek.*

"Happy are the meek," says the beatitude for this choice. But many equate meekness with weakness. In reality, meekness and weakness are at opposite ends of the spectrum. In fact, the Greek work for meekness actually means "strength under control." The word is used to describe a wild stallion that is tamed and taught to be ridden. That stallion still has all its strength, but now its strength is under control, ready for its master's use. God doesn't ask you to be weak, but He does ask you to lay down your pride and be meek. Meekness is surrender; it is submitting; it is agreeing to do what God wants done in your life.

Maybe you're not ready to take this life-changing choice. Your pride may still be keeping you from committing your "life and will to Christ's care and control." Perhaps you need a greater dose of pain. If that's what's needed, God may allow this to happen in order to finally get your attention.

2. GUILT

Guilt is another thing that will keep us from walking across that line and into God's arms. We may be ashamed to ask God to help us: *"Problems far too big for me to solve are piled higher than my head. Meanwhile my sins, too many to count, have all caught up with me, and I am ashamed to look up.*"[5] Have you ever felt that way? Have you ever felt ashamed to look up? Our guilt can make us ashamed to ask God for help.

Maybe you've tried to make deals with God: "God, if You just get me out of this mess, I will never do it again!" Now, you may be embarrassed to ask Him for help. Or you may think God doesn't know all the things you've done wrong and won't forgive you. You're wrong; He knows. Even though He knows it all, there is no sin that God cannot or will not forgive. He wants to forgive all your guilt. That's why Christ went to the cross!

3. FEAR

Are you afraid of what you might have to give up if you surrender the care and control of your life to Christ? Fear takes many forms.

1. Sometimes we're afraid to trust God. There's a story about a guy who falls off a cliff. Halfway down he grabs on to a branch, and he's hanging on for dear life—he can see five hundred feet down and five hundred feet up. He cries out, "Somebody help!" Suddenly, he hears the voice of God, "This is the Lord, trust Me, let go, and I'll catch you." The guy looks back down at the five hundred feet below and back up again. Then he calls out, "Is there anybody else up there?"

Sometimes we turn to God only as our last resort—we're afraid to let go and trust Him. Right now you may be hanging on to that branch for dear life, saying, "Things aren't that bad. No problem, really. I'm fine." No, you are not fine. You are just afraid of letting go and trusting Him.

2. Sometimes we're afraid of losing control. But the truth of the matter is that we're all controlled by someone or something at all times. To some extent you're controlled by the way your parents brought you up. You're controlled by the opinions of other people. You're controlled by hurts you can't forget. You're controlled by your hang-ups and habits.

Part of our control issue is fear of losing our freedom. But do you know what real freedom is? True, lasting freedom is choosing who controls you. When you give the care and control of your life to Christ, He sets you free. God said, *"I have swept away your sins like the morning mists. I have scattered your offenses like the clouds. Oh, return to me, for I have paid the price to set you free."*[6]

3. *Sometimes we're afraid of becoming a religious fanatic.* Maybe you've been afraid to open your life to the care and control of Christ because you think He might turn you into a fanatic, a religious nut. But Jesus does the exact opposite: He brings sanity where insanity has had its way.

The Bible tells a story of a man who was filled with demons. He lived in the cemetery, among the tombs, and was so wild and out of control that the local people had tried to bind him up, but he was too strong for them. The demons tormented him—like some of your inner "demons" may torment you—and he cried out day and night and cut himself with stones (it's interesting that cutting has resurfaced as a current destructive way to deal with inner pain). But when he saw Jesus, he *walked across that line to him.* The Bible says, *"When Jesus was still some distance away, the man saw him. He ran to meet Jesus and fell down before him."* After Jesus called the demons out of that man, the people found him *"sitting there fully clothed and perfectly sane."*[7] No . . . Jesus does not turn us into religious fanatics; He puts us in our right minds and makes us *perfectly sane.*

So what are you afraid of? What are you holding on to that makes you think, *I can't let go?* Is it a relationship, an ambition, a habit, a lifestyle, or a possession? God's Word asks this: *"How does a man benefit if he gains the whole world and loses his soul in the process? For is anything worth more than his soul?"*[8]

When you make this third choice, you give up everything to God's control. God takes what you give Him, He cleans it up, and He turns it around. He adds new meaning, new purpose, new significance, and new vitality to your life, and He gives it back to you in a whole new way.

Don't worry about the specifics of what you may have to give up. If you focus on the specifics, you'll never make the greater decision, which is taking the step toward a personal relationship with Jesus Christ. Just come to God and say, "God, I don't even know what I don't want to give up. I just know I don't want to live this way anymore, and I know I want my life to be under Your control. God, here is a blank check. Here's my life." All you have to do is trust Him. He will take care of the rest.

4. WORRY

Worry causes us to confuse the *decision-making* phase with the *problem-solving* phase. Consider the process of buying a house. First, you make the initial *decision* to buy the house. That's only the beginning. There are several more *problem-solving* steps that must be taken before you can actually move in. You need to go to the bank and apply for the loan. You need to get an appraisal and complete the escrow. Then you have to contact the moving company and set up the utilities. All of this has to be done before you spend the first night in your new home! If you focus on the "problems"—the individual tasks involved in making your dream a reality—you may never make the decision to buy the house. Make the decision; let God worry about problem solving.

5. DOUBT

Have you ever thought, *I want to believe, but my faith is too small?* If so, you need to know the story found in the Bible in Mark chapter 5, about a guy named Jairus.

One day Jairus came to Jesus with a need: "Jesus, I know You can heal people, and my daughter needs to be healed."

Jesus said, "If you have faith, then she will be healed."

Jairus was an honest guy, and so he told Jesus the truth: "Lord, I've got a lot of doubts. I want to believe; help me with my unbelief."

Jesus said, "That's good enough." And He healed the girl.

Maybe you need to say with Jairus, "God, I want to believe that You will help me with my life; help me with my unbelief." *That's good enough.* You don't have to have a big faith to decide to give Christ the care and control of your life. As a matter of fact, *"If you have faith as small as a mustard seed . . . nothing will be impossible for you."*[9]

It's not the *size* of your faith that matters; it's the *who* or *what* you put your faith in that matters. You can have a giant faith and put it in the wrong things—like money and possessions—and come up empty. Or you can have a little faith and put it in our big God and get amazing results.

The bottom line is this: don't let any of these five things keep you from making this third choice. Do not let your pride, your guilt, your fear, your worry, or your doubt stop you from committing your life and will to Christ's care and control. First you make the decision, then you go about solving the problems. Your decision: "I open my life to the care and control of Christ. I don't know how it's all going to work out, but I know it's the right thing to do. So I'm just going to do it."

BEGINNING TO MOVE FORWARD

The Christian life is a decision followed by a process. All this third choice is asking us to do is make the decision. The process will follow! At the end of this chapter, you'll read the stories of Lisa and Charlie, and you'll see how their lives changed when they made the decision to ask Christ to take the care and control of their lives. But for now let's see what it means for you to *step across that line and into the arms of Jesus.*

It all begins with a simple two-step process. You can easily see this process by comparing it to the strategy our military forces used in World War II. In the Pacific when they freed an island from Japanese occupation, they used the same strategy on every island, and it worked every time.

> *It's NOT the size of your faith that matters; it's the WHO or WHAT you put your faith in that matters.*

PHASE 1: SOFTENING UP

First, the planes would fly to the island that had been taken captive, and they would start dropping bombs and various explosives. This part of the strategy was called the "softening-up period." Many of you are in the softening-up period right now. All kinds of explosions are going off in your life, sending fragments everywhere. You're saying, "Life isn't working anymore, and quite honestly, it hasn't been for a long time." You may have come to the point where you're saying, "Yes, I need something beyond myself. My hurts, hang-ups, and habits are softening up my pride, guilt, fears, worries, and doubts. I need help. I need God in my life."

PHASE 2: ESTABLISHING A BEACHHEAD

In the second phase, the marines would establish a beachhead. It may have been only twenty yards deep and two hundred yards wide, but they would get a presence on the island. By establishing the beachhead, had they completely liberated the island? No. The beachhead was just the beginning. It was from the beachhead that they began to fight the battles. Sometimes they would move one hundred yards forward, and sometimes they would get pushed back fifty. Sometimes they won the battle, and sometimes they lost. But everybody knew that once they had established a beachhead, total liberation of the island was inevitable. In the history of World War II, once the marines landed and established a beachhead, they never lost an island. It was just a matter of time until the entire island would be set free.

When you make this third choice, God establishes a beachhead in your life. The Bible calls it conversion, or being born again. Does it mean that everything in your life is perfect? Absolutely not. But it means that God has a presence in your life; He's got a beachhead. For the rest of your life, He will be setting you free from your hurts, hang-ups, and habits—little by little. It's a process. But first you have to trust God to take care of you.

HE WON'T LET YOU GO

Are you worried that in this battle of life you won't be able to hold on? Don't worry. *It's not your job to hold on*. God will do the holding, and He won't ever let you go! God's Word assures us, *"And you also were included in Christ when you heard the word of truth, the gospel of your salvation. Having believed, you were marked in him with a seal, the promised Holy Spirit."*[10] When you put your faith in Christ, you are brought into fellowship with Him—you become *His*. And even beyond that, you are marked with a seal—a sign to all that you belong to Him. He will not let you go! You are His beloved child.

We understand the protective feeling a parent has for his or her child. If you were to help your small child cross a busy street, you would grab hold of his or her hand. As you were walking across the street, your child might, as little children do, want to let go. But no matter how much your child wanted to let go of your hand, you wouldn't let go. Why? Because you are a loving parent.

There are times in your life when you might say, "God, I don't think I want to be under Your care right now." Sometimes you might want to take back control and let go of God's hand. But once we grab on to His hand, God holds on tight. He says, "I'll hold on so you don't have to worry about it."

I made the decision to ask Christ into my heart when I was thirteen years old. When I went to college, I chose to follow my own way. In fact, for the next nineteen years I followed the world's way. But no matter how hard I tried to run, how many times I sinned, or how many poor choices I made, God never let go of my hand. My way left me empty and broken. When I was finally ready to truly repent and surrender, God was right there with me. It was then I truly understood His unconditional love and freely given grace.

Whatever God *asks* you to do, He will *enable* you to do. Just rely on Him as He holds tightly to your hand: "*God who began the good work within you will keep right on helping you to grow in his grace until his task within you is finally finished on that day when Jesus Christ returns.*"[11]

STEPPING ACROSS THE LINE

We've talked a lot about making the choice to commit our lives and wills to Christ's care and control. Let's see how you do that, step by step:

1. ACCEPT GOD'S SON AS YOUR SAVIOR

The first thing you need to do is admit that you need to be saved and accept Jesus as your Savior: The Bible says, "*Believe in the Lord Jesus, and you will be saved.*"[12] What does this mean? It means committing as much of your life and will to Christ as you can, at this moment. Is that good enough? Yes, *that is good enough.*

2. ACCEPT GOD'S WORD AS YOUR STANDARD

Once you make the choice to commit your life and will to Christ, you have—from now on—a manual to live your life by. Some people say, "This life is a test; it is only a test. Had it been an actual life, you would have been given an instruction manual to tell you what to do and where to go."

What they're missing is that we *do* have an instruction manual: it's the Bible. God says it is your standard by which you evaluate life. *"All Scripture is inspired by God and is useful for teaching the faith and correcting error, for resetting the direction of a man's life and training him in good living."*[13]

3. ACCEPT GOD'S WILL AS YOUR PURPOSE

The first thing we need to say as we rise each day is, "Lord, You woke me up this morning. This obviously means You have another day planned for me, a day with a purpose. What do You want me to do with it?" In the psalms, David says, *"My God, I want to do what you want. Your teachings are in my heart."*[14] Inspired by David, you can say, "God, I don't even have to understand everything right now. But, I choose to live my life on Your terms because You made me for a reason. You have a purpose, and I want to fulfill that purpose." As you grow with God, His will becomes your strategy for life.

4. ACCEPT GOD'S POWER AS YOUR STRENGTH

This becomes your power statement: *"I can do everything God asks me to with the help of Christ who gives me the strength and power."*[15] No longer do you have to rely on your own energy. God gives you His power to be all He wants you to be.

Are you ready to step across that line? Jesus extends His invitation: *"Look! Here I stand at the door and knock. If you hear me calling and open the door, I will come in, and we will share a meal as friends."*[16] Jesus is standing at the door of your life, saying He wants to come into your life. But He is a gentleman; He will not beat the door down. In this third choice, we need to open the door and let Him in, and the key that unlocks that door is willingness.

Being willing means changing our definition of *willpower*. Our willpower needs to become the *willingness to accept God's power*. We don't need more self-will; we've already tried to run our lives on our own willpower, and it has left us broken and empty. Now it's time to exchange willpower for the willingness to accept God's power to run our lives.

If you are ready to make this choice and commit your life to Christ's care and control, just answer the following questions:

1. Do you believe Jesus Christ died on the cross for you and proved He was God by coming back to life?[17]

2. Do you accept God's free forgiveness for your sins?[18]

3. Do you want to switch to God's plan for your life?[19]

4. Are you ready to express your desire for Christ to be the director of your life?[20]

If you answered yes to those four questions, it's time to make your decision a reality by making the choice.

MAKE THE *Choice*

ACTION 1: *Pray about It*

It's time to ask Christ into your life. You can do that by praying this simple prayer:

> Dear God, I believe You sent Your Son, Jesus, to die for my sins so I can be forgiven. I'm sorry for my sins, and I want to live the rest of my life the way You want me to. Please put Your Spirit in my life to direct me. Amen.

Congratulations! If you prayed that prayer for the first time, welcome to God's family! Please do not feel you need to understand everything about the commitment you just made. Understanding will come as you grow and mature in your walk with Christ. For now, let these words be your comfort: Jesus says, *"Are you tired? Worn out? Burned out on religion? Come to me. Get away with me and you'll recover your life. I'll show you how to take a real rest. Walk with me and work with me—watch how I do it. Learn the unforced rhythms of grace. I won't lay anything heavy or ill-fitting on you. Keep company with me and you'll learn to live freely and lightly."*[21]

There's more good news! *"What this means is that those who become Christians become new persons. They are not the same anymore, for the old life is gone. A new life has begun!"*[22] As you complete the remaining five choices, your life will never be the same. Your new life has begun!

If you have previously asked Christ into your heart, use this prayer time to commit to continually seek and follow His will for your life.

ACTION 2: *Write about It*

Take some time to reflect on the commitment you just made—whether it was your first commitment to Christ or a renewed commitment to continually turn everything over to His care. Committing to Christ is the most important decision you will ever make. You will never be alone again. As you begin your journaling for this chapter, start off by answering the following questions, which will help you organize your thoughts and emotions:

1. Go back to choice 1, page 24 under "Action 2: Write about It." Reread your answers to questions 1 through 3. Write about how you feel different about them today.

2. How do you feel, now that the burden of trying to control all the people, places, or things in your life has been lifted from you?[23]

3. What does the following phrase mean to you? *"The old life is gone. A new life has begun!"*[24]

4. What are some of the first things you will ask God to do in your new life?

5. What are you having a difficult time letting go of? What is stopping you from turning these things over to God's control?

ACTION 3: *Share about It*

It's important that you share your decision to ask Christ into your life with others. Follow God's direction found in His Word: *"If you confess with your mouth, 'Jesus is Lord,' and believe in your heart that God raised him from the dead, you will be saved."*[25] Each time you share your decision, it reconfirms your commitment. Your sharing also lets others know the reason for the freedom and joy you now have in your life.

Celebrate the "Good News" of your commitment with the person you have chosen to be your accountability partner. Let him or her know how you are feeling and what led you to turn the care and control of your life over to Christ. Be sure to share the things you are having a difficult time letting go of (your answer to question 5 on page 24).

Ask your accountability partner to pray with and for you. As you pray together, thank God for your willingness to make the one-time decision to ask Christ into your life as your Lord and Savior. Pray that you will daily choose to seek and follow God's will for your new life.

You've made it through the third choice. You are well on your way to a happier, healthier life—one lived in your Father's will, by His power and not your own.

Lisa's STORY

My name is Lisa. I'm a believer who is recovering from overeating and sexual abuse. I am also married to a recovering sex addict. This is my story of how taking the third choice of recovery—to commit my life and will to Christ's care and control, accepting Christ as my Lord and Savior—has freed me from my past hurts, hang-ups, and habits.

My parents split up when I was nine years old. My mom left in the middle of the night, taking nothing with her, including my brother and me. We didn't see her again for about one year. When we were reunited with Mom, her new boyfriends abused me, both physically and sexually.

It was not uncommon for me to see my mom being beaten by her men friends. I can remember the feeling of being totally helpless to stop it. Even when I called the police, she would send them away. Once Mom even ended up in the hospital. I saw her and her boyfriends pull knives on each other and threaten to kill each other.

While fighting with my mom, one of her boyfriends smashed an ashtray on the kitchen counter and cut his hand with the glass. He took me and my brother to our room and spread blood all over the door. He said that if he heard us, or if we came out of the room, he would kill us. From our room we could hear Mom screaming and crying.

Then one day, while I was home alone with him, he molested me. I was twelve years old. After that I began to shake anytime he, or any adult man, would get near me. I frequently had horrible nightmares. I learned that love meant being abused and giving sex. I started doing drugs, drinking, and being promiscuous at age fifteen. I would do anything to try to stop the pain and to be loved by someone, anyone.

I got married when I was nineteen, and that was the last day I saw my mom. Not because she didn't approve of my marriage, which she didn't, but because she was murdered five days later. She was stabbed to death in her home in the middle of the night. Whoever did it set fire to her home in an attempt to cover up the murder. Today, more than twenty years later, her murder remains unsolved. It was undoubtedly a result of the many violent relationships my mom chose with men.

My first marriage was short-lived but produced great rewards, my two sons, Eric and Jason. My husband was volatile and a periodic blackout drinker. He would call me in the middle of the night from wherever he was drinking. He would tell me to get up and leave, because he was bringing his new girlfriend home. He was very controlling and told me what clothes to wear, how to fix my hair, and whether I could work or not work. He would not allow me to have any friends.

After our divorce I stayed single for four years. I dated and chose to sleep with many different men. I became pregnant two times during this destructive period of my life. My way of dealing with the first pregnancy was to have an abortion. I gave my second baby up for adoption. I cannot begin to share the shame and guilt I felt over those two decisions. Today I know the cost of my sin. The only way I can live with my past mistakes is through God's grace and complete forgiveness.

My second marriage was worse than the first! I chose the same man, just a different name and face. He drank and did drugs. He called me foul names and frequently threatened to hurt me. I always thought I was doing okay because neither of my husbands ever actually hit me. I gauged the relationships by my childhood experiences, and they were no way near as bad as my mom's! I lived out my belief that love equals abuse and sex. I tried a new way to ease my pain: I found the joy of chocolate! My two new best friends were "Ben & Jerry."

In May 1992, I walked into Saddleback, a large church that met near my home. I was in the middle of my second divorce from an alcoholic, abusive, sexually addicted husband, and I had not been in a church in about ten years. I don't remember what the title of the message was, but I do remember I thought Pastor Rick was speaking right to me. How did he know what I was going through? I cried through the whole service. I felt warmth and love from the church members, and after the service I realized I had found my new church home.

I had just met Peter, a guy who had a newspaper route at the same warehouse where I worked. He was cute, sweet, and made me laugh. We began meeting after our routes for coffee and donuts. I soon learned that Peter drank and that a wall in his room was covered with pornography. But by this point in my life, I thought all men were like this, so it seemed normal to me. Besides, I thought I could eventually love him enough to change him!

I invited Peter to church one Sunday, and he agreed to go. He was very apprehensive because he had been raised in a legalistic Christian church. He had walked away from God long before he met me. At this point he had really long hair and earrings. He smoked, drank, and there was the pornography. He was sure they would not even let him in the front door of the church. He was shocked to be greeted and welcomed, and he loved the church as much as I did. However, because we were living together, we eventually felt too guilty to keep attending. Peter decided we should stop going, and as his good codependent girlfriend, I agreed.

It did not take long for our relationship to become pretty miserable. I began to resent Peter's pornography and drinking. I was working two jobs while Peter worked part-time and took care of my eight- and ten-year-old sons. He took them to and from school, cleaned house, and did the laundry. Sometimes I would come home from work and find that he had spent the whole day watching adult videos.

My resentment and anger grew. I finally found a way to let Peter know how I felt. I made the choice to have an affair with an old boyfriend. I wanted to hurt Peter as much as his "magazine girlfriends" had hurt me. I had tried everything to be whatever Peter wanted in a woman. I even rented the videos for him. However, deep down, I felt degraded and unloved. I was not pretty enough, thin enough, or sexy enough to compete with the women in the videos.

As our relationship continued to fall apart, we remembered Saddleback, the church we had loved so much. We knew they had pastors on call for counseling. We called and made an appointment. That weekend we attended church again for the first time in about six months. Pastor Rick was doing a series of messages about recovery. A man gave his testimony about being an alcoholic and how God had transformed him and saved his marriage. God had given him a vision for a Christian recovery ministry; he called it Celebrate Recovery. It had started at Saddleback about a year earlier. During this sermon series on recovery, Pastor Rick had people share how God was transforming their lives through Celebrate Recovery. By God-incidence (my new word for coincidence), the man who gave his testimony that Sunday "just happened" to be the pastor on call when Peter and I came into the church office for help. His name was Pastor John Baker. We shared everything that had happened in our relationship and how we wanted to get married in the church.

Pastor John was very compassionate and lovingly confronted us about the way we were living. He told us that if we wanted to get married in the church, we needed to stop living together. He said that we had to remain abstinent until after we were married. During our session, I talked about being sexually abused as a child. I also told Pastor John that there was a period of time in my childhood that I could not even remember. John recommended that we both begin attending the church's recovery program and that I see a Christian therapist.

The day before my appointment with the therapist, I had a conflict with Peter. We had been trying to be abstinent, but were still sleeping in the same bed. Talk about insanity! I woke up in the middle of the night with Peter not wanting to take no for an answer. The next day I confronted Peter and told him I thought he was a sex addict. I had heard about it on a radio program while driving home from work. All of Peter's behaviors fit the description of someone struggling with sexual addiction. Peter completely denied that sexual addiction was his problem. He just had a "high sex drive." I remembered hearing that from my first husband too.

I asked Peter to go with me for my first counseling appointment. I told him I wanted him to come because I was afraid to go by myself. The truth was, I had told the counselor that the only reason I was making an appointment was because my boyfriend thought I needed help—but I didn't. We arrived, and I spilled out my whole life story to this sweet woman. She listened and showed so much compassion that I believed I could trust her. At the end of our session, Peter said, "By the way, do you know anything about sexual addiction?" It was her specialty—another God-incidence! She gave Peter some material about sexual addiction and told him to read it.

After reading the material, Peter admitted he was a sex addict and wanted to get help. He began attending secular Sex Addict meetings because the Celebrate Recovery sexual addiction group had not yet started. At Celebrate Recovery he attended the Chemically Addicted group and began to get sober from alcohol.

It took me a while to know I needed to attend Recovery too. I thought as long as Peter "got fixed," he would stop being a sex addict and then we could get married. I believed the only problems I had were the lousy men I kept picking.

My therapist recommended I start attending the Celebrate Recovery group for sexual abuse. I went, under protest. Then I realized I could check up on Peter and make sure he was going to his group. I loved that idea! The first night I was petrified. I could not "share." I was very shy and hated it when people would look at me when I talked.

After a month or so of attending the group, a woman shared my life story through her own words. It was her life, but it was exactly like mine. I could not believe it! I felt like it was a sign from God that I was safe and that I could safely share too. I opened up for the first time. I told the women in that group about experiences I had never told anyone. I had believed these things were in the past and no longer affected me. The pain and tears were overwhelming, and at times I did not think I could continue. However, being a part of that group and sharing openly with these women was a life-changing event for me. They knew all about me and still loved and accepted me.

Within the next few months, Celebrate Recovery started a Sexual Addiction group. Peter began getting sober from his sexual addiction, as well as from alcohol. We committed to being abstinent, even though we were living together. Peter made a room in the garage, and his mom even sent him a heated blanket so he could be warm out there in the winter. We quit smoking, too, but I was not about to give up my chocolate!

One night we had an argument about continuing to live together even though we were being abstinent. Peter was still struggling with employment, and I did not think he was trying hard enough to get a job so he could move out. The argument continued late into the evening, and finally Peter stormed out of our apartment. He was so angry. I did not know what he was going to do. It was 11:30 at night, and I was worried and angry.

He returned home at 1:00 a.m., announcing that he would be moving out the next day. My first question was "What's her name?" Peter laughed at me and said he had walked across the street to Saddleback Church. He went to the three tall wooden crosses that were on the property. One of them had the nails representing Jesus's death on the cross. Peter told me how he'd sat there and prayed and cried. He wrote a list of all the things he wanted to turn over to God, including his need for a place to live and our desire to get married in the church. He shoved the list on the bottom nail of the cross and walked away crying. Immediately he saw someone and thought it was an angel, but it was the night security guard. He asked Peter why he was crying and if he could help. Peter explained our situation and the man said, "I just rented a big house and I have an extra room; you can come live with me for free until you get married." Definitely God-incidence!

Peter moved out, and we started premarital counseling at the church. We were married December 17, 1994, at Saddleback Church. Pastor John, who had counseled us that first day we came to the church for help, performed our ceremony. Our whole new Celebrate Recovery family was a part of our special day. They provided the food for the reception, helped with wedding decorations, and served in a hundred different ways. It was one of the most incredible days of my life. My sons were involved: Jason walked me down the aisle, and Eric was the best man. Peter said vows to them during our ceremony. There was not a dry eye in the church.

For the past thirteen years since our wedding, Peter and I have continued to grow in our intimacy with each other and with God. I finally realized that having true joy and peace in my life was not going to be found in sex, drugs, food (even chocolate), or any human man. I could only find it in a personal relationship with Jesus Christ. That's what the third choice did for me. When I made the decision to . . .

CHOICE 3

Letting Go

Consciously choose to commit
all my life and will to Christ's care and control.

Through my relationship with Jesus, I have been able to forgive those who abused me, ask forgiveness from those I have hurt, and realize that Jesus forgave me on the cross more than two thousand years ago. Now I can forgive myself and break my cycle of despair. I can live my life in response to God's grace, not in pursuit of it.

I am forever grateful for what God has done in my life. He has given me a church family to love me, hold me accountable, and to do this life together with purpose and passion. It has been the thrill of my life to help other couples who have struggled with issues similar to ours. God has turned my sorrow and pain into joy and a purpose for living.

The following has become one of my life's verses:

"He turned my sorrow into joy!
He took away my clothes of mourning
and clothed me with joy."[26]

Charlie's STORY

My name is Charlie, and I am a believer in recovery from sexual addiction, alcohol, and drugs. I grew up in a small West Texas oil town with devout Christian parents. Both my mother and father were involved in the local school system. They were also very involved in our church. They served as Sunday school superintendent and on the board of elders. At home, however, my mother was cold and unaffectionate, and my father was a strict disciplinarian and used corporal punishment often. I used to hide in the closet when my father would rage about one of his disappointments in my behavior.

I had two older sisters. When Linda, my oldest sister, was eight years old, she contracted an infection while hunting with my father. The doctor recommended a minor operation to treat the infection. In 1949, small hospitals in Texas did not always test for allergies to anesthetics. Linda was allergic to ether and died immediately, even before the operation began. Her death became the "pink elephant" in our house that no one was ever allowed to talk about. As the years went by, my mother silently blamed my father. He bore his shame and guilt deep down and treated Linda's memory as if she were a saintly martyr.

Linda had been my father's favorite child. My older sister Ann, who excelled in academics and intellectual abilities, was my mother's favorite child. That left me to take care of myself. In an effort to carve out a place for myself in the family, I tried making good grades. I made all A's and was an honor student. But one of my teachers, who had also taught my sister a few years earlier, told me in front of the class, "Charles, you are smart, but you are sure no Ann!"

Since excelling in academics was not enough, I also tried achieving acceptance from my father through athletics. I lettered in football, basketball, track, and baseball. My father had been a star athlete at Texas A&M University. No matter how well I did, his critique of my performance let me know that I once again failed to measure up.

I got my growth spurt early and was six feet tall and a hundred and seventy pounds in the ninth grade. I started dating high-school girls and hanging out with the varsity football players. The football legends of West Texas seemed to always have a reputation for wildness, heavy drinking, fights, carousing around, and then setting records on the football field. I grew to find the acceptance I had always sought by having the prettiest girl in school as my girlfriend. Not only did I get validation from her, but also from everyone else. They seemed to think that I must be someone special to have her as "mine."

My junior year in high school, I got my girlfriend pregnant. I believed I was in love, and between her parents and mine, we convinced her to marry me. It was the only honorable thing to do. Although I was still in high school, I worked nights at a truck stop and weekends at a mobile-home factory. One Sunday morning I came home to find the house cleaned and a note from my wife saying that she had left the state with no forwarding address. She wrote that she had never loved me and that our child did not need a father. I was devastated by her abandonment.

I then faced my new future and pursued sports once again. However, the school board had a rule stating that students who had been married could not participate in extracurricular activities. So my father helped get me into New Mexico Military Institute to play football. Before taking me to Roswell, New Mexico, my father reminded me of the consequences of my prior decisions. He said, "You may be able to leave this town, but your mother and I still have to live and work with these people!" Talk about shame and guilt. I was stuck in the cycle of despair. The Eagle Scout and athletic hero had just been run out of town on a rail.

It was in military school that I chose to start smoking pot, using drugs, and staying drunk, all while maintaining a 3.8 GPA. Strangely enough, when I was "high," I felt like I was finally in control. But when I sobered up, I felt like a true outcast. I did everything I could to live up to the reputation of a tough, wild football player you never want to cross or confront. No one ever knew when I would fly off the handle.

I continued my quest to be accepted by my father by playing football at Texas A&M University, his alma mater. I continued my heavy use of drugs and alcohol. I injured my shoulder and knee in the beginning of my junior year and had to drop out of football.

I had disappointed my parents once again. I then moved in with a girl from my English and theater class. She wanted an Aggie football player, even an injured one, and I wanted someone to accept me and fix my life. We thought we both found what we wanted. We got married and had two children. After ten years of living with an alcoholic and adulterer, my wife had had enough, and we got divorced. Every time things went wrong, I blamed her and sought someone else to validate me. After this divorce, I went on to repeat the same pattern again with wife number three and child number four.

All this time I attended church faithfully. I was on the board of deacons, taught Sunday school, and lived a double life—one respectable and the other a dark secret. I thought I could hide my dark side from everyone else. I knew I could never live up to my father's performance criteria. So how could I ever really be good enough for my heavenly Father's love and acceptance?

In August 1997 I hit my rock bottom. As I drove my 1976 Ford LTD into Bakersfield, California, I blew out the engine at three o'clock in the morning. I sat in a fleabag hotel for three days waiting to see if my only means of transportation could be fixed. Needless to say, I had a lot of time to look at my life. After years of making poor choices, I had no material possessions, three failed marriages, four estranged children, no job, no friends, no food, and no money. All I had was a lifetime of trying to fill the hole in my heart with sex, alcohol, drugs, pornographic videos and magazines, countless affairs, fast money, fast times, high-risk jobs, and living on the edge. All the things I sought to ease the pain, I came to realize, only made things worse.

I could no longer go on living this way. I could not bear the guilt, the pain, the shame, and the disappointment. I was a hopeless failure in my own eyes and, I thought, in God's. I came to see my life as it truly was; I didn't believe it could get any better or any worse, for that matter. When

I found out that my car was a total loss, I called a man who used to work for me who lived in Vista, California. I asked him to pick me up at the Greyhound bus station in Carlsbad. I had just enough for bus fare.

By this time I admitted I was powerless over my addictions and compulsive nature and that my life had become unmanageable. I contacted a therapist through my company's insurance program. He was a Christian who did wonders helping me see the roots of my addictive and codependent nature. I told Vicky, my new girlfriend, about my excitement in this new process. She told me about the Celebrate Recovery program she was attending. I didn't truly believe this type of program could help me, but if this was how I could get a date, then okay. I drove up from San Diego every Friday night for a year—a 160-mile round trip!

At first I thought I had never seen such a collection of whining, warped, pathetic people in all my life. After all, there was not so much a problem with me, but just with the people and circumstances around me. Then the light seemed to come on. I had already been through a secular twelve-step, court-ordered program. It did not work for me. I decided to give Celebrate Recovery a try. I got a sponsor, the Bible, and the Celebrate Recovery Participant Guides and really started working the program.

After working through the first two choices, I was more than ready for choice 3:

Letting Go

CHOICE 3

Consciously choose to commit
all my life and will to Christ's care and control.

I had tried it all and came up empty. I cannot begin to explain the freedom and the peace I experienced when I was finally able to let go and let

God have control and care of my life. I opened my heart and my mind and allowed all the feelings of the pain of my past to come out. I learned to rely on Jesus to guide me through this difficult time. I analyzed my past honestly, letting the truth be the truth. My accountability partner was very important in helping me stay balanced. I still have a tendency to focus on my poor choices and beat up on myself. But with each passing day I understand Christ's grace and complete forgiveness just a little bit more.

I would like to say that everything is rosy in my life now, without trouble and pain, but it's not. However, today when those trials come my way, I have a different reaction to them. Because of the decision I made in choice 3, all my life's joys, victories, trials, and hurts are now under Christ's care and control. He has restored my health, my career, the relationships with my family, and most of all, an intimate love relationship with Him.

My twenty-one-year-old daughter recently returned to college in Las Vegas. We communicate regularly through e-mail and phone calls. I was able to console my oldest son, Jasen, when his mother died of brain cancer just a short time ago. He is now on his second combat tour in Iraq as an Army officer. My son Scott has spent time with us in the summer for the last two years for his birthday. God has reconciled my relationship with my parents. After years of working in the semiconductor industry, I now have a wonderful job implementing Celebrate Recovery in a drug and alcohol treatment center! My identity is no longer in what I do for a living but in who I am: I am God's child. God has shown me that He will protect and provide for me. My faith is now in Christ and no longer in my own abilities. I continue to fill my life with God's Word and God's people instead of self-destructive patterns and behaviors. By God's grace I have led several Celebrate Recovery step studies, helped with the Men's Codependent group and the Prayer Team, and have had the honor of serving at the Orange County Rescue Mission. God has put incredible joy and peace in my life.

I would like to thank that girlfriend, Vicki, who brought me into this program when I thought I did not need it. She is now my wife! I thank God for teaching me that to have the gift of recovery, I must give it away. I will

always be thankful to the men of my group who are the first true friends I
have ever had, who know all there is to know about me and still like me.
My greatest thanks goes to God, with whom I now have an intimate love
relationship that is real and personal. I know I cannot use imperfect parents
as an excuse for not living up to God's standards. None of us are perfect in
the way we parent. Today I do have a perfect Parent who is teaching me
how to be loving, forgiving, and patient, just like Him: my heavenly Father.

I would like to close with one of my life verses.

> "You did not receive a spirit that makes you a slave again to fear,
> but you received the Spirit of sonship.
> And by him we cry, 'Abba, Father.'
> The Spirit himself testifies with our spirit
> that we are God's children."[27]

Lisa and Charlie both had to go through a lot of pain and heartache
before they finally made the decision to turn the care and control of their
lives over to Christ. Some of you are probably saying to yourselves, "I've
tried this before and it didn't take. I've tried giving my life to God and it
just didn't work." It most likely did not work because you were not truly
committed. Like Lisa and Charlie, when you finally choose to surrender
it all, to commit your life and will to Christ's care and control, then and
only then can God do His life-changing work in you.

R
E
C

Openly examine

and *confess* my faults to myself,
to God, and to someone I trust.

V

E

R

Y

"Happy are the pure in heart." [1]

Coming CLEAN

The HOUSECLEANING Choice

Have you ever tried to outrun your past?

A convention of Arkansas State troopers was asked to submit the best excuse they'd ever heard for someone trying to get out of a speeding ticket. The winning entry was submitted by a trooper who clocked a semi-tractor truck speeding down the interstate. The trooper pulled in behind the truck and turned his lights on, but the truck kept going. The trooper got right up on his bumper, but the truck kept going. The trooper turned on his siren, but the truck went even faster. Finally, the truck ran out of gas and rolled to the side of the highway.

The trooper got out and walked up to the trucker's window. The driver rolled down his window, and the trooper asked, "Did you see my lights?"

"Yes sir, I did," the trucker responded.

"Did you see me following you right on your bumper?"

The trucker answered, "Yes sir, I did."

"Did you hear my siren all those miles?"

"Yes sir, I did," the trucker answered.

Finally, the trooper said, *"Then why didn't you pull over?"*

101

"Well, to be honest, about two years ago my wife ran off with an Arkansas state trooper. I was afraid you were trying to bring her back!"

Wouldn't it be nice to live our lives in such a way that we could be unafraid of our past catching up with us? Is that even possible?

THE JOY OF A PURE HEART

The beatitude we're learning about in this choice says, *"Happy are the pure in heart."* A pure heart is one that is free and clean of impurities. It is a heart free of all the junk that weighs us down, washed clean of all the hurts, hang-ups, and habits that plague our lives. Those who are truly pure in heart aren't afraid of their pasts. They don't spend their todays looking over their shoulders at yesterday. But for many of us, the hope of a "pure heart" was given up long ago.

If we are ever to know the JOY of a pure heart, we'll have to learn how to let go of our guilt and shame and how to gain a clear conscience.

Is the happiness of a pure heart even possible for you? The answer is in the next few pages. In this chapter, we'll learn about *coming clean*. It won't all be easy, but it is broken down into steps—and the results will change your life forever. The truth is that we all have regrets. We've all done things that we wish we could go back and change. But we can't. We feel guilty, and we carry that guilt with us—sometimes consciously, but most of the time unconsciously. We deny our guilt, repress it, and blame other people for it. We make excuses, and we rationalize. But no matter how hard we try to run from it, we feel its effects just the same.

If we are ever to recover from the hurts, hang-ups, and habits in our lives and know the joy of a pure heart, we'll have to learn how to let go of our guilt and shame and how to gain a clear conscience.

A young man called in to one of those call-in radio talk shows hosted by a psychologist and said, "I'm consumed with guilt and don't know what to do with it. How do I get rid of this guilt?" The answer offered by the talk-show host was very upsetting: "You can't get rid of guilt. You just have to learn to live with it." That is not the answer! This guy actually told the hurting young man to rationalize his guilt. We can rationalize all we want. We can say, "It's okay, everybody's doing it, it was a long time ago . . . ," but in our hearts, we know what we did was wrong.

In this chapter, the good news is that you will find the key to relief from your guilt. If you take the steps needed to complete this choice, you will know the happiness of a *pure heart* as you share the words of the psalmist: "*What happiness for those whose guilt has been forgiven. What joys when sins are covered over! What relief for those who have confessed their sins and God has cleared their record.*"[2]

Before we start working on steps to overcoming guilt, it's important to understand the negative effects guilt has on our lives.

WHAT GUILT DOES TO US

1. GUILT DESTROYS OUR CONFIDENCE

Guilt and confidence cannot exist in the same person. Guilt is the fear that I'll be caught or that people will realize I'm not all that I say I am. Guilt makes us feel insecure because we're always worried that somebody will find out the truth about us. And if they do, will they still like us?

Sir Arthur Conan Doyle, writer of the Sherlock Holmes novels, was quite a prankster. One day he played a prank on five of the most prominent men in England. He sent an anonymous note to each man, which simply said, "All is found out. Flee at once." Within twenty-four hours, all five men had left the country.

Guilt is like a dark cloud hanging over our head. We're constantly worried that someone will find the skeleton in our closet—that deep, dark secret that only we know about. It is like carrying a heavy weight around our necks. It robs us of our confidence.

2. GUILT DAMAGES OUR RELATIONSHIPS

Guilt sabotages our relationships by causing us to respond in harmful ways. We sometimes overreact out of impatience or anger, or we explode without reason because of some buried guilt.

Guilt can also cause us to indulge people unwisely. Parents often feel guilty over poor choices they have made and overcompensate by indulging their children.

Guilt can cause us to avoid commitment. We wonder why we won't let people get close to us. We allow ourselves to get just so close but no closer. One of the main reasons is guilt. Past relationships push their way into the present and taint the future. Many marriage problems are the result of guilt over things that happened prior to or early in the marriage. That guilt from the past causes marriage problems today.

3. GUILT KEEPS US STUCK IN THE PAST

Instead of dealing with the current problem, some people remain stuck in the past. Their guilt over something they did holds them prisoner. Guilt tries to keep us focused on what's behind us by replaying the past in our minds over and over. We replay all the things we wish we could change.

It's like driving a car by always looking in the rearview mirror. A rearview mirror is helpful, because it gives us perspective. Looking at our past gives us perspective, too, but if we look *only* at our past, we never get to see the present or look forward to the future. Some people focus on the past to the extent that their rearview mirror gets bigger than their windshield. With this kind of driving, forward progress is nearly impossible. In fact, a crash is likely in the near future.

Spiritual growth is the process of expanding that windshield and shrinking the rearview mirror so you can get on with the present.

Feeling guilty cannot change the past, just like worry cannot change the future. Feeling guilty just makes our today miserable. Over time, guilt can make us physically sick. When we swallow our guilt, our stomachs keep score! And if we don't talk it out with God and others, we will continue to take it out on ourselves and others.

Choice 4 is the one that brings our painful past out in the open so we can deal with it, be cleansed of it, and then move on to health and happiness. This fourth choice may be a scary one, but it's a step that separates those who just want to *talk* about getting healthy from those who really want to *get* healthy:

Coming CLEAN

CHOICE 4

Openly examine and confess my faults

to myself, to God, and to someone I trust.

At the end of this chapter, you'll read the true story of CJ and Linda and how their individual lives, as well as their marriage, were dramatically changed as they made this choice. You will see that their journey was not easy, but you'll also see that the results were nothing less than miraculous.

If you want to change your life, if you want to get well, if you want to grow and let go of your past guilt once and for all, you will have to come clean and make this fourth choice.

The following five steps will help you move past your guilt. While the procedure is fairly simple; it isn't easy to actually *do,* and it requires a lot of courage.

MOVING PAST GUILT

1. TAKE A PERSONAL MORAL INVENTORY

This may sound a bit scary, but taking a personal moral inventory will be one of the most productive and cleansing things you can do—like cleaning out a closet. When you clean out a closet, you uncover things that may have been stuffed in a dark corner for years. That stuff may even be stinking up your house. But you've ignored it because the thought of closet cleaning is just too overwhelming. However, when you clean out your closet, you also discover some unexpected treasures—favorite pieces of clothing you thought had been lost or some great article you had forgotten about.

That's how it is with our personal "closet" inventory. We may have all kinds of messes stuffed inside us that we've tried to ignore—some that may even be stinking up our lives. However, we'll also discover some great things about ourselves that we'd forgotten or never even realized. Once we actually get around to doing it, taking a personal moral inventory can transform our lives.

We'll get into the specifics of how to do the moral inventory in our "Make the Choice" section, but for now let's look at the following acrostic to help us understand how this inventory works:

M – Make time to begin your inventory

O – Open your heart and your mind

R – Rely on God's grace

A – Analyze your past honestly

L – List both the good and bad choices and events in your life

The inventory begins with *making* some time to be alone with no interruptions. And you need to take your time; don't rush it. Next, *open* your heart and mind to God and let Him reveal what you need to see: *"Search me, O God, and know my heart; test my thoughts. Point out anything you find in me that makes you sad and lead me along the path of everlasting life."*[3] As you begin to see the truth about yourself, you can *rely* fully upon God's grace, knowing that He has forgiven you—no matter what your inventory uncovers. As you *analyze* yourself, you must be ruthlessly honest—no more pretending. And finally, be sure to not only look at the negative things in your life but also *list* the good. It's important to keep your inventory balanced.

Why is it important to do this inventory in writing? Because writing forces you to be specific. Thoughts disentangle themselves when they pass through the lips to the fingertips. If you don't put it down in writing, it will remain vague. Just saying, "God, I've blown it in life," is not specific enough. We've all blown it. We need to get specific, and we need to write it down.

When I wrote down my moral inventory, I saw for the first time how, over the years, my poor choices had hurt all those most important to me. It was truly a moment of clarity. I understood how my drinking hurt my wife, my children, and all those close to me. Although it was painful to go through, the end result was worth every minute of it. My past was no longer a secret, and I could choose to continue my healing journey and do my part in restoring all the relationships that I had damaged.

2. ACCEPT RESPONSIBILITY FOR YOUR FAULTS

Honestly accepting responsibility for ourselves is not an easy thing to do, but God has created us with the ability to see ourselves for who we are: *"The LORD gave us mind and conscience. We cannot hide from ourselves."*[4] Accepting responsibility for our faults begins with one *do* and three *don'ts.*

1. *Do be radically honest.* The truth of the matter is, we ourselves are the greatest barrier to the healing of our own hurts, hang-ups, and habits. Our healing starts with us being radically honest and saying, "I'm the problem." We can't keep saying, "If I could just change relationships, jobs, or locations, then everything would be fine." The problem with that kind of thinking is wherever you go, there you are!

2. *Don't rationalize.* We can't keep saying, "It happened a long time ago" or, "It's just a stage" or, "Everybody does it." We need to be honest and face the truth about ourselves. God's grace can cover us, no matter what the truth is. We don't need to minimize our actions by saying, "It's no big deal." If it's no big deal, why do we still remember it twenty years later?

3. *Don't blame others.* We blame others by saying, "It was mostly their fault." It may have been mostly their fault, but God holds us responsible for whatever part is our fault. It's time to stand tall and accept responsibility for our part in our life's problems.

4. *Don't deceive yourself.* We just need to admit where we messed up. *"If we claim to be without sin, we deceive ourselves and the truth is not in us."*[5] If we really want to stop defeating ourselves, we have got to stop deceiving ourselves. God will help us if we just ask Him.

SPECIAL NOTE: If you have been physically or sexually abused as a child or adult, I want you to know that I am sorry that you suffered through that abuse. There is no way I can know the pain it caused you, but I want you to know that I empathize with your hurt. When you start writing down your list of wrongs, simply put the words **"NOT GUILTY"** for the abuse that was done to you. *No part of that sin committed against you was your fault.* Renounce the lie that the abuse was your fault. Do take responsibility for how you may have hurt others because of your reactions to your past abuse.

Don't you think it's time to finally deal with your guilt so you can get on with life? As you complete your moral inventory, you will be able to look at your list and say, "Yes, that's me—the good, the bad, and the ugly. I accept responsibility for my faults."

3. ASK GOD FOR FORGIVENESS

"If we freely admit that we have sinned, we find God utterly reliable and straightforward—he forgives our sin and makes us thoroughly clean from all that is evil."[6] You can't find a better promise than that! If we freely admit it, God will forgive us.

God's nature is the basis for forgiveness. There is no sin so severe that God cannot forgive: *"No matter how deep the stain of your sins, I can take it out and make you as clean as freshly fallen snow."*[7]

A woman came in to see her pastor and said, "I'm depressed. I've been in bed for weeks, and I no longer have the energy to get out of bed and live."

Sensing her deep pain, the pastor asked her, "Is there something in your life you really regret?"

She began to pour it out. "Yes. My husband travels. I had an affair and got pregnant and had an abortion. I have never told my husband about it."

The pastor shared God's promise that no matter how deep the stain of our sins, God can take it out and forgive us.

Distressed, she replied, "It just doesn't seem fair. Somebody's got to pay for my sin!"

"Somebody already has," the pastor assured her. "His name is Jesus Christ. That's why He died on the cross. He died for that sin and every other one you've committed and confessed and ones you're going to commit."

She cried and asked, "How do I ask God for His forgiveness?"

You may be asking the same question. Here's how:

1. *Don't beg.* You don't have to beg for God to forgive you. He

wants to forgive you. God wants to forgive you more than you want His forgiveness. He is a forgiving God.

2. *Don't bargain.* Don't say to God, "If You'll just forgive me, I'll never do this again." If you say you will never do it again, and that's your area of weakness, you're probably setting yourself up for failure. You don't have to bargain with God to get His forgiveness.

3. *Don't bribe.* Don't say to God, "If You will forgive me, I promise to do a bunch of good things. I'll go to church; I'll tithe; I'll help the poor." God doesn't want you to try to bribe Him. He wants you to admit your faults and sins to Him and turn from them to the purpose He has for you.

4. *Do believe.* Do believe that He will forgive you. He forgives our sin and makes us thoroughly clean from all that is evil.

When we freely admit that we have sinned, we will find God utterly reliable. To admit or confess means that we agree with God about the sin in our lives. We are saying, "God, You're right. What I did or am still doing is wrong." That's what it means to confess. And you will be forgiven!

4. ADMIT YOUR FAULTS TO ANOTHER PERSON

God tells us that it is absolutely essential to share our moral inventory list with another person: *"Admit your faults to one another and pray for each other so that you may be healed."*[8] How does this verse say we are we healed? By admitting our faults to one another.

Why can't we just admit our faults to God? Why must another person be involved? Because the root of our problems is relational. We lie to each other, deceive each other, and are dishonest with each other. We wear masks and pretend we have it together. We deny our true feelings and play games largely because we believe, "If they really knew the truth about me, they wouldn't love me." We become more isolated than ever.

We keep all of the junk of our past inside, and we get sick. There's a saying: *We are only as sick as our secrets.* The hurts, hang-ups, and habits that we try to hide end up making us sick, but "revealing your feelings is the beginning of healing."[9]

When you follow God's instruction to "*admit your faults to one another,*"[10] when you risk honesty with another person, all of a sudden, a wonderful feeling of freedom comes into your life. You begin to realize that everybody has problems, and

> *When you risk* HONESTY *with another person, all of a sudden, a wonderful feeling of freedom comes into your life.*

many have the same ones you do. There is something therapeutic about admitting your faults to another person. It's God's way of freeing you.

Maybe you're beginning to open your heart to the possibility of sharing your inventory list with one other person, but have some questions: Who will I tell? What do I say? When do I do it? We're going to answer those questions right now.

Whom Do You Tell?

How do you choose who to tell? Do you just go out and broadcast your sins to everybody? No. Telling the wrong person or people could cause big trouble. You don't just indiscriminately tell your problems to anyone. You need to find a safe person to share your inventory with. Hopefully, you found that person as you completed the action steps in the first three chapters. If not, here are some additional suggestions that will help you find the right person:

1. *Ask someone you trust*—someone who can keep a confidence and is not a gossip. You don't want to finally share the secrets you've bottled up for years and then read about them in next week's *National Enquirer*!

2. *Ask someone who understands the value of what you're doing*—someone who values and understands the journey of a changed life.

3. *Ask someone who is mature enough not to be shocked*—someone who has been transparent with you about his or her life.

4. *Ask someone who knows the Lord well enough to reflect His forgiveness to you*—a pastor, your accountability partner, your ministry leader, a trusted friend, or a Christian counselor. Most genuine Christians would be honored to have you share your inventory with them.

What Do You Say?

1. *Before you say anything, find a place to meet without interruptions.* You will be sharing some tough issues, and it may not be easy to get the words out. You need plenty of time, and you don't need any distractions.

2. *Be up-front in saying that you need to share your moral inventory list.* You may start off by saying, "I just need someone to listen to me as I verbalize some things I know are wrong in my life—some of the things I've done and felt; my hurts, hang-ups, and habits."

3. *Be specific.* The secret you most want to conceal is the very one you need to reveal. The revelation of that most painful secret will bring you the most healing. Then you will experience God's abundant grace and finally be free! You will experience relief and freedom like never before. By taking this action, you step out of the darkness of your secrets and into Christ's freeing "light of life." "*When Jesus spoke again to the people, he said, 'I am the light of the world. Whoever follows me will never walk in darkness, but will have the light of life.'*"[11]

When Do You Do It?

There's one answer to this question: *As soon as possible.* Don't procrastinate.

You may be thinking, "I'll finish the rest of the book, and then I'll come back and share my moral inventory with another person." Or, "I need to think about this one for a while. Maybe I'm not quite ready to take this step yet."

That's okay. You may just need a little more pain.

God is waiting to free you from your past. He's waiting for you to come clean so you can move toward healing and joy. Make this healing choice, do it now, and God will bless you and protect you!

5. ACCEPT GOD'S FORGIVENESS AND FORGIVE YOURSELF

"All have sinned and are not good enough for God's glory, and all need to be made right with God by his grace, which is a free gift. They need to be made free from sin through Jesus Christ."[12] This passage tells us that we have all have missed the mark. We all have done things for which we need God's forgiveness. We're all in the same boat. We've all sinned. We've all made poor choices. We all have hurts, hang-ups, and habits, just in different areas and degrees.

Forgiveness takes place invisibly. What actually happens when God forgives us? How does forgiveness work?

1. God forgives instantly. He doesn't wait. The moment you ask, you're forgiven. It's done. He never makes you wait or suffer for a while. He loves you way too much. Humans do that, but God doesn't. This is the confidence we can have: *"Let us, then, feel very sure that we can come before God's throne where there is grace. There we can receive mercy and grace to help us when we need it."*[13] Doesn't that sound exactly like what you need?

2. God forgives freely. He freely takes away your sins. You don't deserve it; you can't earn it; you can't work for it. It's free. *"All need to be made right* with God by his grace, which is a free gift. They need to be made free from sin through Jesus Christ."[14] God is the one who makes us right—by His grace and for free.

3. *He forgives completely.* God's forgiveness is not in stages; it is not partial; it is absolutely complete. He wipes our sin out. The Bible says, *"Therefore, there is now no condemnation for those who are in Christ Jesus."*[15] How great it feels to live with *no* condemnation, to live with the knowledge that God loves us in spite of all our faults!

Now all that's left is to *do it.* In the three action steps for this chapter, we'll help you deal with your guilt, come clean through a personal inventory, and accept God's gracious, full, and free forgiveness.

SPECIAL NOTE: If you are experiencing a lot of pain and distress over completing your inventory because writing down the events of your past is just too difficult to do on your own, I understand. I suggest you go to www.celebraterecovery.com and find a Celebrate Recovery near you. There you will find help and support in completing your inventory. You will find people who have dealt with the same hurts, hang-ups, and habits that you are going through. You will find a safe place!

MAKE THE *Choice*

ACTION 1: *Pray about It*

Facing your past and being honest about your guilt is not easy. You need God's help to take each step in this choice. Prayer is the best way to tap into His power. You can pray your own words or use these . . .

> *Dear God, You know my past—all the good and bad choices I have made and all the good and bad things I have done. In working through choice 4, I ask that You give me the strength and courage to list the items called for in the "Write about It" section below so that I can come clean and face the truth. Please open my eyes to the truth of my past—the truth of how others have hurt me and how I have hurt others. Please help me reach out to others You have placed along my pathway to healing. Thank You for providing these individuals to help me keep balanced as I do my inventory. As I come clean in this choice, I thank You in advance for the forgiveness You have given me. In Christ's name I pray. Amen.*

ACTION 2: *Write about It*

Take a minute to review what you wrote in chapters 1–3 in the "Write about It" sections. It's important that you complete each chapter to the best of your ability before moving on to the next. The Bible encourages us in our efforts: *"Let us examine our ways and test them, and let us return to the LORD."*[16]

Take an 8½ x 11 piece of paper and divide it into five columns. You will need several sheets of paper to complete your moral inventory:

THE PERSON	THE CAUSE	THE EFFECT	THE DAMAGE	MY PART
1.	1.	1.	1.	1.
2.	2.	2.	2.	2.
3.	3.	3.	3.	3.

Column 1: *The Person*—In this column, list the person or object you resent or fear. Go as far back as you can. Remember that resentment is mostly unexpressed anger, hurt, or fear.

Column 2: *The Cause*—It has been said that "hurt people hurt people." In this column, list the specific actions someone did to hurt you.

Column 3: *The Effect*—In this column write down how that specific, hurtful action affected your life both in the past and in the present.

Column 4: *The Damage*—In this column write down which of your basic needs were injured. *Social*—Have you suffered from broken relationships, slander, or gossip? *Security*—Has your physical safety been threatened? Have you faced financial loss? *Sexual*—Have you been a victim in abusive relationships? Has intimacy or trust been damaged or broken?

Column 5: *My Part*—In this column you need to honestly determine and write down the part of the resentment or any other sin or injury that you are responsible for. Ask God to show you your part in a broken or damaged marriage or relationship, a distant child or parent, or maybe a job loss. List the people you have hurt and how you specifically hurt them.

PLEASE NOTE: If you have been in an abusive relationship, especially as a small child, you can find great freedom in this part of the inventory. You will see that you had *no* part, *no* responsibility, for the cause of the resentment. By simply writing the words **"NONE"** or **"NOT GUILTY"** in column 5, you can begin to be free from the misplaced shame and guilt you have carried with you.

ACTION 3: *Share about It*

In your "Write about It" action step, you spent some serious time listing some difficult truths. Now it's time to share those truths aloud with your trusted friend. In your next meeting, go through your five columns and share it all. This is the second part of choice 4—that you "openly confess your faults to someone you trust."

Take your time and have the courage to go through each column in your list:

- *The Person*—the one or ones you resent or fear

- *The Cause*—the reason you hurt

- *The Effect*—both past and present effects of the hurt

- *The Damage*—how you were hurt (socially, sexually, or made to feel insecure)

- *My Part*—here you take ownership for your role in the problem, large or small

Remember, saying the words aloud untangles the thoughts in your head, giving them shape and enabling you to face them productively. After you've shared these five topics, take a minute with your friend to thank God for His full forgiveness.

SPECIAL NOTE: Be careful to safeguard your inventory; this list is no one's business but yours, God's, and the special person you choose to share it with.

STORIES OF
Changed Lives

CJ and Linda's STORY

CJ: *We would like to share with you how God's miracles can take the hearts of a hardened alcoholic and a resentful codependent and turn them into grateful, joy-filled servants' hearts.*

My name is CJ; I'm a believer who struggles with alcoholism. My family was influenced by a strict German father. We didn't express our feelings or emotions; we certainly never talked about them. Love and God were not discussed. My dad was a yeller, so anger was a fearful emotion for me. My religious background started in a Midwestern rural church. I learned about an Old Testament God. My God and my father were much the same—angry and to be feared. This dysfunctional background set the stage for my avoiding emotions. I left home at eighteen and moved to the West Coast. It was during this time that I met Linda. After being inducted into the air force, I found I couldn't live without her. We were married in 1952.

Linda: *My name is Linda; I'm a believer who struggles with codependency. At eighteen, I was the happiest bride there ever was. We had each other. We thought we didn't need anything else—we were so much in love! When I married, my mother's parting words of advice were, "Remember, CJ is the most important person in your life now; put his needs first, and don't bother him with your problems. Take good care of him; and by the way, never buy lettuce with brown leaves." That was premarital counseling in the '50s. I now had all the information I needed to be the best wife, best lover, and when the time came, the best mother. I would fulfill all CJ's needs, and of course, he would fulfill all mine.*

My skills as a mother were tested by the birth of our daughter a year

118

later, our first son the next year, and our second son five years after that. But these were years of happiness for me. So many things to be done and so many people needed me to do them. I felt loved and needed. I chose to fill my life with my home and taking care of my husband and children. It was very important to me to do all the things I should be doing, never saying no, because what would people think?

The years passed and our lives got busier. CJ spent a lot of time at work. Our children were growing up, with their own problems and challenges. I was feeling less like the perfect wife and perfect mother, and certainly less like the perfect lover. Soon crises came into our lives, starting with the loss of CJ's job. It was harder and harder for us to talk or share, and we grew further apart. I remember just wishing my responsibilities and pain would go away. But I couldn't leave for fear of what my children and husband would do without me to take care of them. It never occurred to me to share my pain with anyone, and it certainly never occurred to me to share it with God. All I could ask myself was, "What am I doing wrong? Why is this happening to me?" I thought that if CJ and the children would just change, I'd be okay!

CJ: I was ill equipped for marriage and, certainly, as a father. I always put other priorities ahead of my wife and family. As family issues became more painful, I chose to numb my feelings with alcohol. During the early years of our marriage, my drinking had been "social." Slowly, drinking became part of everything I did—going out to dinner with friends, parties, working in the yard, social functions at work, weekends—you name it.

Drinking became the priority in my life. I soon began to disrespect Linda, my family, and myself. My morals began to break down, and lusting crept in as Satan pounded me with this sickness. My marriage vows, which I had once honored, were slowly disappearing, and soon I found myself breaking those vows. My heart became hardened, and I turned away from the God I grew up fearing. I was now a full-blown alcoholic, with all the denial to go with it. When I spoke, I wasn't tactful or truthful; I was a practicing liar. As time passed I even began to believe my own lies!

119

Linda: *About this time CJ made a decision to accept a job in Orange County. That meant we would have to sell our home of twenty-two years and move. That felt scary for me but also exciting. I thought it might be a new beginning. After we moved, we even visited some churches, but they were always too big or too small or the people weren't friendly or they met in a gym, and that didn't seem like church to me. CJ's job kept him away from home more and more. I began to feel a loneliness I had never felt before, an empty spot in the middle of my heart that I tried to fill with many things.*

CJ and I were on different tracks; I felt we were traveling in opposite directions. I felt unloved and certainly not cherished. My life became a dark place filled with anger, confusion, self-doubt, and distrust. I didn't allow myself to see the facts that surrounded me. Our lives and our love had changed. Alcohol was more and more a part of CJ's life, and anger was more a part of mine.

Though I had ignored the signs for a long time, I could no longer deny the fact that there was another woman in my husband's life. My main feeling was, Why has this happened to me? Why is God letting this happen to my perfect marriage? I promised God and CJ that I would change, that I wouldn't be angry and criticizing, and that I would be a better wife. I bargained with everything I could. Time passed, but nothing changed. The arguments became more frequent. The pain grew greater, the words harsher, the silences longer, the shouting louder, and the desperation deeper. Periodically I prayed, telling God I would turn it all over to Him if only He would make it all go away . . . if He would just make CJ quit drinking and make our lives whole again. But I would then proceed to do things my own way—never listening for an answer to my prayer or giving control over to God. My isolation was great. I put on my masks and went out to meet the world, hoping nobody would see my guilt and shame and try to reach out to me.

I thought I was fooling everybody, even myself. But our friends and family were seeing the negative changes in our relationship. I felt totally alone. The possibilities were so frightening. I was so angry with God, feeling even He had deserted me.

CJ: At about this time, even though we didn't know it yet, God was about to give us some healing choices. Our grandson came to live with us. He began attending a big church called Saddleback. Linda and I began to attend with him. I would check the church bulletin to see if any Alcoholics Anonymous meetings met there, but conveniently found none. I wondered what Celebrate Recovery was, but I was sure it didn't relate to me.

Linda: Our daughter and our younger son came to the house to talk to us one morning. My daughter told me she was worried about me. I had almost ceased to communicate with her. She cried, "I don't know how to talk to you anymore, and I miss you." Our son told me, "It feels like you and Dad don't have a relationship anymore, and we're worried about that." I took a deep breath, swallowed my tears, and admitted aloud for the first time they were right. I hastened to add they needed to be talking to their dad. That if he would just stop drinking, we might be able to build a life together again.

CJ: They also confronted me on my excessive "closet" drinking. I made a commitment to them, and on Friday evening, February 29, 1996, I went to Saddleback Church. I made the longest walk of my life across the parking lot to the Celebrate Recovery meeting. I told my small group that I had twenty-four hours of sobriety. A man in the circle by the name of Big Al jumped up and said, "Congratulations." Then he grabbed me and gave me a big hug. I really was unsure about that move! I soon learned to love those hugs, and I haven't turned one down since! Big Al assured me that if I kept coming back, I would begin to see some of God's miracles in my life. I agreed that night to start attending a men's step study the next week. The first question in the workbook was, "What do you have control over in your life?" My list was long, but after about thirty minutes of heated discussion, it came down to simply nothing. I have control over nothing, except to get on my knees before God! This was my first step in admitting I was powerless.

Linda: I didn't go with CJ that first evening because I thought this was his thing. He's the one who needed to get well, and that was my denial. I had noticed in the church bulletin there was a group for codependents. But I really didn't want to go sit with a bunch of ladies and tell them about my life. Maybe they wouldn't like me if they knew all those things about me. CJ's joy began to be noticeable to me. It seemed like each time he went to a meeting, he came back home with a greater joy. It did seem that when we went to church on Sunday that I felt some of that joy. Pastor Rick was talking to me so many mornings, and I heard things that began to give me hope. So I decided I would try Celebrate Recovery. The people were friendly. The music was great, and there were some good hugs. However, I wasn't sure about letting total strangers into my life, but I made the choice to try.

CJ: I pray the same prayer every day in my "quiet time," in my car, at night, wherever I might be: "Dear God, I have tried to do it all by myself, on my own power, and I have failed. It is my prayer to daily turn my will over to You, to daily seek Your direction and wisdom for my life. Please continue to help me. Amen."

I had completed the first three choices. During this time I was very fortunate that I had become very close to two men in my step study group. They became my accountability partners. At the time, I didn't know how important they would become as I began to work on the fourth choice:

CHOICE 4

Coming **CLEAN**

Openly examine and confess my faults

to myself, to God, and to someone I trust.

Being the procrastinator, I didn't have a notebook or a good place to write or a proper format, and so on. My accountability partner said, "Just start." But where do I start? I finally figured it out: I asked God. Every day God brought more memories from the past, many of which I hadn't thought about for several years. Some days I couldn't touch my notebook. But as I was able to record each episode, I felt that much closer to God.

My heart became much lighter as the bonds and chains were lifted, one by one. As I worked on my fourth choice, the one thing that kept me going was my step study group. They pushed; they shared their encouragement, love, support, and, most of all, their tears. My two accountability partners became my bastions of help. These two guys, my step study group, and my wife's patience helped me work this choice. Each day, the light became brighter, and the guilt, shame, and resentments began to lessen and disappear. I began to experience a personal relationship with my loving and forgiving Savior, Jesus Christ, who loves me in spite of myself and the things I have done. I began to realize what the word grace truly meant. I love the peace I found in God's Word: "Come, let's talk this over! says the Lord; no matter how deep the stain of your sins, I can take it out and make you as clean as freshly fallen snow. Even if you are stained as red as crimson, I can make you white as wool!"[17]

Linda: Then it happened! On a warm evening, I was sitting outside on the patio reading a book. I remembered as I was reading that there were some things I needed to do. So being the compulsive list maker that I am, I reached across the table and picked up a notebook to pull out a sheet of paper. I opened the notebook to a page with writing on it. My eyes fell on words I could not have imagined. I knew I had a choice to close that page and read no further, but I didn't.

My eyes filled with tears. My heart was pounding in my chest. It was like my love and my life were all on that page and had been wiped out with one big swipe. I had opened to CJ's journal notes for his fourth choice. It was all there—some things I knew, some I didn't. The tears swelled, and the anger was gigantic. I was like a volcano waiting to erupt. There was no reasoning in my mind or my heart. Deep inside, I knew I had read what

I shouldn't have. I also knew I had to face it, tell CJ, and deal with the consequences.

I knew I had to make amends for my invasion of such a special privacy, but how could I do that when I was in the midst of such anger and hurt feelings? My love was rejected, my self-worth was in shambles, and my life was in chaos. When CJ came home, I told him what happened, still so angry and full of resentment. All I could think of was to strike out and hurt.

I remembered being at church one Sunday when Kay Warren, Pastor Rick's wife, spoke. She shared that she had gone through a time when she was in such pain that she couldn't come to the Lord in prayer. But she had others who could pray for her during that time. I knew what Kay felt, but thought, I don't have others to pray for me. So I isolated myself in anger, stayed away from my Celebrate Recovery group, and looked for answers, but found none. I couldn't pray; I didn't have the words. I had never felt so alone. Had God forsaken me? Or perhaps I had forsaken God. His Word tells us: "You began your life in Christ by the Spirit. Now are you trying to make it complete by your own power? That is foolish!"[18] I had forgotten what I had learned in the third choice—to rely on God's power. I was trying to do it all on my own. I forgot to pray for God to give me the strength to change, to forgive, and to endure.

CJ: First, I was angry. What right did she have to do such a thing? Even though it was really my fault for not being more careful with my workbooks and journal. Second, I was scared. As fragile as our relationship was at that time, this would crush all hope. I was sure it was "couch" time for me! I called my accountability partner and got a huge "Oh my! CJ, what have you done? Oh, my!" I received love and support and a renewed commitment from my step study group to handle their books and journals very carefully. There were many prayers for God to help Linda understand. After many days of prayer, God granted me the wisdom to know that it was in His hands and that He would take care of it. God was listening, and God is great. I began to realize that there could never be any more lies between

Linda and me. She knew it all. God touched her heart, and as I continued to work my program, Linda's heart softened.

Linda: *Without my knowing it, there were many prayers being said for God to soften my heart. CJ's accountability partner suggested that CJ call Pastor John to help us work through what had happened. Pastor John met with us, and we both talked and shared our feelings. He was so encouraging and helped me feel better. He prayed with us and suggested that I reach out to someone in my group and make some special friends I could share with. I left with hope in my heart. Soon after that, I had a call from John's wife, Cheryl, asking me to meet her for coffee before Friday evening's Celebrate Recovery meeting. As we walked into the coffee shop, I saw CJ's accountability partner. We visited awhile and then parted, with him saying, "CJ's doing heroic things, you know," and I said, "I know."*

I felt blessed. For the first time that evening as Cheryl and I visited, I felt safe and opened my heart to her. I shared some of my pain and my doubts about forty-four years of marriage that had brought me to this place in time. As Cheryl and I ended our time together, she said something she may not even remember; but it made the first small crack in my hardened heart. She said, "I think you're doing heroic things too!" I thank God every day of my life for those simple words. They were the beginning of a "journey to my heart."

This is surely not the way I would recommend anyone to work a fourth choice, but it was the beginning for me. I can't tell you that all the anger and pain has magically left, but God's grace and love does work miracles on an angry, resentful heart. There have been many prayers—mine, CJ's, and others—to help me to trust God and CJ . . . prayers to help me to reach out, to give up the useless defense of anger, and to embrace Christ and the love and forgiveness He offers each of us.

I returned to the love and safety of my codependency group. This time I was determined not to isolate but to give of my hope, strength, and experience, sharing how God has worked in my life. In return, He has blessed me in more ways than I can express. He blessed me with a growing friendship with the women in my group. I have found encouragement and love in a safe place to grow and share.

My help and my strength have come from God. My accountability partners have loved me, helped me, and kicked me when I needed it. We have cried and shared and prayed our way through the eight choices, always together.

There are days when I call my accountability partner and say I need to talk. She will gently listen as I pour out my pain—sometimes as a mother whose child is hurting, sometimes as the wife of a recovering alcoholic, and sometimes as a frustrated perfectionist who wants to have every bit of dust out of the corners before her friends come to dinner. She reminds me to get out of God's way and let Him work His plan. She helps me be joyful when God is working miracles in a child's life, be grateful to have a husband to laugh and share with, and to lighten up and not worry about whether my house is clean.

CJ: As I worked through the choices, Linda began to walk next to me, hand in hand. I cannot begin to express how much love has been opened between us. It has been eleven years since I started the Celebrate Recovery program. With God's help I have not had the need for a drink since! That's all I really expected from my recovery. I felt that at my age, I couldn't change my behavior or mend my damaged relationships. But God has given me so much more than I thought possible. As the years of my recovery have passed, Linda has seen the changes God has made in me. He has softened her heart and allowed her to reach out her hand to me. After all the years of pain, lies, and disrespect, God opened the doors of forgiveness. As we have progressed, one day at a time, we have redeveloped a relationship and respect for one another. We renewed our marriage vows on our fiftieth wedding anniversary. Pastor John performed the service, and all of our family and Celebrate Recovery friends shared the day with us.

After all these years of marriage, I finally began to understand what intimacy is all about, and little by little it has become a part of our lives. God's miracle. Resentments and differences still arise, but we now have a way to work through them together. With God's help we continue daily to work on listening to each other and communicating in a loving manner.

Pastor Rick has challenged us to say, "God, use me!" We have and God has. We humbly thank God for opportunities to be used as servants and leaders in Saddleback's Celebrate Recovery and to work with other churches to help them start their own recovery programs.

Linda: God has richly blessed CJ and me in our lives, our love, our church, our family, our friends, and our commitment to our personal savior, Jesus Christ. He has given us friends who lift us in prayer in times of trouble and in times of celebration. We have prayed together and loved and cried and laughed together. I thank God for the fourth choice and for all that has happened in our lives on a daily basis. We feel joy in the good and bad, knowing that He truly will wipe away every tear from our eyes. The following scripture has become a daily affirmation of God's love for us:

> "After you have suffered a little while, our God,
> who is full of kindness through Christ,
> will give you his eternal glory.
> He personally will come and pick you up, and
> set you firmly in place, and make you stronger than ever."[19]

CJ and Linda's story is a powerful testimony of what God can do when we complete choice 4. They had to put back the pieces of their individual lives before they could begin to rebuild their marriage. When we make this fourth choice, we become free from the hold our secrets have had on us. We have the assurance that God has completely forgiven us, and we can move forward in our healing journey and our relationships.

R
E
C
O

Voluntarily submit

to every *change* God wants to make
in my life and humbly ask Him
to remove my character defects.

E

R

Y

"Happy are those whose greatest desire is to do what God requires." [1]

Making CHANGES

The TRANSFORMATION Choice

Imagine that you're in a boat and the autopilot is set for east, but you decide you want to change directions and go west. You take hold of the wheel, and you push and pull with all your might. Finally you manage to force the boat west. As long as you hold that wheel steady by *your* strength, the boat keeps going west; but pretty soon, you get tired of fighting against the boat's inclination, and you finally let go of the wheel. Now, once again, you're heading east—because that's the direction the boat is programmed to go.

But you still want to go west, so you muster up your willpower again, grab the steering wheel, and force the boat west. Yet the whole time you're having to struggle and fight because you're going against the pre-programmed inclination of the boat. So again you get tired and you let go of the wheel, and the boat automatically turns back east.

That's how it is when you try to fight against your own internal autopilot. By your own willpower, you try to force new behavior. You try and you try, but pretty soon you get tired . . . and you let go. You go off the diet, get involved in another unhealthy relationship, start smoking again, go back to gambling. You revert back to the way you have always acted.

If you want to change, the only solution is to reprogram your autopilot.

Because you have already worked through choices 1 through 4, you are now ready for the *transformation* choice. You are ready to submit to God and allow Him to change you. The Bible has this to say about the transformation choice: "*Offer yourselves as a living sacrifice to God, dedicated to his service and pleasing to him. . . . Let God transform you inwardly by a complete change of your mind.*"[2] God is ready to transform you by changing your mind; He is just waiting for you to submit to His loving hand.

The beatitude paired with this choice says, "*Happy are those whose greatest desire is to do what God requires.*" And one of the things He requires is *change,* and that change begins with your submission to His power. Will the changes be easy? Will they happen overnight? Of course not. But the promise of this beatitude is that when your greatest desire is to do what God requires, you'll be *happy.*

You know God has forgiven you; now He wants to change you. He loves you too much to leave you the way you are.

In this chapter we will learn how to *cooperate with God in His process of changing us.* But first, we'll look at the *origin of our character defects* and *why it is so hard for us to get rid of them.*

WHERE DO OUR CHARACTER DEFECTS COME FROM?

Our character defects come from three sources: biological, sociological, and theological. We'll examine these three sources through our *chromosomes*, our *circumstances*, and our *choices*.

1. OUR CHROMOSOMES

Do you know that your mother and father each contributed 23,000 chromosomes to your development? From your parents, you inherited some of their strengths and some of their weaknesses. You inherited many positive traits from them, but you also inherited some of their negative characteristics. You inherited some physical defects, as well as some emotional defects. This explains your predisposition toward certain problems.

However, this predisposition doesn't give you an excuse to act out inappropriately. You are still responsible for your own behavior. For instance, you may have a tendency toward a hot temper, but that doesn't give you an excuse to go out and punch somebody. You may have a tendency to be lazy, but that doesn't mean it's okay for you to lie on the couch all day. You may have a tendency, genetically, toward certain addictions, but that doesn't excuse you for choosing to become addicted to prescription drugs.

God LOVES you too much to leave you the way you are.

Our genetics, or our natures, contribute to our character defects; and while they don't provide us with excuses, they do provide some understanding.

2. OUR CIRCUMSTANCES

The circumstances of how you were raised and what you saw as you grew up, even your current circumstances, contribute to your character. Much of how you behave and relate you learned from watching others. When you were very young, you learned from watching your parents. As you grew you learned from watching others—your peers, your teachers. You developed certain patterns and habits; many of them were attempts to protect yourself, to handle hurt and rejection, and to cope.

The truth is, many of your current character defects are actually self-defeating attempts to satisfy your unmet needs. You have a legitimate need for *respect*. If you didn't get respect early in life or don't feel you have it now, you may settle for attention instead. You've figured out how to get attention in various ways, some positive and some negative. You also have a legitimate need for *love*. If you didn't get the love you needed as a child (and perhaps you still feel unloved), you may have learned to settle for superficial relationships or one-night stands. You also have a need for *security*, but if you grew up in an insecure environment or are in one now, you may be seeking security through the accumulation of possessions.

Our circumstances, past and present, help us understand the character defects that haunt us today.

3. OUR CHOICES

The choices you make are the most significant source of your character defects, because they are the one thing you can do something about. You can't control or change who your parents are. You can't go back and change the environment of your childhood. But you can, with God's power, change the choices you make.

You develop your hang-ups because you repeat negative choices. And if you choose to do something long enough, it becomes a habit. Once it becomes a habit, you're stuck. When a person makes the choice to take that first drink, he or she never thinks addiction will eventually follow. But after a series of choices to continue to abuse alcohol, the habit or addiction begins to own that person's life. Our choices may have been influenced by our chromosomes or our circumstances, but ultimately we are responsible for the choices we make.

WHY DOES IT TAKE SO LONG TO GET RID OF OUR CHARACTER DEFECTS?

Why is it so hard to change the defects in our lives? There are four main reasons:

1. BECAUSE WE'VE HAD THEM SO LONG

It's human nature to want to hold on to what's familiar, even when that familiar thing is causing us pain. Most of us have had our hang-ups and habits for a long time—they may have taken years to develop. Many were developed in childhood. Many are painful and self-defeating, but we hold on to them because they are familiar.

They're comfortable like an old pair of shoes. They may have big holes in the soles and they allow our feet to get wet, but we hang on to them because we're used to them; we feel comfortable in them. A lot of our character defects are like old shoes—they're comfortable. Since we've had them for so long, we have a hard time letting them go.

2. BECAUSE WE CONFUSE OUR DEFECTS WITH OUR IDENTITY

We often confuse our identity with our character defects. We say, "That's just the way I am." We identify ourselves by our defects when we say, "It's just like me to be a workaholic or overweight or anxious or passive. It's just like me to be fearful or lose my temper or to lust."

Our words and thoughts become self-fulfilling prophecies. If you say, "I'm always nervous when I get on planes," what's going to happen the next time you get on a plane? You're going to be nervous.

Sometimes we so closely identify ourselves by our defects that we worry, "If I let go of this defect, will I still be me? This has been a part of me for so long, who will I be if I ask God to remove it?"

In the small group meetings at Celebrate Recovery, when someone shares, they introduce themselves by saying, "Hi, I'm Bob, a believer who struggles with anger." Or, "I'm Nancy, a believer who struggles with overeating." Notice that their identity is in their belief in Christ. Their hurts, hang-ups, and habits do not define them. They do not allow character defects to become their identity.

3. BECAUSE EVERY DEFECT HAS A PAYOFF

We have a hard time letting go of our defects because each one has a very real payoff. The payoff may be temporary relief from pain. It may be attention or control. Our defects may give us an excuse to fail or allow us to compensate for the guilt in our lives.

If a negative behavior is repeated, you can be sure there's a payoff. The payoff may be self-destructive, but it brings some sort of perceived benefit.

A mom who is struggling with her anger might politely say to her children, "Kids, come to dinner." When they don't come, she asks them again. When they still don't come, she yells, "Kids come down to dinner, or you are going to get me mad, and you know what happens then!" Then they come. Unconsciously, the kids have set up their mother to yell and get mad, and Mom has figured out that yelling works. There's the payoff.

4. BECAUSE SATAN DISCOURAGES OUR EFFORTS TO CHANGE

Satan constantly tries to fill our minds with negative thoughts. He is the accuser. He whispers in your ear, "This will never work; you can't do it; you'll never change." Some of you have been reading this book and thinking, "This is good stuff. I'd really like to get rid of this habit. I'd like to stop hating that person. I'd like to stop hurting from that past experience out on the schoolyard. I'd love to change." Then you put the book down, and Satan starts in on you: "Who do you think you are? You think you're going to change? Forget it! Other people can change, but not you. You're stuck. It's hopeless. Don't even think about it." And worse than that he says, "If you change this about yourself, who will you be? If you change, you'll self-destruct; something bad will happen to you."

The Bible says that Satan is a liar: *"There is no truth in him. When he tells a lie, he shows what he is really like, because he is a liar and the father of lies."*[3] But counteracting Satan's lies is the truth that sets us free. Jesus said, *"You will know the truth, and the truth will set you free."*[4] As you grow in God's truth and voluntarily submit to the changes He has in store for you, you will discover the happiness of doing what God requires.

At the end of this chapter you'll read the stories of Dovey and John and how they found freedom when they faced the truth about their character defects and voluntarily submitted to the changes God wanted to make in each of them. For now let's discover the exciting news of how we can cooperate with God as He works the change process in our lives through choice 5:

CHOICE 5

Making CHANGES

Voluntarily submit to every change

God wants to make in my life and humbly ask Him to remove my character defects.

HOW DO WE COOPERATE WITH GOD'S CHANGE PROCESS?

Remember the illustration we opened the chapter with—about the autopilot setting on the boat? Again, the only way to change the direction of our lives—long-term—is to reset our autopilot. That's what the *transformation* choice is all about. Remember also the verse that says,

"*Be transformed by the renewing of your mind.*"[5] Transformed. Renewed mind. If we want to change our lives, we've got to reset the autopilot on the way we think. Our thoughts determine our feelings, and our feelings determine our actions.

What character defects are you trying to stop by using your own willpower? Are you tired yet? Have you figured out that you can't do it on your own until you reset your autopilot? By God's power, your mind can be changed and your autopilot can be reset.

We can't think about living an entire lifetime of victory, but we can focus on victory for JUST ONE DAY.

After I made the fourth choice, all of my sins and the wrongs of my past were no longer a secret. I was finally willing to allow God to change me by removing the defects of my character. I was willing to have Him reset my autopilot. I had to allow God to transform my mind— its nature, its condition, its identity.

I thought my major defect of character was my sin addiction to alcohol. But I learned that it was only a symptom. God showed me that my biggest character defect was my nonexistent self-esteem. As a young boy in high school I never felt good enough for anyone—my teachers, my coaches, my parents, my girlfriends, my teammates, anyone. I attempted to cover up that poor self-image with the world's largest ego. Believe me, that is not a very comfortable way to go through life. I carried my character defects with me until I finally got into recovery.

In this fifth choice, God changed me. He helped me rebuild my self-worth based on His unconditional love for me. I stopped trying to measure up to the world's standards and always failing and falling short. Today I attempt to live my life pleasing to God. Not much changed in my life—Just everything! If you would like to read my entire story, go to www .celebraterecovery.com.

The following seven focus points will show you how to *cooperate* with God as He works to change your autopilot and gets you heading in the right direction.

1. FOCUS ON CHANGING ONE DEFECT AT A TIME

You may have thirty different things you know need changing, but the wisdom of Proverbs tells us, *"An intelligent person aims at wise action, but a fool starts off in many directions."*[6] Trying to tackle all thirty problems at once is like those little bugs that fly around in all directions, never making any real progress but stirring up a lot of motion. Ask God to help you focus on changing one defect at a time. Otherwise you'll feel overwhelmed and discouraged, and you won't be able to change anything at all.

Focus on one specific change at a time, such as your anger, anxiety, workaholism, dishonesty, or your tendency to control people. In "Action Step 1" at the end of this chapter, you'll look through your moral inventory from chapter 4 and ask God which item on the list is causing the most damage to your life, today. He can help you focus on one defect at a time.

2. FOCUS ON VICTORY ONE DAY AT A TIME

God didn't promise to give us all the groceries we need for the entire year so we can stuff our refrigerator full and then forget about Him. When Jesus taught His disciples to pray, He said, *"Give us today our daily bread."*[7] He didn't say, "Give us this month our daily bread." He didn't ask for one week, one month, or the rest of His life. Why? Perhaps for two reasons: first, God wants us to lean on Him day by day; and second,

He knows we can't handle looking forward to a whole lifetime all in one chunk. We need it broken down. We can't think about living an entire lifetime of victory, but we can focus on victory for just one day.

It's like the old saying: "How do you eat an elephant? One bite at a time." You take a lifetime problem, remembering you didn't get it overnight, and you break it down into bite-size pieces. You seek victory one day at a time. God gives you enough strength to change for one day. He takes care of you one day at a time, as you put your trust in Him.

We live in a world of instant everything: mashed potatoes, coffee, microwave popcorn, even information. And we want instant spiritual maturity. One day we are a total mess, and we want to be Billy Graham the next. It doesn't happen that way. There's another old saying: "Life by the yard is hard, but by the inch, it's a cinch." You grow by inches. You experience victory day by day. Jesus tells us, *"Don't be anxious about tomorrow. God will take care of your tomorrow too. Live one day at a time."*[8]

Don't set a deadline for yourself; just work on it one day at a time. Some character defects you'll be working on for the rest of your life.

Ask God to help you just for today: "Lord, just for this day, I want to be patient and not get angry. Just for today, protect me from going to those Internet sites. Just for today, help me think pure thoughts instead of lustful ones. Just for today, I want to be positive instead of negative." Ask God to help you just for today, and take it a little bit at a time. This keeps you from making rash vows like, "I promise never to do it again, from here to eternity." Such promises doom you to failure. Remember, one day at a time. Bite-size pieces.

Each night thank God for whatever change or victory He has worked in your life, no matter how small.

3. FOCUS ON GOD'S POWER, NOT YOUR WILLPOWER

Can you remember your last New Year's resolutions? Even if you can remember them, have you followed through and actually done them? Probably not. Studies show that within six weeks, approximately 80 percent of us will break our New Year's resolutions.

You already know that willpower isn't enough. If your own willpower worked, you would have already changed. The truth is, your self-will can't help you change because *you* don't have the power to do it. In fact, depending on your own strength will actually block your recovery. It's like trying to turn that big boat by your own willpower when it's set on autopilot to go the opposite way. You struggle and you try, but in the end you are defeated because you just get worn out with the effort of fighting those strong opposing forces. As soon as you get tired, as soon as you let up just a little, the autopilot will pull you right back on the course you've always been on.

God's Word gives us some profound insight: *"Can . . . a leopard take away his spots? Nor can you who are so used to doing evil now start being good."*[9] Forget it. You'll never change by your own willpower. Here's the good news: *"I can do everything through him who gives me strength."*[10]

Try to imagine God literally taking away your character defect. Let's say you are working on your temper. Imagine taking your temper out and opening up the garbage can. Imagine putting your temper into the garbage can, sealing the lid, and taking the garbage can out to the curb. Then imagine the garbage truck pulling up by the side of the road. See the sign on the side that says, "God & Son, Doing Business with People Like You for 2000 Years."

Watch them pick up the garbage, dump it in the truck, and smash it down. Then watch as the truck turns around and speeds off, taking your defect with it. Some days you will need your garbage picked up about every hour. Talk to God about it: "God, it's going into the garbage." Then let God take it away. Willpower doesn't work. You have to trust God's power, not your own. He can help you change your character defects if you submit to Him and pray, "Lord, I know I can't change on my own power, but I'm trusting You to change me."

4. FOCUS ON THE GOOD THINGS, NOT THE BAD

The Bible says, "*Fix your thoughts on what is true and good and right. Think about things that are pure. Think about all you can praise God for and be glad about.*"[11] What you focus on is what you move toward. What you focus on dominates your life. If you focus on the bad, it will dominate your life. If you say, "I'm not going to think about sex, I'm not going to think about sex," guess what you are going to think about? Sex! So what's the answer? You change the mental channel of your mind. If you're watching an inappropriate show on TV, you don't just sit there and keep saying, "I'm not going to watch this; I'm not going to watch this." No, you pick up the remote control and change the channel.

This is where the power of God's Word comes in. Did you know that there are more than seven thousand promises in the Bible? These promises are the perfect channel to change to. When you get these promises into your mind, you can change your channel to something good at any time. You can change your channel by learning to memorize Scripture. Memorize one verse a week, and by the end of the year, you'll have fifty-two verses memorized. When they're in your mind, you can change the channel on any negative thoughts the enemy or others give you.

Did you know that every time you think a thought—positive or negative—it sends an electrical impulse across your brain, and that impulse creates a path? Every time you think the same thought, the path gets deeper and reinforces that brain pattern. Some of us have negative ruts in our minds because we've thought the same negative things over and over. But we can also create positive pathways in our mind. Every time we think about a scriptural truth, we reinforce that positive brain pattern. The only way to replace the negative ruts is to think God's Word over and over.

As you focus on what you can be and what God wants you to be, you will move in the right direction. Whatever has your attention has you. Jesus tells us, *"Stay alert, be in prayer, so you don't enter the danger zone without even knowing it. Don't be naive. Part of you is eager, ready for anything in God; but another part is as lazy as an old dog sleeping by the fire."*[12]

Stay focused on the good and not the bad. According to what Jesus said in the verse above, that means staying alert to the danger that's out there and being diligent in our positive focus instead of being *"as lazy as an old dog sleeping by the fire."*

5. FOCUS ON DOING GOOD, NOT FEELING GOOD

If you wait until you feel like changing, you'll never change. The enemy will make sure you never feel like it. But if you'll go ahead and do the right thing, your feelings will eventually catch up with you. It's always easier to act your way into a feeling than to feel your way into an action. If you don't feel loving toward your spouse, begin to act loving, and the feelings will come. If you wait until you feel like it, you may have a long wait.

The old phrase "Fake it 'til you make it" applies here. Do the right thing even though you don't feel like it. Do it because it's the right thing to do. Eventually, your feelings will catch up. Anytime you try to change a major part of your life—a character defect, flaw, personality trait, or weakness—it won't feel good at the start. In fact, it will feel awkward. Even more, it will feel bad for a while. Why? Because it won't feel normal. Sometimes we are so used to feeling abnormal that normal doesn't feel good.

Let's say you're a workaholic, and you decide to *do* the right thing whether you *feel* like it or not. So you go home at five, and you don't take work home in your briefcase. The first time you try this, it feels really weird. The first time you try to relax, you find that you don't know how to relax because you've worked so hard for so long. If you're an overeater, a drinker, or a smoker, the first time you try to break your habit, you feel weird because there's nothing in your mouth. It'll feel funny for a little while, and it may not feel right. But if you do the right thing, over and over, eventually your feelings will catch up with your behavior.

As we focus on doing what's right, we must draw on the power of the Holy Spirit, whom God has placed in all believers. Scripture makes a powerful promise about our reliance on the Holy Spirit: *"If you are guided by the Spirit you will be in no danger of yielding to self-indulgence."*[13] The guiding of the Holy Spirit works in direct opposition to self-indulgence. So as we *do* what's right, His power works in us to bring our heart and feelings in line.

6. FOCUS ON PEOPLE WHO HELP, NOT HINDER YOU

The Bible says, *"Do not be fooled: 'Bad friends will ruin good habits.'"*[14] In other words, if you don't want to get stung, stay away from the bees. If you know what type of people tempt you, just stay away from them. If you're struggling with alcoholism, don't say, "I think I'll go down to the bar with a friend just to eat some peanuts." Bad idea. If you're struggling with pornography, you don't hang out with a friend who has pornographic magazines lying all over his apartment. You don't get around people who mess you up.

On the other hand, you *do* need to hang around people who will help you make positive changes in your life. Again, the Bible has words for us: *"Two are better than one. . . . If one falls down, his friend can help him up. But pity the man who falls and has no one to help him up! . . . A cord of three strands is not quickly broken."*[15] There is power in numbers. If you fall you'll need the kind of friends who can help you up.

7. FOCUS ON PROGRESS, NOT PERFECTION

Some of you may be thinking, "I've been reading this book for a while now, and I don't see a whole lot of change yet." Don't worry about it. It's progress we're after, not perfection. Life change is a process. It's a *decision* followed by a *process*. To the Philippians, the apostle Paul said with total confidence, *"I am sure that God, who began the good work within you, will continue his work until it is finally finished on that day when Christ Jesus comes back again."*[16] If you have turned the change process over to God and have resolved to cooperate the best you can, God *will* work change in you through the power of His Holy Spirit.

Don't fall into the trap of thinking that God will only love you once you reach a certain stage. God loves you at each stage of recovery and growth. God will never love you any more than He does at this very minute. And He will never love you any less than He does right now. A father does not expect his seven-year-old to act like a seventeen-year-old. The seven-year-old still makes messes and acts like a child, but the father is pleased with and loves his seven-year-old child.

God is pleased with whatever growth and progress you have made. Just as a parent thrills at his or her baby's first steps, your heavenly Father thrills at each and every step of your growth—no matter how small. It's the direction of your heart that pleases Him as you say, "God, I voluntarily submit to the changes You want to make in my life. I humbly ask You to remove my character defects."

MAKE THE *Choice*

ACTION 1: *Pray about It*

In this chapter we've talked a lot about character defects—where they come from, why it takes so long to get rid of them, and how we can cooperate with God to change them. You may be feeling a bit overwhelmed, so let's just pause and take a breath. We're not trying to fix everything at once. Remember the question, "How do you eat an elephant?" You do it one bite at a time. That's how you'll face your character defects—one defect at a time. So in this action step, we're going to put into practice one of the seven ways to cooperate with God. The first focus step listed earlier is "Focus on changing one defect at a time." Look back at the moral inventory list you made in chapter 4. Through prayer, ask God to help you review this list and choose a place to start. You can pray, using your own words or follow along with the prayer below:

> *Dear God, thank You for Your forgiveness. Now I am ready and willing to submit to any and all changes You want to make in my life. By Your grace, I am ready to face it and deal with the defects one by one.*
>
> *I have defects that have hurt me and defects that have hurt others. I've lived with some of these defects for so long that they have become a part of who I am. I have tried by my own power to fight against my defects and have failed over and over. I now ask that by Your power and*

the power of Your Holy Spirit that You transform my mind, my heart, and my actions.

I need Your help in knowing where to start. I cannot handle all my defects at once. I can only face them one at a time. Show me, Lord, where should I begin? Help me as I look over my inventory list. Which character defect is the most damaging to my life? Where do I need to start? I am ready to follow Your lead. Amen.

ACTION 2: *Write about It*

In addition to writing in your journal, this action step will provide you with some Bible promises to help you focus on the *good* things, not the *bad*.

To begin, you'll need several 3 x 5 index cards. On one side of the card write a positive Scripture verse. On the other side write a practical application of the verse in the form of a personal affirmation. Here's an example:

On side one, write:

There is no condemnation for those
who belong to Christ Jesus.
(Romans 8:1 NLT)

Turn it over and write:

God does not condemn me for my
_____. He loves me just as much on
my bad days as on my good days. I can
make it through today without _____,
because Christ gives me His strength

Here's another example:

Side one:

> *Where God's love is,*
> *there is no fear,*
> *because God's perfect love*
> *drives out fear.*
> (1 John 4:18 NCV)

Side two:

> Today is going to be a better day than yesterday, because God is helping me get stronger. Yesterday, I was worried about _____. Today, I'm not afraid because God loves me!

Some other verses you might use are:

+ *If anyone belongs to Christ, there is a new creation. The old things have gone; everything is made new! (2 Corinthians 5:17 NCV)*

+ *Those who know your name will trust in you, for you, Lord, have never forsaken those who seek you. (Psalm 9:10 NIV)*

+ *Trust in the Lord with all your heart and lean not on your own understanding; in all your ways acknowledge him, and he will make your paths straight. (Proverbs 3:5–6 NIV)*

+ *Commit to the Lord whatever you do, and your plans will succeed. (Proverbs 16:3 NIV)*

+ *Come to me, all of you who are tired and have heavy loads, and I will give you rest.* (Matthew 11:28 NCV)

+ *Do not worry about anything, but pray and ask God for everything you need, always giving thanks. And God's peace, which is so great we cannot understand it, will keep your hearts and minds in Christ Jesus.* (Philippians 4:6–7 NCV)

+ *Without faith no one can please God. Anyone who comes to God must believe that he is real and that he rewards those who truly want to find him.* (Hebrews 11:6 NCV)

Write out a whole stack of these. Every night when you go to bed, read the verses and affirmations and think about them. When you wake up in the morning before you get out of bed, read them again. Put them in your pocket or purse and read them throughout the day. As you think positive thoughts, your autopilot will be reprogrammed and new positive ruts will be created in your mind. In about four to five weeks, you will begin to notice a difference in how you feel.

As you write in your journal . . .

+ Keep a record of how this simple exercise changes the way you feel about God, yourself, and others.

+ Write about the defect God has guided you to focus on first. Then record the progress (and setbacks) you are experiencing as you cooperate with God to focus on changing this one defect.

+ Spend time journaling about your efforts to "focus on *doing* good, not *feeling* good." It helps to write down the daily struggles and victories you have as you try to do the right thing, even when you don't feel like it.

As the weeks pass, you will see in black and white how you are overcoming certain defects of character. You will also begin to see other defects that you and God still need to work on. Having it all written down helps as you share your progress with your accountability partner.

ACTION 3: *Share about It*

If you shared your moral inventory list (your hurts, hang-ups, and habits) with your accountability partner, you've taken a big step in this sharing relationship. If you haven't shared it yet, you need to do so before you go any further. It is important to complete one choice completely, to the best of your ability, before moving on to the next. This is especially true with sharing your moral inventory. Your accountability partner can't help you work on your defects of character if he or she does not have all your information.

If you have shared your moral inventory, then you are ready to:

+ Share the one defect God has guided you to focus on changing first. Be honest about the character defect, how it has hurt you and how it has hurt others.

+ Share the progress God is making in your life in changing this defect. Be honest about your level of cooperation.

+ Share about your efforts to act yourself into a better way of feeling. Share the negative feelings you're trying to replace, and share the positive actions you're taking even though you don't yet have the feelings to match.

Remember the promise in Proverbs, *"As iron sharpens iron, so one man sharpens another."*[17]

Dovey's STORY

My name is Dovey, and I am a believer in Jesus Christ who struggles with codependency. Most of my life, I have felt that Christ was the rock and leader of my life. In the last eight years I have learned how important that foundation is. I learned to turn my life and will over to His care and allow Him to change me. The hope the Lord promises, by taking the bad things and using them for good, has been affirmed in my life.

I was born and raised in Southern California. I had a close and loving relationship with my mom and dad. Family life was happy most of the time. When I was two my grandmother died, and we moved into her house, along with a female relative. When I was three my brother was born. I was excited to get a baby brother, but I also remember feeling jealous of his blond curls and blue eyes. I thought he was beautiful like my mom. I was just the opposite. I had low self-esteem at an early age! When my brother started walking, he acted like Dennis the Menace. I learned early that my perfect behavior won praise, love, and respect.

When I was five we moved to a nice neighborhood into a charming cottage-style house by the best schools. Our relative again moved with us. I don't remember my parents fighting, but my dad did move out into an apartment for about a month. My only memory of this time was going to visit his apartment and seeing an 8x10 framed picture of another woman. Today I still wonder why he would subject me to this. The way I coped with all this was to attempt to block it out or minimize it. I learned to do this with other painful issues later in my life.

My dad returned home, and life went back to normal. My mom was a stay-at-home mom and devoted all her time to taking care of all of us. She

149

was a great cook, a designer seamstress, and worked hard to keep the house clean and comfortable. She always put herself last, rarely buying clothes or anything for herself. My dad was also a hard worker, both on his job and in keeping the house and cars in good repair. My mom and dad both taught me the value of hard work and perseverance. When my dad got home from work, my parents would have their nightly cocktails, but I never remember seeing them drunk. I can't ever remember them having heart-to-heart talks, but instead, they stayed very busy or watched television.

My dad discouraged my mom from seeing her family, but he insisted that his relative continue to live with us. We spent every weekend with another relative and her husband. These women were part of my day-to-day family and, unfortunately, were not positive role models. One was an unhappy, overweight woman, in a continuing relationship with her high-school boyfriend who was married. My parents never told us that there was anything wrong with this; they just felt sorry for her. She also brought pornographic magazines into the house. Childish curiosity caused me to peek at these, but they made me feel sick and uncomfortable.

The other relative and her husband were even more destructive to our family. The husband was a professional gambler and an alcoholic and made a lot of money through the card club that he kept open by paying off government officials. His wife called all the shots with my dad. My father allowed this because of his Armenian cultural beliefs. Nothing made you break ties with family. I also believe that my dad equated wealth with importance, no matter how that wealth was gained. My dad's relative would go into full manipulation or rage if my dad did not do whatever she wanted. He would allow me to go out to dinner with them at 10:00 at night to avoid a conflict with her.

They eventually had a daughter of their own. She was subjected to much emotional, verbal, and physical abuse. It was not uncommon for them to break into full-blown fights during our family gatherings—involving every foul word, throwing heavy objects, or the woman chasing her husband with a knife. I will never understand why my dad did not remove us as soon as conflict broke out, but he didn't. As children, my brother and I just got used to it. We really didn't know what normal was! We learned to accept abuse as normal. Why did people who said they loved you behave this way?

My mom took me to Sunday school every week at a small Baptist church, which I am very grateful for. This is where I learned about Jesus, the love He had for me, and the love I had for Him. He became my safe refuge. My parents did not go to church and did not depend on God, although they would say they believed in Him. I was baptized, committed my life to Christ, and served in my youth group. I wanted to go into the ministry, but in the sixties, I felt that was not encouraged for women. I did believe if I followed His ways, He would take care of me and remove the chaos from my life. Because of my relationship with Jesus, I was able to stand up to my family in my teen years about things I knew were wrong.

When I was eleven, the husband of my dad's relative was arrested. It was front-page news in our city paper. During his trial, he committed suicide. His wife became even more emotionally unstable, and finally, after an ugly display, my dad had to cut off our relationship with her. For a while, all was well. But when I was thirteen, I received some shocking news from my mom. She told me that she had been married once before and had two other children. She had left the children when they divorced, because she felt she had no way to care for them. This was unbelievable coming from my sweet "Donna Reed" mom! I didn't know what was real and what wasn't. I learned not to trust or expect any security.

Although my relationship with my dad was okay, he had unexpected moments of rage. These were not usually directed at me but at my mom or brother. When this would happen, my mom would never speak up for herself. She knew it would make his anger worse. My role in the family became the "rational peacemaker." On many occasions I would have to talk my dad "down" off one of his irrational binges. I also learned how to be a people pleaser and stay in his good graces. I avoided being a target at all cost.

During high school I became more focused on doing all the things I thought would bring me praise and, more important, a secure future. I was determined to do certain things to ensure that my future did not look like my past. I made good grades, was president of our Baptist Youth Fellowship, went to college, and tried to live the best godly life I could. My big mistake was looking to affirm myself through male attention. I really loved the fact that I always had a boyfriend, with someone always in the wings if I wasn't being treated perfectly. I realize now I was trying to fill my heart with love and raise my self-esteem.

After I graduated from college, I felt I was ready to make a life for myself. I found a great job and was feeling good. I soon started dating my husband-to-be, Tim, and all seemed perfect. We had known each other casually since we were twelve. My impression of him was that of a super-clean-cut basketball player from a good family. A regular Pat Boone! As I got to know him, I was excited that we had similar goals and morals. He had a very positive outlook and loving nature. He told me his family did not believe in Jesus, but he had come to believe in Him through religious education classes in his elementary school. He didn't feel close to his family, which was fine with me, because it gave us more time at my parents'. I didn't realize it then, but I was repeating my old family habits. He fulfilled everything on my perfect-husband list. We had a romantic, fun, whirlwind courtship and were engaged in six weeks!

During our engagement, I realized Tim drank a bit, but I thought all young men did. I didn't know what normal was. We got married in December of 1972. I became pregnant a few months later. The stress for Tim of being a father and breadwinner caused a time of upheaval in our marriage that would come and go in the years to come. Tim's drinking escalated and so did his verbal and emotional abuse. He struggled with depression and escaped to another relationship. I focused on caring for our daughter and trying to stuff my great pain and feeling of betrayal. I had empathy for Tim's depression, as I was well aware of his unhappy childhood. But the only thing I knew how to do was pray and go to church. I constantly looked at myself and wondered what I had done to cause him to lose love for me. I tried to do everything I could to fix it: "If only I had kept

the apartment perfect." "If only I would lose weight." My self-worth was at
an all-time low. When I look back, I am amazed that I allowed myself to
be treated so shabbily. But I didn't believe God wanted me to divorce. Also,
I had watched my mom put up with so much pain, past and present. This
was normal, right?

Over time our relationship improved, and Tim started attending church
off and on. We still struggled with Tim's issues of drinking and temper
outbursts. Then in 1986 Tim decided to stop drinking, still denying that he
was an alcoholic. However, his pain from his childhood didn't stop. Without
a recovery program or counseling, we still struggled with his anger and
"trading of dependencies."

After each incident of verbal abuse directed at our daughter or me, or
broken promise involving his sexual addiction, my husband would ask for
forgiveness. And I gave it. I thought it was easier to try to forgive than to
set boundaries or to carry out consequences. I continued to repress and stuff
my anger, which led to resentment, depression, and a lack of ability to offer a
truly intimate relationship.

Our daughter and I continued to attend church, and I got involved in
women's ministry. Over time Tim started to attend church regularly again,
and things seemed to be better each day. I really thought our problems
were behind us. In 1999 our daughter was getting married and we hit our
50s—fertile ground for midlife crisis and untreated addiction meltdown! I
started noticing signals that all was not well. Tim began isolating himself
more, and I noticed an escalation in girl watching and flirtation. Being the
good codependent that I was, I did all I could to control the situation. I
continued to ask him, "Is something bothering you? Are you behaving in
ways you shouldn't? Why are you watching TV by yourself instead of as a
family?" Of course, his response was "Everything is fine. You are imagining
things; you're paranoid." I could only accept these answers, go into hyper-
vigilance, and make sure to be with him as much as possible to try and head
off any problems. I honed my quiet controlling behavior to a new level!

One day when I was feeling particularly anxious, knowing all was not well, I pleaded with God to help me. He so clearly provided me with the answer: "Release him." Confused by thinking that God wanted me to divorce, I answered, "I can't do that now; this isn't a good time. My dad is dying, and my daughter is getting married." Again, God clearly directed me, "Release him." This time I understood God's direction. Nothing I did or could do would help Tim. All of my enabling and trying to control had only gotten in God's way. I painfully learned we had to "kiss concrete" (hit our bottom) to allow us to come out of denial and let God and His people help us heal.

A few weeks later, we did hit bottom. We will never forget the day. That was a traumatic day, but also a day that was the turning point in our family. Tim made an appointment with a Christian psychologist. The counselor informed us that Tim was a "dry alcoholic" who had traded addictions. Since Tim had quit drinking on his own with no recovery program, he still had the addictive personality. Our counselor felt there was little hope for our marriage, because so much damage had been done repeatedly and so much trust had been lost. I have to admit, I completely agreed with him at the time. All trust and respect had been destroyed in my heart and mind. I just didn't think I could go on after twenty-six years of being hurt and lied to. I think the only reason I had for trying was to hold the family together, one day at a time. My dad was dying from congestive heart and kidney failure, and my beautiful and treasured daughter was starting her new married life. Little did I realize that Tim and I were starting our new married life too. The chains of dysfunction that had run through our family were about to be broken.

Our psychologist told us to go to Celebrate Recovery. He recommended books for us to read. We completely immersed ourselves in recovery. The more we learned and understood about addiction, healing from past wounds, and poor relationship skills, the more we wanted to understand. We started the Celebrate Recovery Participant Guides and joined a Monday night step study. Then on Tuesday nights we went to the class on boundaries, Wednesdays we were home reading and working on our recovery material, Thursdays with our counselor, Friday nights at Celebrate, and Saturday nights at church. Every morning Tim would get up at the crack of dawn and go to a recovery meeting.

We knew we had to totally reprogram our old ways of thinking and relating. We were ready for the next step, which was:

CHOICE 5

Making CHANGES

Voluntarily submit to every change

God wants to make in my life and humbly ask Him to remove my character defects.

We were devoted to doing all the work it would require. We actually looked forward to it. There was great freedom in the new and intimate relationship we were forming with God, each other, and the other members of our Celebrate Recovery small groups. One of our greatest blessings was that our daughter and her husband started attending Celebrate Recovery with us. They also completed the step studies for themselves. I won't say that every day was easy or pain free. It wasn't! I learned that I had an idealized version of my family life in my head. I knew that hurtful events had occurred and that I had the habit of minimizing them to minimize my pain. I also learned that I tried to control everything I could, in a fruitless attempt to keep chaos and injury out of my life.

Day by day, the Lord healed my broken heart, and He showed me how my life had gotten to this point, and the part I played in it. He has brought wonderful ladies into my life who love me and let me love them. This kind of friendship was something I had lost during the years of trying to keep secrets and hide the problems in my family. God has healed and grown my marriage into a deep friendship, built on newfound truthfulness, respect, intimacy, and playful romance. He healed my daughter and son-in-law's emotions and hearts. This is an awesome treasure, for it promises a break in the chain of our family dysfunction and a rich and loving future for our grandchildren. God has proven to me that He will bring good out of bad in a dramatic way!

We were so grateful for all the Lord had given us that we wanted to give back. We now share our experiences with others and encourage them to come to Celebrate Recovery. Tim and I became leaders and co-lead groups on Friday nights and Monday night step studies. I continue to grow as I serve in this way. The Lord has truly restored the years that were lost.

John's STORY

My name is John, a believer who struggles with alcohol and pride. I would like to share with you how God has used my Saddleback church family and Celebrate Recovery to change my life in ways I never would have thought possible. Twelve years ago I was struggling to make ends meet. I had become a blackout drinker on the verge of losing the two people who meant the most to me, my wife and my little girl. I was self-centered and totally consumed with resentment over the unfairness of life. My pride and my arrogance would not even allow for the possibility that maybe, just maybe, some of my unhappiness was due to the poor choices I had made. No, it had to be somebody else's fault that life had lost its meaning. Here's the scary part of my story: As far as the outside world and most of my friends were concerned, nothing was wrong with John. I was still suiting up for work every day in corporate America. As a salesman in the high-tech networking field, I was your typical hard driver, trying to control everything and everyone in the pursuit of my goals and my desires. "Whatever it takes" had become my motto. Stress was part of the landscape, and a "couple" of drinks at the end of the day were well deserved. I thought, "If things don't work out at home, I could always get a divorce. No big deal, right?" I was really out there!

When I think back on the emptiness I felt at that time, I am appalled at how lonely I was. I had so many walls up around me, even my wife couldn't get inside. Everything I had tried in the pursuit of happiness had failed to provide any lasting sense of fulfillment and purpose. What had gone wrong? As I look back on my story, I see nothing earth-shattering about my circumstances—no broken home, no going to bed hungry at night, no abuse as a child. In fact, I had a very normal middle-class start in life, grew up in a good Christian home, and attended church every week. My problem was that at a very young age, I became determined to earn God's approval and the approval of everyone else. Unfortunately, living for the approval of others is all about ego and self-gratification. I have been in total denial about this for most of my life. I thought I was just trying to please others. In reality, I was only concerned about what I could do to make myself look good. When I was a teenager, people in my church started telling me that I'd take over for Billy Graham someday, and it was music to my ears. I figured, *If that is true, then God must think I'm really neat.* So instead of finding a relationship with God based on trust and forgiveness, I found a religion based on performing for God. In fact, I set out to be the one person in the world who would never let God down.

Always trying to do everything by the book, I married a good Christian girl from a good Christian home and planned to enter full-time ministry. At this stage, God had become nothing more than an intellectual exercise, and my relationship with Him had been reduced to a set of legalistic standards. I graduated from seminary with a 3.8 GPA, a master's degree in theology, and a major case of clinical depression.

Entering therapy, I found that much of my self-imposed demand for perfection was due to my major character defect of an inflated sense of self. But instead of accepting the truth that I was no better and no worse than the next guy, I used psychobabble to blame it all on my parents. I was always ready to blame somebody else for whatever was wrong with me. Even worse, my image of God had turned into a belief that He was unpleasable. I used that as an excuse for satisfying all of my pent-up demands for ego gratification. Instead of realizing that He already loved me as much as I wanted Him to, I threw out the proverbial baby with the bathwater. I gave up on trying to please God. I gave up on entering the ministry.

Entering corporate America, I quickly earned the adulation of my company and celebrated my first year of success on the French Riviera. I was being rewarded for being my company's salesman of the year, and I felt like a movie star. With everyone telling me I was on my way to the good times, I felt I could live life on my own terms. God never gave me a standing ovation, but now everyone else was doing just that. What more did I need?

Riding high in 1984 with plenty of money and a big home, I found myself needing constant reassurance that I really was something special. I was coming up empty, but I was still convinced I could live life on my own terms. Surrounded by women who were openly available, I saw them as a way to meet my narcissistic craving for self-confirmation that I was something special. I began to commit adultery after nine years of marriage. I was so consumed by my own neediness, I hardly noticed my wife's broken heart when I finally told her what I had been doing behind her back. But, consistent with my "take care of number one" approach to life, I found excuses for everything. My lousy excuse for being unfaithful to my wife was that she was not "attractive" enough. Blaming her for everything gave me a way to justify my divorce.

At this stage, I found a gorgeous girlfriend who looked good on my arm, and I went into party mode. Alcohol and cocaine were the order of the day. In a short two years, I managed to run up a $60,000 credit-card debt. I couldn't pay off the debt because the drugs and alcohol had taken their toll, making me totally ineffective at work. Of course, the bankruptcy wasn't my fault! That was my ex's fault for taking me to the cleaners. Excuses and alcohol always gave me a way to deny the pain and what I had become: isolated, self-centered, and egotistical. I took all the gifts God had given me and convinced myself that I didn't need His help with anything. Like the prodigal son in Luke, I wound up in a pigpen.

In spite of all the drunken hurt and heartache I caused in her life, that gorgeous girlfriend became my wife. A few years later, our daughter was born. Danielle's arrival gave me an inkling that there was more to life than just living for me. However, by this time, my love affair with alcohol had taken over my life. I would try to pace my drinking around my little girl's bath. I thought she would be safe if I was only "buzzed." After she went to bed, I'd complete the process, and my wife would have to put me to bed. Finally, in early 1994, my wife told me, "Enough is enough." That was my first wake-up call. I knew I had to get my life together or I would lose both of them. I stopped going out to bars, but I continued to drink at home. Drinking allowed me to black out every night and perpetuate the denial of my emptiness. Mornings were miserable as I dragged myself into work. I tried to get over the guilt of not being able to remember any detail from the previous night. In my denial, I still managed to justify the memory loss as a simple case of being overly tired. I mean, everybody forgets how they got to bed the night before, right? "Blackout" was never a consideration.

Although I was reluctant to turn to God, He remained faithful to me. He was waiting for me to come home. At my wife's urging, we started going to Saddleback Church in March of 1996. From the very first day, we met people who have demonstrated God's love for me in critical ways and who have literally made the difference between life and death. That first Sunday, I was looking for any excuse to conclude that this place was just a bunch of phonies. As we walked up to the two-year-old childcare, I thought to myself, If my daughter shows any resistance to this place, we are out of here. Instead, a lady named Julie reached out her arms to my little girl. Danielle took one look at her and almost jumped from my arms into hers. God used Julie that day to reach out to my family. I thank God for her heart.

I sat in church that first Sunday, waiting for somebody to tell me I needed to donate my hard-earned money to God. But then I read this in the church bulletin: "Please do not feel obligated to participate in the offering!" What kind of weird place was this, anyway? For the first time in my life, I actually enjoyed church music. It wasn't too fast; it wasn't too slow. As hard as I tried, I could not find fault with Pastor Rick Warren's message, and the love there was almost tangible. In all my church attendance and seminary, I'd never really grasped the truth that I mattered to God! Then one Sunday in May, a man from the church's Celebrate Recovery program gave his testimony as a part of Pastor Rick's message. Like me, Jon was a functional alcoholic. His story, and the ministry of this church, made me start to hope again that a relationship with a God of love could give my life some real purpose. Jon, I thank God always for your testimony.

June 11, 1996, was my first day of sobriety. I came to my first Celebrate Recovery with a feeling that I had no place else to go. I found a bunch of men who had nothing but love, compassion, and understanding in their hearts. One man in particular helped me enormously that first night. I was humiliated and deeply embarrassed over even being seen with a bunch of avowed alcoholics. I mean after all, this is John we're talking about. I wasn't like the rest of those guys. Unfortunately, or fortunately as the case may be, all my education and all my posturing failed me that night. I couldn't even complete a four-word sentence as I tried to explain who I was and why I was there. God sent Kenny to my rescue. He completed those sentences for me and made it okay for me to be there. Kenny was the first man to show me acceptance simply because I was me. He was much more eloquent that night than I have ever been with all my fancy degrees. Kenny, I thank God always for your love.

On the eighth day of my recovery, I wrote this in my journal: "I am still searching for a God who I hope is there. Perhaps my God is too small; perhaps He is not there. I fervently hope that is not true, because I have no place else to go." I had tried everything else. Even though I was losing my grip at work because of the alcoholic haze, and in spite of the cost of the things I destroyed when I was drunk, I knew my drinking was just a symptom of my real problem. I was in a life-and-death search for the God who could make sense out of my life. Sixteen days into my recovery, I met with Pastor John and he shared a Bible verse with me that finally cut through all of my denial: "'Be still, and know that I am God!'"[18] I finally heard God say to me, "It's okay now; you can stop trying to maintain the façade that you've got it all together. You don't have to make excuses for your life any longer. That is why I died for you. Be still, relax, and accept My gift. You're free!" At long last I finally came home to my Abba, my Daddy in heaven. I finally began to understand that God's purpose for my life all along was to simply have a relationship with Him. What a concept—I was made to be loved by God! Pastor John, I thank God always for your openness to being led by God. And I thank God for how He used that meeting with Pastor John to open my eyes to the truth of His love.

As I started to embrace the process of recovery in this place, my first reaction was to complete the Celebrate Recovery program in record time.

The obsessive-compulsive habits of overachieving were not going to die on their own. Thankfully, I found an accountability partner, a mentor, who had the wisdom to see right through that defense mechanism. He spent his entire time slowing me down and just loving me. When I finally completed my moral inventory and openly confessed my faults to my accountability partner at the end of four hours, I told him there was one other thing I had not written down. As I watched his eyes intently for any flicker of condemnation, I openly confessed something that had haunted me since early childhood. Instead of condemnation, and with tears in his eyes, John communicated the unconditional love and forgiveness of Jesus. John, I will always thank God for your love.

I am alive again! I am amazed at the peace I feel as I learn to let go of my own control and allow God to direct me. By God's grace I've been sober for eleven years. God has restored my relationship with my wife. He has renewed my productivity at work and made it possible for me to be a daddy to my little girl. Danielle does not even remember a daddy who drank every night. In the middle of writing my story, Danielle walked into my room and asked if she could write something. She wanted to write, "Daddy is the greatest dad God has ever created!" That alone is a blessing beyond compare. My wife, Sheila, has become my best friend, something that all of my arrogant manipulation had never been able to realize. We're still learning how to accept each other as high-maintenance people who do have bad-hair days on occasion. But we are learning how to forgive each other and make allowances for the differences that come up in any relationship.

Like the prodigal son returning home, I have been welcomed back into the family of God with far more love and forgiveness than I ever thought possible, and certainly more then I deserve. About a hundred days into my sobriety, Pastor Rick decided to trust me and asked me to share my story with my church family. I've got to tell you, looking back on that, I wouldn't have trusted me with a hundred days of sobriety. But God used that opportunity to humble me. The fact that I was sharing my story in the light of day forced me to realize the miracle that had happened in my life. Only God could have effected the changes that had taken place in such a short time. Pastor Rick, I will always thank God for your trust. I truly knew I was ready to have God change me. I was ready for Him to begin to remove my defects of character. I was ready for:

CHOICE 5

Making CHANGES

Voluntarily submit to every change

God wants to make in my life and humbly ask Him to remove my character defects.

Today I still struggle with my pride on a daily basis. It's still very easy to fall back into the old pattern of thinking that if I perform flawlessly, I will be able to control the outcome. But by surrendering my life to Jesus on a daily basis, staying connected and accountable to my church family, and giving back what God has so freely given me, I am reasonably happy and at peace with myself and others for the first time in years! Philippians 2:3 says, "Do nothing out of selfish ambition or vain conceit, but in humility consider others as better than yourself." Humility isn't thinking poorly about yourself; humility is not thinking about yourself at all.

Shortly before my dad died, he gave me a new insight on what it means to take up my Lord's towel of service on a daily basis. I asked him what he wanted to do when he got to heaven. In times past, this once-proud man would have said he wanted to help the apostle Paul teach the book of Romans. This time he simply said, "I hope my Lord will trust me to go on errands for him." Like my dad, I hope to go on errands for my King wherever that may lead. God has given me a second chance to answer the call I received so long ago to go into full-time ministry as my career. This has been the miracle to end all miracles.

God's purpose for my life is still unfolding. But, as He gives me the opportunity to share my experience, victories, and hopes with people, I am reminded of what Jesus said:

> "Anyone who intends to come with me has to let me lead.
> You're not in the driver's seat; I am. Don't run from suffering;
> embrace it. Follow me and I'll show you how.
> Self-help is no help at all. Self-sacrifice is the way,
> my way, to saving yourself, your true self.
> What good would it do to get everything you want and lose you,
> the real you? What could you ever trade your soul for?"[19]

At Celebrate Recovery, I know beyond a shadow of a doubt that this path I am on would be impossible without the power of God in my life. Not drinking anymore is the tip of the iceberg. Getting rid of my defects of character will be a long process, but as Jesus said, "With man this is impossible, but with God all things are possible"[20]

Changed lives! That is what this book is all about. How exciting and encouraging it is to read real stories like Dovey's and John's. You know God wants to change your life too! All you need to do is let go and start working on this fifth choice!

R
E
C
O
V
E
R
Y

Evaluate all my relationships.

Offer *forgiveness* to those who have hurt me,
and make amends for harm I've done to others,
except when to do so would harm them or others.

"Happy are those who are merciful to others." [1]

"Happy are those who work for peace." [2]

Repairing RELATIONSHIPS

The RELATIONSHIP Choice

I love collecting "church bloopers"—funny mistakes made in the church bulletin or spoken during announcements from the pulpit. But sometimes the corrections are funnier than the original bloopers. One Sunday morning during announcements, the pastor said, "I need to make a correction to an announcement from last week's bulletin. It read: The church will host an evening of fine dining, super entertainment, and gracious hostility. It should have read: The church will host an evening of fine dining, super entertainment, and gracious hospitality. Sorry, folks, we are a loving church, not a hostile one. We love hurting people."

He then went on to say, "I just have one announcement for this morning. The peacekeepers meeting scheduled for this afternoon has been canceled due to a conflict."

Sometimes in our attempts to make amends and correct a wrong, the situation is made worse. In the above example, the corrections were attempts to make right something that was wrong. Though the results were not what was desired, the sentiment was right.

In this choice we'll work on making "corrections" in some of our relationships by doing some relational repair work. And we'll do that by working through a two-part process: We'll start off by *forgiving* those who have hurt us, and then we will work on *making amends* to those we have hurt.

There are two beatitudes that guide us in our sixth choice:

"Happy are those who are merciful to others."
"Happy are those who work for peace."[3]

When we are *merciful* to others, we are willing to forgive them, whether they deserve it or not. That's what mercy is about—it's undeserved. And when we *work for peace,* we put out real effort to make amends where we have wronged another, and we work to bring harmony back into that relationship. This choice and these beatitudes are all about repairing relationships. In this chapter we'll look back on our lives for the purpose of evaluating, not regretting. We'll learn how to repair the damage that others have done to us and that we have done to others.

Let's begin with forgiving others for the wrongs they have done against us. But *why* should you do this and *how* do you do it? These are good questions.

REPAIRING RELATIONSHIPS BY FORGIVING THOSE WHO'VE HURT YOU

WHY SHOULD YOU FORGIVE OTHERS?

There are at least three reasons, and believe it or not, the benefits are all yours.

1. Because God Has Forgiven You

If God has forgiven you, shouldn't you forgive others? The Bible says, *"You must make allowance for each other's faults and forgive the person who offends you. Remember, the Lord forgave you, so you must forgive others.*"[4] When you remember how much God has forgiven you, it makes it a whole lot easier for you to forgive others. The Bible also says, *"Get rid of all bitterness, rage and anger, brawling and slander, along with every form of malice. Be kind and compassionate to one another, forgiving each other, just as in Christ God forgave you."*[5] You forgive as Christ forgave you. You will never have to forgive anybody else more than God has forgiven you.

When you have a hard time forgiving someone else, it's usually because you don't feel forgiven. It is a fact that people who feel forgiven find it easier to be forgiving. If you don't feel forgiven, look again at these two verses: *"Remember, the Lord forgave you . . ."* and, *"Forgive each other, just as in Christ God has forgiven you."* If you accepted Christ in choice 3, you are *forgiven!* It is a done deal. Now He asks you to turn around and forgive others.

2. Because Resentment Doesn't Work

The second reason you need to forgive those who have hurt you is purely practical: resentment doesn't work. Holding on to resentment is *unreasonable, unhelpful,* and *unhealthy.*

Resentment is unreasonable. The Bible says it plainly: *"To worry yourself to death with resentment would be a foolish, senseless thing to do."*[6] Why is holding on to resentment foolish and senseless? The practical answer is that *"you are only hurting yourself with your anger."*[7] Resentment hurts you much more than the person you resent. Think about it. When you are angry and resentful toward someone, you're not hurting them; you're hurting yourself. You're the one who's stewing, spewing, stressing, and fretting. You're the one who's losing sleep and being distracted from the joys of life. It's not bothering them at all! They're sleeping great. They probably aren't even aware of all the huffing and puffing that's going on inside you. They're oblivious to it all.

Someone may have hurt you ten, twenty, thirty years ago, and you're still hurting yourself over it. It's still making you miserable, but they've forgotten all about it. From a purely practical point of view, resentment is totally unreasonable—it's an irrational waste of energy, making no sense at all.

> *Nothing* DRAINS *you emotionally like bitterness and resentment.*

Resentment is unhelpful. Resentment cannot change the past, the problem, or the person who hurt you. It doesn't even hurt the person who hurt you; it only hurts you. Resentment certainly doesn't make you feel better. Have you ever known anyone to say, "I feel so much better being resentful"? Of course not! Resentment just makes you mad and unhappy.

Resentment is unhealthy. "*Some people stay healthy till the day they die. . . . Others have no happiness at all; they live and die with bitter hearts.*"[8] Resentment is like a cancer that eats you alive. It's an emotional poison with physical consequences. Have you ever said, "That guy is a pain in the neck"? Did you ever stop to think that your resentment against him may actually be causing that real pain in your neck?

Did you hear the one about the guy who walked into his doctor's office and said, "I need some more pills for my colitis"? The doctor asked, "Who are you colliding with now?" Resentment has emotional and physical consequences. It can lead to depression, stress, and fatigue. Nothing drains you emotionally like bitterness and resentment. Continuing to replay the hurt you received from that teacher, relative, business associate, or former husband or wife allows them to continue hurting you emotionally and physically today! It simply prolongs the hurt. It's a kind of emotional suicide. In the beatitudes paired with this chapter, Jesus shows us a better way: *"Happy are those who are merciful to others"*[9] and, *"Happy are those who work for peace."*[10] Mercy and peace.

3. Because You'll Need Forgiveness in the Future

We will all need God's and others' forgiveness in the future. *"When you are praying, first forgive anyone you are holding a grudge against, so that your Father in heaven will forgive you your sins too."*[11] Resentment blocks you from feeling God's forgiveness. The Bible says you cannot receive what you are unwilling to give: *"Forgive us our debts, as we forgive our debtors."*[12] It can be dangerous to pray the Lord's Prayer. In it, you are praying, "Lord, forgive me as much as I forgive everybody else." You want nothing short of His complete and full forgiveness, so the obvious implication is that you must extend nothing less to those who have sinned against you.

The story has been told about a man who went to John Wesley and said, "I can never forgive that person. Never."

John Wesley replied, "Then I hope you never sin. Because we all need what we don't want to give." Don't burn the bridge you need to walk across.

HOW DO YOU FORGIVE OTHERS?

Forgiving others is not easy. How do you forgive those who have hurt you? These three Rs can show you how: *Reveal, Release,* and *Replace.*

1. Reveal Your Hurt

You have some options when it comes to dealing with your hurts. You can *repress* them and pretend they don't exist, but they do. You can *ignore* them and try pushing them out of the way. That never works because those hurts always pop out in some form of compulsion. You can *suppress* them and say, "It's no big deal; it doesn't matter. They did the best they could." No they didn't. These people hurt you. Or you can do what works: You can *admit* them. You can reveal the truth that you hurt.

You can't get over the hurt until you admit the pain. Why is it that we don't want to admit that the people we love have caused us pain? Perhaps it's because we have the misconception that you can't love somebody and be angry with them at the same time. The truth is, you can.

A woman in a counseling session insisted, "I forgive my parents; they did the best they could." But the more she talked, the more obvious it became that she really hadn't forgiven them. She was angry with them, and she was denying her anger. The truth was, her parents hadn't done the best they could. None of us do the best we can. Your parents didn't, and if you're a parent, you are not doing the best you can. We're all imperfect, and we all make mistakes. When this woman was able to admit that her parents didn't do the best they could, then she was able to forgive them.

If you want to close the door on your past and get closure so certain people don't hurt you anymore, you can do it. But there's one thing you have to remember: there is no closure without disclosure. First you must admit it, or *reveal* it, by owning up to the truth: "That hurt. It was wrong, and it hurt me."

Once you've revealed the hurt, then you will be in a position to *forgive*. You can't forgive a hurt you won't admit.

2. Release the Offender

The second step in forgiving an offender is *releasing* him or her. You may have some questions about how this works.

When do I release the offender? The answer is that you do it now; you don't wait for the offender to ask for forgiveness. You make the choice to do it independently of the other person. You do it whether the person asks for forgiveness or not, and you do it for your sake, not the other person's. You do it for the three reasons we looked at earlier in the chapter: because God has forgiven you, because resentment doesn't work, and because you'll need forgiveness in the future. So you release your offender and forgive for your own sake.

How often do I have to do it? Jesus was asked this very question by Peter: "'How often should I forgive someone who sins against me? Seven times?' 'No!' Jesus replied, 'seventy times seven.'"[13] Jesus is saying that our forgiveness must be continual. Forgiveness is not a one-shot deal where you say, "I forgive you," and it's done. Those feelings of resentment are going to keep coming back. Every time they do, you've got to forgive again until you have fully released the offender, even if it takes a hundred times or more.

How will I know that I have fully released an offender? You'll know when you can think about him or her and it doesn't hurt anymore. You'll know when you can pray for God's blessing on his or her life. When you can begin to look at and understand the hurt he or she feels, rather than focusing on how you have been hurt—remembering that hurt people hurt people. You keep forgiving and keep forgiving, until thoughts of the person or offense aren't associated with hurt. You may not be able to completely forget, but you can release the offender and let go of the pain.

Is it always wise to release the offender face-to-face? Not always. And in some cases it's not even possible to go back to the people who have hurt you. To bring up old hurts may not be productive for you or kind to them. If your parents hurt you, they may not even know about it, and for you to go back to them forty years later and bring up old pain would just blow them away. You may not be able to find some of the other people even if you wanted to. They may have remarried, moved away, or even died.

What do you do in those situations? There are two techniques you can use. One is the empty chair technique. You sit alone with an empty chair and you imagine the person you need to forgive sitting in the chair, and you say, "I need to say some things to you. Here's how you hurt me," and you lay it out. "You hurt me this way, this way, and this way. But I want you to know I forgive you because God has forgiven me, because resentment doesn't work, and because I will need forgiveness in the future. I am releasing you."

Another technique is to write a letter that you will never mail. In this letter you put down in black and white how you have been hurt: "This is how you hurt me." You've been carrying your hurt so long. Now is the time to unload it, and you can do that by letting it out in a letter. At the end you say, "But starting today, I forgive you because God has forgiven me, because resentment doesn't work, and because I will need forgiveness in the future." And you do it for your own sake. You release your offender so you can experience freedom.

3. Replace Your Hurt with God's Peace

At some point, all this free forgiveness may start to sound unfair. If I forgive this person—especially if I forgive my offender without him asking for forgiveness or without me ever confronting her face-to-face—then he or she gets off scot-free. I've been hurt, and this person suffered no consequences.

We need to relax and let God settle the score. He can do a whole lot better job than we can, anyway. The Bible says, *"We will all stand before God's judgment seat. It is written: 'As surely as I live,' says the Lord, 'every knee will bow before me; every tongue will confess to God.' So then, each of us will give an account of himself to God."*[14] We see here that God is going to settle the score. He's going to call things into account; He's going to balance the books; and one day, He's going to have the last word. He'll take care of it. He's the judge. He's just. When we learn to release our offenders and allow God to be in charge of settling scores, then we will discover the wonderful blessing of His peace. The Bible tells us to *"let the peace of Christ rule in your hearts."*[15] You get to choose what rules your heart. It can be the misery of unforgiveness or the peace of Christ.

The fact is, relationships can tear your heart into pieces. But God can glue those pieces back together and cover your heart with His peace.

When you forgive those who have hurt you, God is free to do the needed repair in your heart.

Before we move on to the second part of repairing relationships, let's review choice 6:

CHOICE 6

Repairing **RELATIONSHIPS**

Evaluate all my relationships.

Offer forgiveness to those who have hurt me, and make amends for harm I've done to others, except when to do so would harm them or others.

With this in mind, let's move on to the second part of relationship mending.

REPAIRING RELATIONSHIPS BY MAKING AMENDS TO THOSE YOU'VE HURT

Repairing relationships is a two-part process: we've talked about *forgiveness;* the second part is *making amends.* Not only have people hurt you; you have hurt other people. *Why do we need to make amends* and *how do we it?*

WHY DO YOU NEED TO MAKE AMENDS?

As painful as making amends may seem, it is absolutely essential. Dealing with the root of your problems means dealing with unresolved relationships. Until you do this, recovery can't happen.

When I got to this choice, I had a lot of work to do. I had quite a long list of names of people to whom I needed to make my amends. Over the years of making poor choices, I had hurt a lot of people. They ranged from former employees and employers, to friends and neighbors. But the most special amends I needed to make were to my family. I had caused them a lot of pain and heartache, but they graciously accepted my amends, and our relationships were restored. Today those relationships are stronger and more loving than I could ever have hoped for or deserved.

After I completed making my amends, God truly blessed me and my recovery. He gave me the vision of starting Celebrate Recovery—a Christ-centered recovery ministry for people struggling with all kinds of hurts, hang-ups, and habits. It is a safe place for individuals and families to find His healing grace.

Making amends is such a big deal that the Bible says, "*If you are standing before the altar in the Temple, offering a sacrifice to God, and you suddenly remember that someone has something against you, leave your sacrifice there beside the altar. Go and be reconciled to that person. Then come and offer your sacrifice to God.*"[16]

One of our beatitudes for this choice says, "*Happy are those who work for peace.*" Making amends is "working for peace." The Bible places a high priority on getting things right in our relationships.

The Bible also says, "*Watch out that no bitterness takes root among you, for as it springs up it causes deep trouble, hurting many in their spiritual lives.*"[17] One of the reasons you can't let go of that hurt, get past that hang-up, or get over that habit is that when you hold on to unresolved relationships, bitterness takes root in your heart and causes all kinds of trouble. These unresolved relationships must be dealt with if you're really going to get on with your recovery and enjoy the happiness that comes from being merciful and making peace, as our beatitude says.

We've talked about *why* we need to make amends; now we'll talk about the hard part: *how to do it.*

HOW DO YOU MAKE AMENDS?

The Bible has a great piece of advice on keeping peace with others: *"If it is possible, as far as it depends on you, live at peace with everyone."*[18] Keep this in mind as you work through the steps of making amends to those you've hurt. Do what you can. The Scripture says, *"If it is possible, as far as it depends on you . . ."* You are only responsible for what you do; you are not responsible for how the person you approach responds to your amends.

How do you make amends to the people you've hurt? We'll show you how:

1. Make a List of Those You've Harmed and What You Did

We'll do the actual hands-on work for this step in the "Make the Choice" action steps, but let's think about a couple of things as we introduce this idea.

First, a word of caution: As you start listing the people you need to make amends to, your mind may immediately jump to "How on earth am I going to pull this off?!" Don't worry about the "how-to's" right now. Don't travel down that mental road of "How will I ever ask forgiveness of my ex-spouse?" or "How can I pay back the money I borrowed from my dad?" Just write the names down; the how-to will come later.

Second, some of you may be saying, "I can't think of anybody I've hurt." In the "Make the Choice" section, you'll find some questions to help get you started. Getting the names and offenses down in black and white is an important first step in making things right with those you've wronged.

2. *Think about How You'd Like Someone to Make Amends to You*

Most of us have heard these words from Jesus before: *"Do to others as you would have them do to you."*[19] So stop and think, "If someone were going to come and apologize to me, how would I want it done?" Here are four things that might affect how you'd want it done:

Timing: There is a time to *let* things happen and a time to *make* things happen. There are right times and wrong times to make amends. You don't just drop a bomb on somebody. You don't just bring up a sensitive topic when they're rushing out the door or as they're laying their head down on the pillow: "By the way, I've got some stuff to deal with, and it involves you." You do it according to what works best for the other person, not when it's best for you. Ecclesiastes says, *"There's a right time and right way to do everything."*[20]

Attitude: Think about how you would like somebody to apologize to you. Here are four things to consider.

First, do it *privately.* Choose your time and place carefully, and consider what will make the other person the most comfortable.

Second, do it with *humility.* Sincerely and simply say what you did wrong. Don't make any justification for your actions or attitude; offer no excuses. Just humbly acknowledge your part in the problem and assume whatever responsibility belongs to you. The other person may have had a part in the problem too, but you're just trying to clear up *your* side of the ledger.

Third, do it *without expectations.* Don't expect anything back from the person you're trying to make amends to. If the other person doesn't acknowledge his or her responsibility or apologize too, who cares? While it is important to consider them regarding *appropriateness* and *timing*, the actual heart change is not about them. It's about you doing what's right.

Appropriateness: There will be some situations when contacting the one you've hurt would be unwise. Remember the qualifier in choice 6: "except when to do so would harm them or others." In some situations, trying to make amends would be inappropriate because it would open up a whole can of worms and probably make the situation worse. You could harm an innocent party, as well as the person you intended to make amends to. You wouldn't want to go back to an old boyfriend or girlfriend who is now married. If you were involved in an affair, it would be inappropriate to have further contact with that person. The more serious your offense, the less likely it would be appropriate to make amends face-to-face. So what do you do? Once again, you can use the empty-chair or unmailed letter technique. The wisdom of Proverbs says, "*Rash language cuts and maims, but there is healing in the words of the wise.*"[21] Consider the situation, consider the person, and try to make amends in the way that's best for him or her.

> "*If someone were going to come and* APOLOGIZE *to me, how would I want it done?*"

Restitution: Make restitution wherever possible. If you've borrowed something and not returned it, return it. If you owe somebody some money, pay it back—even if it takes a long time. Making restitution gives you freedom and confidence.

The Bible tells about a guy named Zacchaeus. He was a tax collector, and in Bible times tax collectors could charge people as much as they could get from them. After paying Rome, they could keep whatever was left over. As a consequence, they were the most hated people in society. But of all people Jesus could have visited, He chose to go see Zacchaeus.

Meeting Jesus changed Zacchaeus's life, and with that life-change, he decided to make restitution for everything he had ever cheated anyone of. In fact, he decided to restore it all fourfold. This guy was willing to put his money where his mouth was by making restitution.

Again, the more serious your offence, the less likely you'll be able to make restitution. There are some things you can't restore. But don't underestimate the power of a sincere apology. Here's what you do: discern the right time, put on the right attitude, be sure making contact is appropriate, then say something like, "I'm sorry. I was wrong. I don't deserve your forgiveness, but is there any way I can make restitution to you?" And you leave it at that.

3. Refocus Your Life

Today can be a new day. Starting today, you can refocus your life on doing God's will in your relationships.

As long as you focus on the past, you allow the past to control you. The good news is this: God wants to deal with all the relational garbage in your life, once and for all. He knows when you can handle it and how much you can handle at a time, so He takes the garbage off one layer at a time. When you committed your life and will to Christ in making choice 3, a layer came off. As time goes on, God keeps dealing with you, working with you, releasing you from hurts, hang-ups, and habits.

As you make this sixth choice, forgiving those who have hurt you and making amends to those you have hurt, God begins to recycle the relational garbage of your life and use it for good. How does He do that? In the book of Job, we find three steps to refocusing—and recycling—

your life, and with those steps comes one amazing promise: *"Put your heart right. . . . Reach out to God, . . . then face the world again, firm and courageous. Then all your troubles will fade from your memory, like floods that are past and remembered no more."*[22]

"Put your heart right." Refocusing your life begins with your heart. This is where you get your attitude right so you can begin to make amends.

"Reach out to God." If you haven't yet asked God into your life, you can do it today. You do not have the strength to make amends on your own. It's too big a job to handle alone. You need to plug in to Jesus Christ. He can daily give you the strength, wisdom, and humility to face your past and make amends where you can. As you reach out to God, He will enable you to reach out to others and make amends.

"Face the world again." As you make amends and clean your slate, *"as far as it depends on you,"* you resume living. Your eyes are open and looking ahead as you courageously and joyfully face the world. You step out and say, "I'm not a victim anymore." You don't withdraw; you don't hide in a shell; you start looking ahead.

"Then all your troubles will fade from your memory like floods that are past and remembered no more." Here's the promise: as we put our hearts right, reach out to God, and face the world again, the memory of our troubles will begin to fade away. Wow. In those few words is the sound of hope.

Wouldn't you like to be free from all that relational garbage? The choice is yours. Peace and mercy await you.

MAKE THE
Choice

ACTION STEP 1: *Pray about It*

You've worked through the first five choices of this book; you've made a lot of progress toward becoming the healthy, whole individual God created you to be. The two-part process in this chapter's choice will bring you even closer to your goal, for in it you will find the healing of relationships—and broken relationships lie at the root of so much of our pain. But the choices in this chapter cannot be made alone. You need God's help to follow through. In this action step, we will ask God to help us both forgive those who have hurt us and make amends to those whom we have hurt. The freedom and hope found at the end of this process will bring you great release. Use your own words to ask God's help, or join in the prayer below:

> *Dear God, You have shown me that holding on to resentment for the wrongs done to me and refusing to make right my own wrongs has crippled me—emotionally, spiritually, and even physically. I ask You today to help me be honest about the hurts I feel. I've stuffed some and ignored others, but now I am ready to come clean and tell the truth about my pain. As I do, I ask that You give me the strength and the courage so I can release those who have hurt me and let go of my resentment toward them. Only by Your power will I be able to do this, Lord.*

I pray, also, that You will give me the courage and discernment to know how to make amends to those I have hurt. Help me to be honest as I look back and remember, and guide me as I find the ways to make restitution, where appropriate.

Finally, I pray that I can begin a new life today as I refocus my life on doing Your will in my relationships. Help me set aside my selfishness and set my whole heart on You—I know I have a long way to go. I want the promise found in Job that all my troubles will fade from my memory and be remembered no more. Amen.

ACTION STEP 2: *Write about It*

Now is the time to get some important issues down in black and white.

Those You Need to Forgive

We'll begin by dealing with those who have hurt you—those you need to forgive. Remember, admitting that someone has hurt you and that you are angry about what he or she has done does not mean you don't love this person. You can be angry with a person whom you love very much.

Here's how you begin: You make a list of those who've harmed you. Write down:

- his or her name and relationship to you

- what this person said that hurt you

- what he or she did that hurt you

- how the hurt made you feel

Put it down on paper so you can look at it. When you do, it loses its fuzzy quality and becomes real. Think about that teacher who embarrassed you or the parent who said, "You'll never amount to anything; you're a failure." That former boyfriend/girlfriend/husband/ wife/friend who was unfaithful to you. Write it all down, and reveal your hurt. This is your Forgiveness List.

Those to Whom You Need to Make Amends

You made your Forgiveness List of those who've harmed you. Now you need to make an Amends List of those you have harmed. Write down:

+ his or her name and relationship to you

+ what you said to hurt this person

+ what you did to hurt him or her

+ how you think you made this person feel

+ why you are sorry for hurting him or her

Once again, when you write it down on paper and get it down in black and white, the offense becomes real. It is no longer vague: "I think I may have hurt her with my words when I was angry." When you write it out, it becomes, "This is how I hurt her with my words when I lost my temper that night." Your Amends List makes your responsibility specific. Go back and review once more the names you wrote down in the moral inventory in choice 4, column 5, page 116.

If you are having trouble thinking of anybody you've hurt, perhaps these questions will get you started:

+ Is there anyone to whom you owe a debt that you haven't repaid? A friend, a family member, a business?

+ Is there anyone you've broken a promise to? A spouse, a child?

- Is there anyone you are guilty of controlling or manipulating? A spouse, a child, a brother, an employee, a friend?

- Is there anyone you are overly possessive of? A spouse, a child?

- Is there anyone you are hypercritical of? A spouse, a child?

- Have you been verbally, emotionally, or physically abusive to anyone?

- Is there anyone you have not appreciated or paid attention to?

- Did you forget a child's birthday or your anniversary?

- Is there anyone you have been unfaithful to?

- Have you ever lied to anyone?

That's enough to get you started. If you still do not have anyone on your list, go back to choice 1 and start all over again!

ACTION STEP 3: *Share about It*

Offering Forgiveness

It is very important that you share your Forgiveness List with your accountability partner prior to sharing it with the person who hurt you. Your accountability partner can help you develop a plan for safely offering your forgiveness to those on your list. Your accountability partner also knows you and can challenge you to include anyone you may have omitted.

It is vital when offering forgiveness that you do not allow the person to hurt you further. Using your accountability partner as a sounding board will help minimize the risk.

Use the empty chair technique with your accountability partner to offer forgiveness when a face-to-face is not helpful or appropriate. You can also share your unmailed letter with your accountability partner, when you determine that a letter is the best approach.

Making Amends

Be sure to also share your Amends List with your accountability partner. An objective opinion can ensure that you make amends with the right motives. The Bible encourages us to *"consider how we may spur one another on toward love and good deeds."*[23] Just as your accountability partner helped you offer your forgiveness, he or she can help you plan the right time and place to make your amends. If you owe someone money, your partner can help you develop restitution plans.

You need your accountability partner to encourage you to make all the amends on your list. Once that is done, there will be no skeletons in your closet. Then you will have come to the point in your life where you can say, "I have nothing more to hide. I'm not perfect, I have attempted to repair all the harmful things I've done in my past. I have made amends and offered restitution for my part."

Carl's
STORY

I'm Carl. I'm a believer in recovery from my hurts, hang-ups, and habits. I want to share about my lifelong struggle with fear and legalism and let you know how my Higher Power—Jesus Christ—is using my weaknesses for my good and His glory. I've spent most of my life pretending I'm braver than I feel. It can be shameful to admit to insecurity, worthlessness, panic, anxiety, and downright terror, and perhaps even more when you're 6'3" and 210 pounds. However, I obviously wasn't always this big, and that's where my story begins.

I was raised in the 1950s by an alcoholic father and a controlling, enabling mother. Child rearing was much stricter in the '50s, but my parents were ultra-strict. There was no physical abuse, but they used rage and fear to intimidate my brother and sisters and me into submission. Because we were isolated from other families, it wasn't until years later that I realized other kids voiced their own opinions in a family setting. Not in my family, you didn't! When complimented on how well-behaved his kids were, my dad would say that children are to be seen and not heard.

There were two incidents when I was six or seven that really get at the genesis of my fear. My family was returning home from visiting my grandparents late one night, when I decided to offer a stick of gum to my siblings. Dad immediately knew I had stolen the gum from my grandparents and confronted me. I admitted my transgression and expected a good spanking when we got home. However, Dad pulled over and asked if I knew what happens to thieves. I said no, and he replied that they have to go to prison. He pointed to a big, dark, scary-looking building and told me it was the prison I would be staying in for the next twenty years. He instructed

187

me to hand over all my possessions and that I should beg God's forgiveness. My brother and sisters and I were screaming in fear. That incident, and a similar one a year later, taught me that the approval of my parents and God was conditional—it was based on my behavior. I know that my spirit was broken. I learned to anticipate my parents' moods and feed them the appropriate response along with a happy face, ready to do a quick 180° if I had guessed wrong. Instead of becoming resentful, I tried harder to please. I craved love and affection, but they were incapable of giving it.

My experiences at home were reinforced by my religious upbringing. I was taught that my salvation was my responsibility, based on how perfect I was. If I led a perfect life but committed one mortal sin and died without confessing it, God would send me to hell for all eternity. What made this scenario even more terrifying was that there was no one to share with. The expectation was perfect adherence to the Ten Commandments, under my own power. Since there was no provision for failure or progress, I could not admit any struggles. So I learned to put on a mask of self-righteous piety, while inside I was consumed by the terror and guilt of my inability to live up to everyone's standards.

My concept of God was based on the model of my dad as the unpleasant parent, so I tried to appease the wrath of both by going to seminary to study for the priesthood. I hoped to escape my feeling of self-condemnation and earn the love I desperately desired. But I wasn't able to do either. From day one, I compared myself with the other seminarians and felt I came up short. Not only did I feel they were more godly than I, but I also felt God Himself viewed me as a hypocrite. I wanted to leave after the first six months, but it took two more years to build up the courage to face my dad's disappointment of not having a priest as a son.

After my seminary experience I met Margaret. We went together for six years and were married for nineteen. Margaret came from an extremely physically abusive family. Conflict was what she was used to, just like total compliance was normal for me. We fought often; and after token resistance, I'd feel afraid and guilty and give in. We both got what we wanted and were miserable. Our sex life was the best part of our relationship, but there was no intimacy out of the bedroom. Over time she gained a hundred and twenty pounds, but I tried to be supportive. When that didn't work, I should have lovingly confronted her. Instead, I had a pity party and started going to prostitutes. Finally after nineteen years, five miscarriages, and countless misery, she left me.

I spent the next three months in severe depression and isolation and sought therapy to deal with my low self-esteem. But the final straw came when my therapist fell asleep during one of the sessions! I decided for the first time in my life to live for myself without regard for others' approval. I partied for the next four years, and for a while I had fun, but the price tag was steep. I got addicted to prostitutes and pornography, tried drugs, and became an alcoholic. No matter how much I used, I couldn't escape the childhood fear that still gripped me. So I tried confronting my fear by making myself physically tougher. I used steroids that I'd smuggled from Mexico, took karate, and worked for four years as a bouncer (complete with tattoos) in a local bar. But all these remedies were only skin-deep. Gradually, I realized how I had traded one form of bondage for another and how empty it all was—and how empty I was.

God reached out to me with the first of many loving people. My buddy Frank, a fellow bouncer, began sowing the seeds that God caused to take root. Then another friend, Andi, invited me to church. For the first time I heard who Jesus really is. I had been taught that Jesus was a victim. Now I was hearing that He had chosen to die and that He did it for me! I also heard about grace; it's amazing! I still love the fact that the Lord used Andi, a beautiful dancer from that drinking establishment, to draw me to Him. He knew where my focus was.

It took a "driving under the influence" arrest to get me into recovery. I started attending Alcoholics Anonymous in November of 1990. I managed to stay sober by going to meetings, but it wasn't until I started attending Saddleback Church that the other miracles started happening. Pastor Rick began a series on recovery, and I was blessed by one of the testimonies.

The following Friday the Lord introduced me to my brothers and sisters in Celebrate Recovery, and I knew I was home at last. They didn't enable me, judge me, or attempt to fix me. Mostly, they gave me what I'd been looking for all my life—unconditional love. They even threw in some hugs as a bonus.

God has sent many loving and courageous individuals to encourage me through difficult times. Lisa, Tim, Lori, Joe, Cathy, Bob, Karrie, and the men in my recovery group have all been there for me. Please forgive me for mentioning the names of people unfamiliar to you. I need to do it, however, to remind myself how blessed I am by their presence in my life and to focus on the fact that God is relational. He designed recovery to be worked in relationship with others. It wasn't until God pulled me out of my isolation through the intervention of these individuals that I started experiencing the freedom that was missing from my futile attempts of recovery through self-effort.

In recovery I found that I had a God problem. My childhood terror of God was based upon fear and punishment for not living perfectly. Then God revealed the amazing truth that freed me from my terror of Him. Philippians 2:13 (NASB) says, "For it is God who is at work in you, both to will and to work for His good pleasure." The proof that He loves me is in the fact of my sobriety! All I did was to stay involved in the process. I kept coming back. He did for me what I couldn't do for myself. He loved me enough to empower the gift that transformed my life!

The Lord has brought me much healing in the area of victimization. When I was growing up, I was a victim. I didn't even have ownership of my own feelings and opinions. I was powerless. I had no problem embracing the first choice. Like Paul, I embraced my weaknesses. Unfortunately, I was stuck there. My fear kept me from seeing this as a positional truth—that I glory in my weakness so that I can rely on the power of Christ. First John 4:18–19 (NIV) says, "There is no fear in love. But perfect love drives out fear, because fear has to do with punishment. The one who fears is not made perfect in love. We love because he first loved us."

In regard to my hurts, the Lord has surrounded me with the loving support of my Adult Children of a Chemically Dependent group. God's love and grace modeled to me by others in Celebrate Recovery gave me the courage and the strength to complete choice 6:

CHOICE 6

Repairing RELATIONSHIPS

Evaluate all my relationships.

Offer forgiveness to those who have hurt me, and make amends for harm I've done to others, except when to do so would harm them or others.

Working this choice has provided closure with my ex-wife. God was also at the center of my amends on three separate occasions.

The first was to the owner of the bar where I worked as a bouncer for four years. I had stolen approximately three thousand dollars during that time. I had stopped working in the bar, but I was doing its plant maintenance. I didn't have the money, but God urged me to step out. Pride had held me back because the owner, Connie, had put me up on a pedestal. I knew that my honesty would destroy her illusions. When I confessed, I expected her notorious temper to explode, along with a demand for immediate repayment. Instead, I received God's mercy and grace. At first she winced, then she said, "I forgive you. Let's forget it and put it behind us."

The second instance was even more difficult because I had stolen thousands of dollars in plants from my biggest supplier. I broached the subject with his office manager. He told me that the owner was likely to refuse to accept my confession and restitution, and would certainly cut off my business. God encouraged me to go forward despite my anxiety and shame at having broken the trust of this friend and business associate. He not only accepted my amends and money order for the full amount stolen, but a couple of weeks later I received a letter of gratitude. Our relationship has been repaired and is now closer than ever.

The third amend was similar to the last one in that it involved the theft of plants. However, I had forgotten this, so the Lord brought it to my attention. It was a small firm in San Diego, and it had happened so long ago that I couldn't remember the name of the firm. I prayed about it but just couldn't bring it to mind. Of course, my old alcoholic way of thinking tried to use that as an excuse to justify avoiding it, but God said "no way" and kept after me. Finally, one day as I was driving, God again laid it on my heart, and I got frustrated. "Lord," I said, "I don't have time to drive to San Diego to pay my money, so would you please help me remember?" No sooner had I finished that prayer, than the firm's delivery truck pulled up alongside me. Is God awesome, or what? And does He ever have a sense of humor! Not only did I make the amends and mail them my check, but I got the chance to witness to them. They were incredulous over why, after more than ten years, I would take this step.

However, the greatest thing God did by allowing me to make amends and offer my forgiveness was the complete restoration of my relationship with my parents. I had been in recovery for more than twelve years and had done all the action steps regarding making amends and offering forgiveness. Yet there was something missing in the relationship with my parents. Maybe I had the expectation that the fruit of intimacy would automatically follow. Instead, there was still a distant formal rigidity. Then God stepped in and shook everything up!

My dad was diagnosed with terminal cancer and was given six months to live. The Lord started working on his heart and mine. For the first time in our relationship, we shared feelings and had conversations about more than what was on television. My dad even told me he loved me!

God then began laying on my heart to share my faith with my parents. In the past, whenever any spiritual experiences would come up, my parents would say, "We are happy that you like your church, but we're content with ours." End of discussion.

Then my mom had to be hospitalized, and as I drove out to see her, the Lord encouraged me to lovingly talk to her about Him. It was difficult to witness to family because I wanted so badly for them to know Jesus the way I do. Well, this time there was no nervousness as I shared Christ with my mom. It went smoothly because He gave me the words and, even more important, the loving heart to meet her where she was. As she accepted the Lord, I saw my mom as my sister in Christ!

One week later I visited my parents again, and the Lord had already prepared my dad's heart. My mom had told him about her decision, and he was anxious to pray to receive Christ himself. Praise God for his unfathomable grace and faithfulness. Not only did God bring about full reconciliation between my parents and me, He blessed me with the ultimate intimacy by allowing me to lead my parents to Him!

This was borne out a month later as the Lord brought my dad home to be with Him, and I can honestly say that I'm truly joyful at this time. I'm anticipating an awesome homecoming when I get to be reunited with my dad and my heavenly Father. Praise be to God!

In regard to my habits, I recently celebrated sixteen years of sobriety. I also give thanks for fourteen years of celibacy. I am so grateful to the Lord for the eight choices that provided the essential structure.

God's power and unconditional love have given me a passion to be used by Him to serve others, despite a lingering childhood fear. That weakness enables Jesus to display mercy and compassion through me. I'm His vessel—especially as a co-leader of my Adult Children of a Chemically Dependent group. I'm also grateful to serve as co-leader in our group for troubled teens. This ministry is especially close to my heart because we use the loving intervention and restoration embodied in Celebrate Recovery to prevent some of those kids from becoming addicts.

I would like to leave you with my life verse. It provides the answer of hope for everyone like me who struggles with perfectionism. Jesus Christ is perfect, so I can relax and let Him be God.

"Therefore, there is now no condemnation
for those who are in Christ Jesus."[24]

My name is Bill. I'm a believer who is in recovery from alcoholism. I am also an adult child of an alcoholic. There was a time when I thought I would never need to admit anything like that. Although I come from a family of alcoholics, I thought I would be different. My dad had a problem with drinking, but I was sure I was different. I believed I was different up until the evening of Friday, February 26, 1999, when a tragedy occurred and my life changed instantly.

My story of growing up is that of an ordinary boy in a military family. My earliest memories are about being lonely. Since my dad was a career marine, we were constantly moving. In the first eleven years of my life, we lived in Illinois, Michigan, North Carolina, Virginia, Wisconsin, Missouri, Hawaii, and California. We never stayed in one place long enough for me to attend the same grade school for two consecutive years. I am the only boy among seven children. Although many people would guess that I was the spoiled one, I actually felt like the odd kid out much of the time. I felt envious of my sisters being closer to each other than to me. It seemed as if there was no one to share my thoughts and feelings with. I became somewhat shy and introverted. I have always felt comfortable remaining silent around others, whether I know them or not. I prefer to listen rather than speak.

My dad was the toughest guy in the world. He was a "by the book" Marine. In my youth he rarely showed emotion toward me. I felt as though he handled me in accordance with some Marine manual. He was a self-made man, having enlisted in the Marines even before completing high school. His first duty was in Korea, where he was shot in the head during combat. Dad survived the ordeal and received a Purple Heart. I figured nothing could kill him. I was always very proud of my dad, and I respected him, even though I could not get close to him.

We had been living in Wisconsin about a year while Dad was away in Vietnam. One morning as we were getting ready for school, the phone rang. Mom answered, and we knew immediately that something was wrong. We quickly learned that Dad had had a heart attack and was in very bad condition. Everyone was crying, and it seemed that life would never be the same again.

He survived the heart attack, and after he recuperated in the hospital for a time, the family reunited at his next station assignment in Hawaii. This is where I first witnessed my father's affinity for alcohol. I would go with him for his Saturday round of golf, and we would go to the bar afterward. He made me promise that I wouldn't tell Mom where we went. On another occasion, I inadvertently caught him standing in front of the open refrigerator chugging a bottle of wine. He saw me and profanely insulted me for looking at him. I was confused by his reaction. I couldn't understand what he saw in the bottle. It seemed only to cause problems with him and Mom.

When his assignment in Hawaii was up, we resettled in Irvine, California. After an attempt to own and operate a beer bar, Dad got a job with the county. As we settled into our lives, I made friends with Ray, a neighbor kid. Ray and his family were Christians, and they attended church regularly and took me along. This was a new and different experience for me. The free grace and forgiveness they spoke about was intriguing, but I had a hard time imagining a father who could forgive unconditionally. Mom and Dad were practicing Catholics. All through grade school, we were required to go to catechism, as well as church every week. I was baptized as an infant, received First Communion at age six, and First Confession at age eight. I knew there was a God and that Jesus was my Savior, but I didn't have a close relationship with Him until I came into recovery. Somewhere around age fifteen, my parents allowed church to be optional, and I opted out. I still prayed to God almost every day, but I didn't want to go to church anymore.

When I was eighteen, I took a job as a clerk at a liquor store while attending college. Although I hadn't had a desire to drink, it was always around. My first experience with drinking came soon enough when some workmates and I went to see The Rocky Horror Picture Show. I chose a large bottle of Grand Marnier from the store's selection to share with the others. I was told it tasted like orange, which sounded a lot better than rum or vodka. So we sat in the balcony and chugged straight from the bottle. It didn't take long before the drinking process reversed itself. And even though I got sick, I had enjoyed my first experience of being drunk. My inhibitions were gone. I was sociable and less self-conscious. I came out of my shell. I was more fun, more gregarious. And I felt like I was more accepted when under the influence. Little did I know.

I finished college with good grades, passed the CPA exam on my first attempt, and landed a job with a prominent national public-accounting firm. I remember trying to impress some of the partners at a Christmas party with my knowledge of wine. I was the center of attention at a big round table, showing them all how to swirl and sample wine. Well, I must have swirled a little too hard, because the wine slipped out of the glass and was strewn in a large circle all around the table. It was not white wine. I later went to work for a local CPA firm in 1984 and stayed there for seven years while rising through the ranks and developing my career.

I met Diane while working at a client's office in Los Angeles. She was so beautiful that I hardly had the nerve to speak to her. Another accountant, who was also my roommate at the time, had his eye on another secretary in the office. Together we asked the girls out. Diane told me she only went along because her friend was so insistent. But we hit it off and saw each other every chance we got. She became my wife in June 1989.

During this time, my family and friends performed an intervention on my dad. I can remember feeling like a hypocrite when it came time to tell Dad how adversely his drinking had affected our lives. The intervention worked for a while. Dad entered a program and abstained from alcohol. Then my parents retired and they went on a long vacation. Sometime during this road trip, Dad decided to start drinking again. In August he became ill and a few weeks later he was hospitalized with liver disease.

The whole family was at Dad's bedside for two weeks. We knew there was little chance for recovery, but we hoped and prayed. Dad was tough enough to survive gunshot wounds and heart attacks. But he would not defeat alcoholism. He died at the age of fifty-five. The entire family leaned on him so much. I still have dreams about him as though he were still around. I miss Dad deeply. But even his death was not enough to make me change my ways. In my denial, I reasoned that my drinking would never get as bad as his. After all, I only drank on the weekends, not every day.

God was trying to get my attention, but I still wasn't ready to listen. I had several dangerous episodes while drinking. The common theme was that I escaped almost completely unhurt. There were some damaged vehicles, but they could and would be repaired. My life went unscathed. What drinking problem?

As time passed, my wife finally went from concern to anger about my drinking routine. She was ready to leave me. I had no alternative but to promise to stop drinking. I kept that promise for three weeks. When confronted with the accusation of being an alcoholic, I explained to Diane, "I am not an alcoholic. I just can't control myself after I take the first drink."

My denial knew no limits until the evening of February 26, 1999. I was returning from a business trip in Houston. I had a few drinks at the airport and on the plane. It was early Friday evening when I arrived in Orange County, California. I called Diane and arranged to meet her and our daughter, Kristin, for dinner at our favorite Mexican restaurant. We had a few margaritas along with dinner. Since Houston, I had been drinking for six hours, had crossed two time zones, and was feeling no pain. We finished dinner and headed home.

Diane drove separately, so she and our daughter got in her car and she asked me if I was okay to drive. I gave the routine reply of "yes." We took separate routes home. It was 8:40 on a Friday night, and I was anxious to get home. I was less than half a mile from my house as I approached the crest of a hill driving way too fast. A red Toyota coming from the opposite direction was turning left. I first saw them as they crossed into my lane. I am not sure if they ever saw me. There was almost no time to react. I lunged for the brake and started to turn the wheel to avoid them. Impact, airbags, screeching, screaming—then silence. I was amazed to find that I could get out of my car. I didn't think the other car fared as well, but I was too dazed to be able to tell. It wasn't long before the sounds of sirens announced the arrival of the police and paramedics. I was taken away from the scene, tested, and booked. Shortly before I was put in Orange County Jail, the officer notified me that there were two people in the car that I hit. A fifty-year-old woman had been thrown from the car upon impact and died immediately. Her husband was pronounced dead on arrival at the hospital.

As I sat there in a jail cell, I knew my life would never be the same. My whole outlook changed in an instant. There was nowhere to hide and no one else to blame. Regardless of what my intentions were, I believed I had committed an unforgivable offense. I made choice 1 right there, right then: I realized I am not God; I admitted that I am powerless to control my tendency to do the wrong thing and that my life is unmanageable.

I made bail the next morning and went home. As I waded through constant feelings of guilt and remorse, my whole family was there to comfort me. After a lifetime of being unable to express my love to them, they were there in my time of need. I could not make sense out of this life-changing event, but I knew this wouldn't blow over in a few days. I knew God could make sense of it, that He had the power to restore me, and that He would if I'd let go.

A week after the accident, the entire family attended service at Saddleback. I had been to church there a few times with Diane and Kristin. This week the message made me weep. They sang, "Oh Lord, Holy Lord," and I identified with every word. "When I thought my life was over, you were waiting there for me. Now I can see that there are good things only suffering can bring."

After the service, one of my sisters was walking by the information tables and saw John, an old friend of mine. He was manning the Celebrate Recovery table that morning. We talked later that afternoon; he told me all about Celebrate Recovery and that a step study group would be starting the next day. I could see that this was no coincidence. John picked me up and drove me to that Monday meeting and stayed with me. A short time later, I asked John to be my accountability partner.

I cannot put into words the guilt and shame I had over the accident. At first the remorse was almost unbearable. There appeared to be no solace for me with the constant thought that I had ended two lives and left their children without parents. This was further compounded by the prospect of losing my job, my driver's license, going to prison, and losing all my possessions in a civil trial. With the help of my family, Celebrate Recovery leaders, accountability partners, and attention to working the choices, I learned what it meant to accept hardship as a pathway to peace. I knew there were going to be consequences for my actions, but I tried not to be frozen by worry. The apostle Paul tells us, "Don't worry about anything; instead, pray about everything. Tell God what you need, and thank him for all he has done."[25] People asked me how I could continue to function with the weight of what I had done and the impending hardship on my shoulders. I focused on surrendering. I prayed for God's will.

I informed my employer of the accident. It would not have surprised me if they had let me go. Somehow God saw to it that I kept my job. The DMV was not so understanding. Shortly after the accident, my driver's license was revoked. My job entailed much travel, and I didn't know how I was going to manage. God did. Every time I needed to be somewhere, He provided me with a way to get there. Thank you to everyone who gave me a ride.

A month after the accident, the arraignment hearing was scheduled. I was placed on house arrest. I was required to be at home at all times except for work, church, and Celebrate Recovery meetings. I wore a bulky, irremovable bracelet around my ankle for more than thirteen months. It was uncomfortable to be sure, though not nearly as uncomfortable as the jail cell would be. I knew God had a plan. He allowed me to hold a job, to be with my family, and to work the choices at Celebrate Recovery.

There were several court appearances throughout the next year. Each time I walked in, I knew I might not be allowed to walk out. Family and friends were always there to comfort and support me. I knew people were praying for me, and I was very thankful. Meeting nights at Saddleback were a safe harbor. There was no judgment, just care, concern, and love.

Finally a sentence was handed down—three years in state prison with credit for the time I was on house arrest and for good behavior. I had a few days to tend to matters and prepare my family for my time away. I can't really explain why, but I knew everything was going to work according to God's will. He was in control. I was apprehensive but not afraid.

While I was in prison, a number of friends were there to look in on my family: John, CJ, and Joe, to name a few. We had known them only a short time, but they showed such a willingness to help and extended themselves to us in our time of need. Joe was especially helpful. He painted and installed a new front door, moved furniture, and was a general handyman for Diane. I am forever grateful to them for acting in such a selfless manner.

Time passed quickly. Before I knew it, I was headed back to Orange County. God used my sister to convince the state that I should be selected from a large number of inmates for a work-furlough program. I was blessed to find a job even before I arrived at the halfway house. Another benefit to the halfway house was that I was permitted to go to meetings. I remember the first Friday back at Celebrate Recovery. That wonderful feeling of being in a safe harbor came over me again. I have never been hugged so hard so many times in all my life. God restored my fellowship.

A civil trial still loomed. I was blessed to be referred to a lawyer who genuinely cared. After working on my case for several months, he admitted to being an alcoholic himself and today is active in the program. God's Word assures us, "We know that God causes everything to work together for the good of those who love God and are called according to his purpose for them."[26] My lawyer was gentle and persuasive during the trial proceedings. On the first day of the formal trial, all parties agreed to a settlement.

But how was I ever going to make my amends to the two children of the couple I had killed? How was I ever going to do what choice 6 asked?

CHOICE 6

Repairing RELATIONSHIPS

Evaluate all my relationships.

Offer forgiveness to those who have hurt me, and make amends for harm I've done to others, except when to do so would harm them or others.

During this time, my lawyer had the opportunity to speak to the oldest son of the deceased. The son told my lawyer to tell me he had forgiven me for killing his parents. This man, whom I have never actually met, modeled a grace for me that I will always treasure. No way do I deserve it, but he forgave me anyway. We often hear in recovery that we have no rights. The question is, why? I now know I have no rights because I have been forgiven. This is the kind of love I hope defines my new life. And someday I hope and pray to be able to personally express to the surviving children how truly sorry I am for causing them such loss and pain. Choice 6 says, "except when to do so would harm them or others." I need to wait and seek God's timing to complete this choice with them.

Within a couple months of my release, my revoked driver's license was returned to me. God provided me with a good job less than three miles from my house. I now have a healthier relationship with my wife and daughter since I have been able to make my amends. We love each other very much and together seek the Lord's will in our lives. Like all our relationships, our path is one of progress, not perfection. In August of 2001, we were baptized together as a family.

Both Diane and I are blessed to be leaders in step studies at Celebrate Recovery. I love this ministry and know that I need it more than it needs me. Each night of fellowship strengthens my faith. I also enjoy being a part of the BBQ team. I come from a long line of eaters, and it gives me pleasure to see others enjoy a meal.

Most important, I continue to seek God's will in my life. I enjoy living with nothing to hide and nothing to prove. I use the "Serenity Prayer" as a framework for each day. As I say it in my daily quiet time, one verse resonates. I meditate on that verse and try to act on it during the day. Some days it works better than others. Needless to say, my life is not perfect, but I am comforted by this scripture:

> "I am sure that God, who began the good work within you,
> will continue his work until it is finally finished
> on that day when Christ Jesus comes back again."[27]

God has seen me through some dark times, and He has restored me. All I had to do was surrender. Give it up. Be willing to be willing. Let go and let God: "The sacrifice you want is a broken spirit. A broken and repentant heart."[28] *I look back and see that through all of my life I have been surrounded by faith, hope, and love. There were times when I did not recognize it, or worse, that I took it for granted. My family has shown me faith through our unity. Our hope is that we all will find the pathway to peace.*

God used Carl's and Bill's willingness to offer their forgiveness and make their amends to restore and repair many of their broken relationships. Completing choice 6 provided them with additional freedom from their past hurts. The shame and guilt of their past mistakes and the harm they had brought to others had been removed. We need to offer our forgiveness and make our amends without expecting any reward for doing so. But as you can easily see from both Carl's and Bill's testimonies, the rewards they received from completing this choice were many and great!

R
E
C
O
V
E

Reserve a daily time with God

Y for self-examination, Bible reading, and prayer
in order *to know* God and His will for my
life and to gain the power to follow His will.

Maintaining MOMENTUM

The GROWTH Choice

A middle-aged woman went to New York and up to the twenty-third floor of an apartment building. She knocked, and a beautiful young woman opened the door. Incense came wafting out, music was playing, she was wearing a sarong, and she was clapping little bells. The young woman asked, "Are you here to see the great Bagone? The one who knows all, sees all, tells all, understands everything, and is in ultimate control?"

The middle-aged woman answered, "Yes, tell Sheldon his mother is here."

Sometimes we need someone to tell us we're just Sheldon. We need someone to say, "Who are you kidding? You're you." God will allow us to relapse, again and again, until we finally realize we can't do it on our own. He'll allow us to fall one, twenty, or one hundred times until we say and truly mean, "God, I can't do it on my own power." God tells us plainly, "'You will not succeed by your own strength or power, but by my Spirit,' says the Lord All-Powerful."[1]

Only God has the power to take away and keep away our old hurts, hang-ups, and habits. If we revert to trying to do it on our own willpower, we're going to relapse.

In the last six chapters, you've been learning about coming out of the dark and exposing your problems to the light of God's love. At whatever level you've been able to accomplish this, God has been healing the hurts, hang-ups, and habits that have messed up your life. Many of you are already experiencing some amazing changes in your life.

In this chapter we're going to focus on helping you maintain your momentum. The fact is, growth is not smooth. The road to healing is bumpy. Some days it's two steps forward and one step back. Just because you are reading this book and attempting to live out these biblical choices does not mean your journey will be problem free.

If you don't keep your guard up, you can easily fall back into your old self-defeating patterns. This is called *relapse*. The alcoholic starts drinking again. The overeater regains the weight. The gambler returns to the casino. The workaholic fills up his schedule again. We all tend to repeat the patterns of our past. It's easy to slip back into old hurts, old hang-ups, and old habits.

In this chapter we'll begin to understand relapse—its *patterns* and *causes*. Then we'll learn how to *prevent* relapse in the first place. Let's first look at the very predictable pattern of relapse. Regardless of the issue, the pattern is usually the same.

THE PREDICTABLE PATTERN OF RELAPSE

COMPLACENCY

CONFUSION

COMPROMISE

CATASTROPHE

PHASE 1: COMPLACENCY

Relapse begins when we get comfortable. We've confessed our problem, we've started dealing with it, and we've made some progress. Then we get comfortable, and one day we stop praying about it, and then we stop working at it. Our pain level has been reduced—not eliminated but reduced—and we think we can live with the reduced level of pain. We haven't thoroughly dealt with our problem, but we don't feel as desperate about it as we once did. We think we don't need to meet with our support group anymore. We don't need to work the choices anymore. We don't need to call our accountability partner anymore. And before we know it, we have become complacent.

PHASE 2: CONFUSION

In this phase we begin to rationalize and play mental games with ourselves. We say things like, "Maybe my problem really wasn't all that bad; maybe I can handle it by myself." We forget how bad it used to be. Reality becomes fuzzy and confused, and we think we can control our problems by ourselves.

PHASE 3: COMPROMISE

When we get to this phase, we go back to the place of temptation. We return to the risky situation that got us in trouble in the first place, whether it's the bar, the mall, 31 Flavors, or that "XXX" Internet site. We go back to that unsafe place like the gambler who says, "Let's go to Vegas and just see the shows." But when we place ourselves in risky situations, we'll likely make poor choices. It may begin with little things, but it won't be long before it all unravels and all the ground that's been gained is lost. That brings us to phase four.

PHASE 4: CATASTROPHE

This is when we actually give in to the old hurt, old hang-up, or old habit. The hate comes back, the resentment returns, or we fall back into the old patterns of behavior. But we need to understand this: the catastrophe is not the relapse. The relapse began in phase 1 with complacency. The catastrophe is simply the end result, the acting-out phase of the pattern.

So why do we fall back? Why do we fall into the predictable pattern of relapse when we know which way to go, when we know the right thing to do? Why do we tend to ignore what we know is right? There are four things that can cause us to relapse.

THE CAUSES OF RELAPSE

1. WE REVERT TO OUR OWN WILLPOWER

The Bible speaks to our foolish tendencies of trying to make it on our own: *"How can you be so foolish! You began by God's Spirit; do you now want to finish by your own power?"*[2] We got off to a good start:

+ In choice 1, we admitted that we are powerless to change on our own.

+ In choice 2, we agreed that only God has the power to help us change.

+ In choice 3, we made a commitment to turn our life and will over to Christ's care and control.

+ In the fourth choice, we examined ourselves openly and honestly and confessed our faults.

+ In the fifth, we voluntarily submitted to the changes God wants to make in our lives.

♦ Then in the last chapter, our sixth choice, we focused on repairing our relationships—offering forgiveness and making amends.

We've submitted, trusted, and committed. We've made room for God to make major changes in our life. But now, if we're not careful, we may start to think, "It's me doing this; I'm making the changes. It's my power." We revert to relying on our own willpower; but the problem is, it didn't work in the first place, and it's not going to work now! We have a few successes, and suddenly we think we are all-powerful and all-knowing, and can handle everything on our own.

2. WE IGNORE ONE OF THE CHOICES

Maybe we get in a hurry and try to move through the choices too quickly. Maybe we decide to skip over a difficult choice. Perhaps the amends step seems too hard, and we rationalize that we can do without that one. "Maybe partial recovery and healing will be enough," we think. But the truth is that we need to follow through on all the choices, or the plan doesn't work. It's been tried and proven countless times over.

There's no quick fix. You didn't get into this mess overnight, and you're not going to get out of it overnight. You need to work through all the choices to the very best of your ability at your own speed. Maintain your momentum. Follow the admonition the apostle Paul gave to some other Christians who had fallen back on their original commitment: *"You were doing so well! Who made you stop obeying the truth?"*[3]

3. WE TRY TO RECOVER WITHOUT SUPPORT

Since the very first chapter, we've learned the importance of someone to share with, someone to hold us accountable. But some of you may still think, "I can do this on my own. Just me and God—that's all I need to get well. I'll read the book, do the first two action steps at the end of each chapter, and I'll be good to go. I don't need an accountability partner, and I certainly don't need any kind of meetings or small group!" Wrong! It doesn't work that way. You're asking for a relapse.

God's Word tells us why having an accountability partner is so important. We've looked at this verse before, but we need to look at it again: *"Two people are better than one, because they get more done by working together. If one falls down, the other can help him up. But it is bad for the person who is alone and falls, because no one is there to help."*[4] The "Share about It" action step at the end of each chapter puts you in touch with someone who can help you when you fall down. Don't neglect this powerful resource. You can't overcome your hurts, hang-ups, and habits alone. When you're tempted and things go bad, who are you going to call? If you do not have anyone to reach out to, you're not going to make it. God created you to be in healthy relationships: *"Let us not give up the habit of meeting together."*[5]

If you try to do these choices on your own, you may see short-term progress and growth, but without the support of others, you will eventually fall into relapse. It's like driving a car at fifty-five miles an hour, then taking your hands off the wheel. You may not crash immediately, but you will eventually. If you don't have a support team when the temptation comes, who will encourage you to do the right thing? If you fall, who will be there to help you up?

4. WE BECOME PRIDEFUL

The fourth cause of relapse is our pride. We get overconfident and start to think we've beaten this hurt, this hang-up, or this habit. We think we've got forgiveness all sewed up and that we've closed the door on our past. Be careful. Scripture tells us that *"pride goes before destruction."*[6] We need to stay humble or we'll stumble. Always remember the lesson of the whale: "When you get to the top and are ready to blow, that's when you get harpooned."

Pride always sets us up for a fall. It blinds us to our own weaknesses and keeps us from seeking help. It prevents us from making real amends and from working through all the choices fully.

The biggest problem with pride is that it causes us to blame other people for our own problems; it prevents us from seeing the truth. Don't let your pride blind you to your own faults and responsibilities. The Bible reminds us, *"If you think you are standing firm, be careful that you don't fall!"*[7] You have been working hard on "getting it all together," but you don't have it all together yet. The secret to lasting recovery is to live in humility: *"Humble yourselves before the Lord, and he will lift you up."*[8] Humility is the best protection against relapse.

> *Pride BLINDS us to our own weaknesses and keeps us from seeking help.*

Several years ago, before the Soviet Union broke up, a German teenage boy flew a private plane into Soviet airspace and landed right in the middle of Red Square. This was the most heavily guarded airspace in the world, and a kid flew right into it. This incident is a parable of life. Your greatest weakness is often an unguarded strength. You may say, "I've got this all together; I haven't had a drink in over a year." Watch out. "I made my amends years ago; my marriage could never fall apart." Watch out. "I could never get addicted to food." You'd best be careful.

"If you think you are standing firm, be careful that you don't fall!" If left unguarded, the "relapse plane" will fly in and land right in the middle of the very area where you think you're strongest.

PREVENTING RELAPSE

The keys to preventing relapse are found in the words of choice 7:

Maintaining MOMENTUM

Reserve a daily quiet time with God

for self-examination, Bible reading, and prayer
in order to know God and His will for my life
and to gain the power to follow His will.

Developing new habits is not easy. New healthy habits are about making daily choices that put us in a place where God can begin His transformation work in us. Someone has accurately said that the most difficult thing about the Christian life is that it is so *daily*. Jesus knew about daily temptation, and He knew how to fight it: *"Watch and pray so that you will not fall into temptation. The spirit is willing, but the body is weak."*[9]

Relapse is part of our human nature. It is human nature to go back to things that mess us up even though we know they mess us up. It's human nature to let past problems revisit us, to allow old hurts, hang-ups, and habits to haunt us. That's why Jesus tells us to *"watch and pray."* Choice 7 is all about putting those "watching and praying" habits in place in order to prevent relapse.

At the end of this chapter, you'll read the very powerful stories of Regina and Steve who discovered the hard way that relapse was a very real threat. They learned that they needed the support of like-minded people, along with the three new habits below, in order to maintain their momentum.

HABIT 1: EVALUATION

The Bible makes it clear that we are to evaluate ourselves: "Test yourselves to make sure you are solid in the faith. Don't drift along taking everything for granted. Give yourselves regular checkups."[10] We're also instructed, "Let's take a good look at the way we're living and reorder our lives under God."[11]

You've already had some practice evaluating yourself in chapter 4, when you did your moral inventory. In this chapter the focus is on *ongoing* inventories and evaluations of ourselves and our progress. First, we'll look at *what* we should evaluate, then *why* we should evaluate ourselves, and finally, we'll look at *when*.

What You Should Evaluate

1. *Physical:* "What is my body telling me?" Your body is a barometer of what's happening inside you. Are your muscles tense? Guess what? You're under stress. Do you have a headache or a backache? Your body is a warning light, telling you that something may be wrong. Periodically you need to stop and ask, "What is my body saying to me? Am I hungry? Am I tired? Am I fatigued? Am I stressed out?"

2. *Emotional:* "What am I feeling right now?" Are you allowing your real feelings to surface, or are you forcing them down? Repressing your real feelings is like shaking up a bottle of Coke and not taking the cap off; it's going to blow eventually. You need to take time for a "Heart Check."

H – am I *h*urting?

E – am I *e*xhausted?

A – am I *a*ngry?

R – do I *r*esent anybody?

T – am I *t*ense?

Do this check frequently, and respond to your emotional needs.

3. *Relational:* "Am I at peace with everyone?" If not, that internal conflict will hold you back on your road to healing. You know when you're having conflict with someone. It's up to you to resolve the part you've played in the conflict as soon as possible. When you allow a conflict to remain unresolved, you also allow painful memories and the people associated with them to live rent-free in your mind. Aunt Bertha may have hurt you fifteen years ago and live a thousand miles away, but if every day you wake up thinking about her, she is living rent-free in your mind, preoccupying your attention and energy. Soon this preoccupation will grow into a major resentment.

> *Celebrate any* VICTORY, *no matter how small, and do it on a daily basis.*

Is someone living rent-free in your mind? Are you holding on to a new hurt? Have you recently hurt someone and not made amends? If the answer to any of these questions is yes, offer your forgiveness or make your amends promptly!

4. *Spiritual:* "Am I relying on God?" Today, moment by moment, are you relying on God? Many of us don't take time to be alone and quiet in the presence of the Lord. We have disconnected ourselves from the most important lifeline we possess. That lifeline is a consistent, regular time with our heavenly Father. How are you doing in your relationship with God? Are you spending time alone with your Father? Are you relying on Him day by day, moment by moment?

Why You Should Evaluate

When you do an inventory at work you count everything. While it's essential to be honest about counting your shortcomings, another important reason to evaluate yourself is to celebrate the positive things in you. "I told the truth at least once today." "Yes, I blew it three times, but I was calm twice." "I at least wanted to be unselfish in that situation." Look honestly at where you are, but always remember to see what's good in your life. Be grateful for what you have done right.

The Bible tells us about a good kind of pride: *"Each one should test his own actions. Then he can take pride in himself, without comparing himself to somebody else."*[12] You can be honestly proud of what God is doing in your life, grateful that God is working with you and that you can see progress. Celebrate any victory, no matter how small, and do it on a daily basis.

When You Should Evaluate

Your evaluation, or inventory, is kind of like cleaning house. There are three kinds of housecleaners: neatniks, end-of-day cleaners, and spring cleaners.

Neatniks live with a DustBuster strapped to a holster and like to clean up messes as soon as they happen. They walk around behind the kids, picking up after them, like those waiters at restaurants who take your plate before you've finished your meal.

End-of-day cleaners look around the house, do a daily cleanup, and keep things in order on a fairly regular basis.

Spring cleaners clean house once a year, whether it needs it or not.

These same cleanup styles can help determine when you should do your personal evaluation.

1. *Spot-check evaluation:* The neatnik can do a spot-check at any time of the day. When you start feeling the pressure build, you say, "What is my body saying to me? What are my emotions saying? Do I have any relational conflict? Am I tuned in to God right now?" You try to deal with

it immediately, because the longer you postpone dealing with a problem, the worse it gets.

Spot-check evaluations help you keep short accounts with God. If you keep short accounts, you will never have to do another moral inventory, because you are dealing with your issues as they surface. It's like taking the garbage out every day. There may even be times when you have to take the garbage out more than once a day because something really stinks. If you let it pile up, your life starts to stink. Sometimes you need to deal with your garbage on a moment-by-moment basis.

2. *Daily review:* This is for the end-of-day cleaners. As your day winds down, find a quiet spot and review your day, confessing your failures and celebrating your victories. Get out your journal and make a list under each of these three headings:

+ Things I did well today

+ Things I messed up today

+ This is how I responded

I have found journaling at the end of each day a key to my "relapse prevention plan." Thank God, I haven't had a drink in over eighteen years. But I can't rest on past victories. That is just what the enemy wants me to do. After all these years, I still write down my daily inventory in my journal. I can see the areas where I have fallen short and missed the mark. I can see the daily victories God is giving me. When I sin (not *if* I sin), I write it down and do my best to make the necessary corrections. Over time I can see unhealthy patterns develop, and with the support of God and my accountability partner, I can put together an action plan to get me back on track.

3. *Annual checkup:* This inventory is like a spring cleaning. You take

some time off, go away for a day, and do an annual checkup. Look at your life, see what's in order and what's not, and do some deep cleaning. Here are some things to review:

+ Your relationships

+ Your priorities

+ Your attitude

+ Your integrity

+ Your mind

+ Your body

+ Your family

+ Your church

HABIT 2: MEDITATION

Meditation may be a new concept to you, but it really isn't all that hard. Here are two simple keys to get you started: the how-to and the blessings of meditation.

The How-to of Meditation

1. Reverse worry. If you know how to worry, you know how to meditate. Worry is just negative meditation. When you worry, you take a negative thought and think about it over and over. When you meditate, you take a positive thought—often a verse of the Bible—and think about it over and over.

2. Listening. Meditation is a form of listening to God for His answers and directions. It's a time for slowing down long enough to hear God.

The busyness in our lives stifles our recovery and growth. Meditative listening is the secret of spiritual strength.

3. *Memorization.* Having God's Word in your heart is a powerful deterrent to sin. *"I have thought much about your words and stored them in my heart so that they would hold me back from sin."*[13] How do you store God's words in your heart? You memorize them. As you think about God's Word and memorize key passages, it will keep you from sinning and prevent relapse. Do you want to avoid temptation? Think about God's Word. It is the owner's manual for life. Your life will become a lot easier when you follow the manufacturer's instructions.

The Blessings of Meditation

The key to growth is to have roots deep down in God's Word. The way you grow roots in God's Word is to meditate on it. As you do that, you will be like *"trees along a riverbank"*: *"They delight in doing everything God wants them to, and day and night are always meditating on his laws and thinking about ways to follow him more closely. They are like trees along a riverbank bearing luscious fruit each season without fail. Their leaves shall never wither, and all they do shall prosper."*[14] Three blessings of meditation leap out from this passage:

1. *Fruit without fail:* Those who meditate on God's Word will bear *"luscious fruit each season without fail."* That's quite a bold promise! If we hold God's Word deep in our hearts and meditate on it, we can be sure that our efforts will bear continued healing and growth; we can be sure of God's transforming power in our lives.

2. *Health:* We also read, *"Their leaves shall never wither."* If you regularly meditate on God's Word, when the heat's on, you won't wither away; and when the drought comes, you won't dry up and blow away. You will remain strong and tall and healthy. You won't have a relapse.

3. *Prosperity:* Finally, *"all they do shall prosper."* Knowing and

meditating on God's Word leads to success and prosperity. This is not necessarily talking about financial prosperity, but prosperity of *life*. Meditating on God's Word will help you know the right thing to do, and then you will end up succeeding in God's purpose for your life.

HABIT 3: PRAYER

Prayer is your way of plugging in to God's power. You pray, "God, I can't do it, but You can."

Pray about Anything!

Most people don't realize you can pray about *any* need in your life. You can pray about a financial need, a physical need, a relational need, a spiritual need, or an emotional need. And you can most definitely pray about the struggles in your life: Jesus said to *"watch and pray so that you will not fall into temptation."*[15] You can take any need, any struggle, to God.

The How-to of Prayer

Jesus tells us how we should pray in what is often called the Lord's Prayer: *"This, then, is how you should pray: 'Our Father in heaven, hallowed be your name, your kingdom come, your will be done on earth as it is in heaven. Give us today our daily bread. Forgive us our debts, as we also have forgiven our debtors. And lead us not into temptation, but deliver us from the evil one.'"*[16]

Notice that Jesus says this is *how* we should pray, not *what* we should pray. He has given us a model, not a rote prayer.

When you choose to put these three new habits into practice— evaluation, meditation, and prayer—you are choosing life and health and recovery.

MAKE THE *Choice*

ACTION 1: *Pray about It*

Praying the Scripture may be another new experience for you, but it's a prayer method that brings amazing blessings. In this action step, we'll pray through the Lord's Prayer. You will see how the eight choices support this great prayer. Even though you haven't yet come to chapter 8, you'll be able to pray this choice, too. As we pray, we'll focus our prayer to avoid the dangers of relapse.

> *Scripture:* "*Our Father in heaven, hallowed be your name . . .*"
> *Choice 1:* Realize I am not God . . .
> *Choice 2:* Earnestly believe that God exists . . .
> *Prayer: Father in heaven, Your name is wonderful and holy. I acknowledge that You hold all power—that You are God and that on my own I am powerless. Without You, I will most certainly relapse into my old hurts, hang-ups, and habits.*
>
> *Scripture:* "*Your kingdom come . . .*"
> *Choice 8:* Yield myself to God to be used . . .
> *Prayer: I pray that Your kingdom will come in my life—that I will yield myself to be used by You, that You can use me to reach out to others with the Good News of Your kingdom and Your healing. Help me to finds ways to serve You and others.*
>
> *Scripture:* "*Your will be done on earth as it is in heaven. . .*"
> *Choice 5:* Voluntarily submit to God's changes . . .

Prayer: *Oh, Lord, I pray that Your will be done in my life. I fight against it so often, but in my heart of hearts, I choose to submit to You. Help me to hold on to that choice. I choose Your will over my willpower; help me not to fall back into old patterns.*

Scripture: *"Give us today our daily bread . . ."*
Choice 3: Consciously choose to commit . . . to Christ's care . . .
Prayer: *Supply me with just what I need for today. Help me to take my recovery one day at a time, not looking too far ahead, but committing all my life and will to Christ's care and control—one day at a time.*

Scripture: *"Forgive us our debts . . ."*
Choice 4: Openly examine and confess my faults . . .
Prayer: *Forgive me, Lord. I have looked at my life and my heart, and what I've seen is not pretty. You already knew that, and I thank You for loving me anyway and for forgiving me so freely. Thank You for the loving support from others that You have provided along my healing journey.*

Scripture: *"As we also have forgiven our debtors . . ."*
Choice 6: Evaluate all my relationships . . .
Prayer: *Soften my heart toward those who have harmed me. Teach me, by Your power, to forgive, as You have forgiven me. And give me the courage, the conviction, and the wisdom to make amends where I have harmed others. Help me not to relapse into old patterns of resentment and bitterness.*

Scripture: *"And lead us not into temptation, but deliver us from the evil one . . ."*
Choice 7: Reserve a daily time with God . . .
Prayer: *Help me to daily spend time with You. I know that time with You is my best defense against relapse and my best offense toward growth. May my time with You create a hedge of protection around me. Amen.*

ACTION 2: *Write about It*

One of the habits we talked about in the Preventing Relapse section is the habit of *evaluation*. Spend some time writing about the four areas we discussed there: *physical, emotional, relational,* and *spiritual.* Use these questions to guide your writings:

1. *Physical:* What is your body telling you? Remember, your body serves as a warning light, alerting you to things that are wrong.

2. *Emotional:* What are you feeling? Try to be honest as you write and not repress or stuff your feelings. Use the H-E-A-R-T check to identify what's going on inside of you:

   H – am I *h*urting?

   E – am I *e*xhausted?

   A – am I *a*ngry?

   R – do I *r*esent anybody?

   T – am I *t*ense?

3. *Relational:* Am I at peace with everyone? Do I need to make amends to anyone? Do I need to forgive anyone? Write honestly about any conflicts you're having and what your responsibility in the conflict may be so you don't relapse into your old habits.

4. *Spiritual:* Am I relying on God? Take a moment to write about where you are in your relationship with God and what you can do to move your relationship to the next level.

ACTION 3: *Share about It*

Share what you wrote in your "Write about It" section with your accountability partner. You can share with him or her daily if you're going through a tough time. Your accountability partner can help you develop a godly plan to resolve each problem promptly. If you acted out and owe someone an amends, share that with your accountability partner too. This person can help you see your part and pray with you about making your amends.

As you share your evaluation and journal with your accountability partner, ask him or her to help you see any unhealthy patterns that are developing and any old hurts, hang-ups, and habits that are resurfacing.

Review the patterns of relapse with your accountability partner: *complacency, confusion, compromise,* and *catastrophe,* and ask him or her to help you look honestly at your life to see if any of these patterns are there. Listen openly, and talk together about ways to turn things around and prevent relapse in the future.

Regina's
STORY

Hi, my name is Regina, and I am a PK (Pastor's Kid). I am also a believer who struggles with drug and alcohol addiction. I was born into what most would consider a perfect home. I was the daughter of a pastor and a stay-at-home mom. I had an older brother to look up to and a younger sister to look out for. As I have examined my life, I realize the perfection I was born into all changed on June 1, 1988. It was on that day that my mother had surgery for breast cancer.

I remember two things, one being the day she came home from the hospital. My father helped her up the stairs into her room and onto her bed. I stood in the doorway staring at her lying in the bed, not wanting to touch or go near her. The second was when my father sat my brother, younger sister, and me down and told us just how sick Mom really was. It was with that talk that I believe I began to change. At the young age of eight, I felt I had to start taking care of myself. My mother, who had always been there to take care to me, was now unable.

As I continued through second and third grade, I was sick a lot. I recall sitting in the nurse's office waiting for my mom to come pick me up and overhearing a conversation the secretaries were having about me. They were talking about how many times I had been sick and that it was all psychosomatic. They thought I just wanted to be home to keep an eye on my mom.

My family moved a lot. My second move was at age nine, and I had to change schools and make new friends. During this time, I had a teacher who was verbally abusive. It was a very difficult time for me, and I can't remember much of it. However, when I think about that teacher, even to this day I get tense. I allowed her actions to haunt me for years. When I used to see women with long red hair like hers, my heart would begin to race and I would tense up, even if they were on TV.

It wasn't long before we moved again, and I once again had to switch schools. This time the new school was at home. I didn't enjoy being home schooled; in fact, I was upset because my brother stayed in public school. However, the home schooling stopped after mom had a seizure as a result of all the cancer medication.

I'll never forget that night. I was lying in my bed. My dad came running down the hall and shut the door to my room. I sat up in bed knowing something was wrong, and I began to cry. I looked through my window and watched the ambulance and fire trucks pull up to our house and take my mom. We never really talked about what happened that night. After that my sister and I went back to public school and had to be accepted into a new group of friends.

I have only a few good childhood memories. Some of them are from our summer trips to my grandpa's farm in Kansas. I learned to love fishing, running, hiking, and watching the animals outside the window in the dining room. However, my dad went on only one summer vacation with the family. He was always working.

I looked forward to our church's summer camp each year. But during my last church camp, my life changed forever. It was the beginning of my long downward spiral. We had just moved again, and I was going into junior high. Because of a lack of kids my age at church, they chose to put me with the high-school kids and make me a camp counselor. Once again, I was put in with new people I had to make friends with, something I still found very uncomfortable. On the night before the rest of the kids were to arrive, they gave the counselors a free night with no curfew. We could stay out as late as we wanted. The group of kids I had become friends with that week went for a walk, so I went along. As we walked, a guy pulled out a bag of marijuana and a pipe. I remember it getting passed to me and not thinking twice about smoking it, even though I'd never smoked anything before. From the first hit, I loved it! It was all I could think about for the next two weeks at camp. I kept asking if we were going to do it again. I was upset when I left because the person who brought the marijuana lived about an hour from me, and I wouldn't see him again.

That September, I started junior-high school. It was almost as if I was attracted to other kids who had smoked marijuana. They became my friends; for the first time making friends was easy for me. As I went through junior high I began to use more and more, once a month, twice a month, once a week, then three times a week or more.

After junior high we moved again. My grandparents moved in with us. This was a blessing as well as a curse. In some sense, it kept me under control. I didn't want to cause my grandpa any grief or stress. He was not well; his heart was weak, and I was always afraid that if he found out about me, it would give him a heart attack. I didn't want to be responsible for his death.

When I started high school, I met more people who used other drugs. There was never a doubt in my mind as to whether I would use new drugs or not; I just did. My secret was still safe; very few people knew about my drug use. I thought I had everything under control. I was living a double life. I was the good church girl, the pastor's daughter, sitting in a front pew every Sunday morning. I still had many of my church friends, but I also had another set of friends that used and dealt drugs.

The change in my drug habits came when I met a guy named Jon. Jon was a marijuana dealer, and I thought he had everything: popularity, money, and all the drugs he wanted. The cops and school security watched his every move, and that's where I came in. I was the good little pastor's kid no one would suspect in a dealing ring, so we became a team. Jon had the contacts, and I had the innocence. I didn't do it for the money, but more for the feeling, friends, and free weed. I had any drug at my disposal now, and I didn't have to pay for it. And as I slipped further into this new life, I began to give up on the old one. I immediately ditched my church friends of eight years. I found that it was easier to sit through classes if I was loaded, so before school, at breaks, and after school I was taking something. My fear of getting caught, however, made my drug dealing with Jon last for less than a year.

Not too long after my dealing stopped, I was sitting in my youth group at church and the pastor quoted this verse: "Do not change yourselves to be like the people of this world, but be changed within by a new way of thinking. Then you will be able to decide what God wants for you; you will know what is good and pleasing to him and what is perfect."[17] An instant conviction set into me. I realized I was going against everything I had been taught and that my life was not an example of that verse. It was with that, that I went to my church's youth leaders and told them I had been using and wanted to stop. They told me to get rid of my "druggy" friends and start hanging out with my Christian friends again. So I did. However, the desire to use began to eat away at me, and not knowing how to get rid of it, I quickly relapsed. It was during the next year that I went to numerous people asking them what I needed to do to stop using. All of them had the same answer: "Pray harder, and read your Bible more." It sounded so simple—"Pray harder, and read your Bible more." They had no understanding of how to help me or how with God's power I could help myself.

It was another two years before I realized why I was going to these people. I was looking for those magic words that would take away my problem. I was looking for a way around working for the solution. I realized staying clean and sober would require personal effort, and I wasn't sure I was up to it. While seeking the answer to my problem, I continued to struggle with my double life. I would read my Bible and pray to stop using. I would quit using for a while and soon find myself relapsing again. However, over time I convinced myself that this was the greatest way to live. I had the two things I wanted most in life: drugs and a relationship with God. Talk about insanity.

Strangely, as my love for drugs grew, so did my love for God. I was even on the youth leadership team at my church. However, the deeper I got into my relationship with Jesus, the more uncomfortable I became with my drug use. I was beginning to be filled with guilt and shame.

Sitting in church one Sunday morning in 1999, the college pastor mentioned a mission trip to Romania. I was sure God was calling me to go! Little did I know the decision to follow God's call on my life would be the beginning of the end of my drug use. It was a few weeks later that I realized I could not use drugs and be a missionary at the same time. I told my pastors about my using and brought all my drugs and paraphernalia to them and asked them to dispose of it. I spent the next few days at one of their houses going through detox. Once again, they told me to "pray harder and read the Bible more." The following Monday I went back to work.

I worked at a veterinarian's office. From the early days on my grandpa's farm, I had loved animals, especially dogs. That day an old dog named Amazing Grace was brought in, and we had to put her to sleep because she had cancer. While we were sitting with the owners in the exam room, I asked them why they had chosen the name Amazing Grace for her. They asked the doctor if he remembered what he said to them ten years before when they brought her in for the first time. He replied, "The same thing I have said over and over again through the years: she is a dud, you should give her back. The price you will pay will not be worth it." The owners of Amazing Grace then looked over to me and said, "What if God had said that about us? He died for us because he could look past the price and see that we're worth it. That's why we named her Amazing Grace, because we showed her the same grace that Christ showed us by dying for us." I walked out of that room with tears pouring out of my eyes, knowing I needed to let God be in control of my life. One more seed was planted in my heart.

I stayed clean for months following that day. I went to Romania and Hungary and loved it! I wanted to see the rest of the world. It was a few months later that I was at a college briefing at a Christian retreat center. I was asked to give my testimony in front of fifteen hundred college students and young adults. That, too, was an experience I will never forget. Person after person came up to me, saying they could relate to my story and struggle with drugs. It was through this weekend that God showed me He would use me in a major way.

Less than a month after that weekend, I relapsed again and went back to my speed addiction. The speed binge that followed was the worst of my drug use. Why was I using after God intervened? I have asked myself that question many times. I found that while I was working toward a goal for God, like a mission trip, I was able to stop using. But when the valley of normal life would return, I wouldn't know how to handle it. I didn't have the tools. Everyone kept saying, "Read your Bible more and pray more." Obviously that wasn't enough!

My life's journey has been filled with these moments. Weekly prayer meetings followed by using drugs. I would serve on the servant-leadership team at my church, continue my Bible studies, then use again. At my job at the animal hospital, I was promoted to an orthopedic technician in surgery. I was making great money. At the end of the day, I would go home, use again, and pass out.

It wasn't long before the reality began to set in that I would not be able to live without drugs. Just weeks before I was going on my next mission trip to Israel, I took a bottle of ketamine, which is an anesthetic induction drug, from the animal hospital. I used two or three times that week, then on a Thursday afternoon I went to a weekend of prayer and meditation with my church's college group. On Friday, after five hours of silence, our group came together to pray. As I sat there with my eyes closed, I had what I can only explain as a vision. I saw myself standing alone, and then I saw the hand of God reach out to me. When He did so, I took a step back. With every step God took toward me, I took a step back, and this continued until I was running away from God and He was chasing me. That scared me! Mostly because I didn't know what it meant. I look back and realize I should have taken it a bit more seriously.

When I got back to work that Tuesday, I walked through our treatment room and grabbed a needle and syringe. When I got home that night, I relapsed again. I can remember those first few seconds of being high, and then I remember nothing. I don't know how much time elapsed, but I slowly began to realize that something was wrong. I knew something had happened to me. I was lying in darkness, and I could see only a light above my head. There were people all around me; they were working on me and talking to each other. I couldn't see or hear them, but I knew they were there. I drifted in and out of consciousness for quite some time. As the ambulance pulled up to the emergency room, I began to come to and was able to talk. The medics proceeded to tell me what had happened. My mother used a hammer to break into the bathroom, where she found me unconscious and barely breathing. I lay in the emergency room for hours. About twenty-five friends and family came to see me there. That was almost harder than the overdose itself. I didn't want people to see me like that, and most of all, I didn't want my sister to see me like that. I still remember what she looked like at the end of the bed. She just stood there staring at me; the fear was still in her eyes, even though she already knew I was going to be all right. I told her I was sorry she had to see me like that. I don't remember if she said anything in return, but her look of disappointment will haunt me for the rest of my life. Another person who stands out in my mind is the nurse; she never looked at me with disappointment. Instead, she stood over me and told me that the waiting room was filled with people who loved me and that was more than most drug addicts had going for them.

As a result of that night, I lost my job at the animal hospital. I was also facing possession charges. I had finally hit bottom. It was a decision between life and death! I lost the job that I thought was a lifetime career. I had no idea what I would do for work; I didn't want to do anything if I couldn't work with dogs. I knew I needed help, but I didn't know where to get it. Okay, pray more and read the Bible more; those things helped me, but there had to be more! I tried with all my willpower, but I could not stop from relapsing on my own.

A few days after I OD'd, a family friend told me about Celebrate Recovery. I was at a complete loss as to how I was supposed to live. I walked into the Celebrate Recovery Women's Chemically Dependent group that

Friday night. Celebrate Recovery and Saddleback Church have been home ever since!

Just weeks after the overdose, I went on my mission trip to Israel. I was scared to death that I wouldn't be able to make it through those few weeks having to stay sober in another country. But I made one of the most important decisions of my life while I was there. I was in Ein Gedi, an oasis in the Israeli desert. All I could see were two mountains covered with dead plants and rodents. I had trouble believing there was an actual oasis between the mountains, but I was told that if I kept hiking, I would find it. They were right; it was the most amazing thing I'd ever seen—different colors of green, the deer, and sights of waterfall after waterfall, seemingly flowing from nowhere. I spent that night at a Bedouin camp, and in the morning when the sun rose, so did I. I climbed the mountain outside our tent and began to reflect on my hike at Ein Gedi. There had been no sign of life as I walked up to those mountains, but I began the hike anyway, because I did what people had told me to do—just keep walking. That is when I thought about recovery. I chose in that moment to believe what people had to say about recovery: if I just started the walk, I would see the miracle at the end.

When I got home from Israel, the Lord provided me with a job and a support system. I started right back into Celebrate Recovery on Friday nights, bought the Celebrate Recovery Participant Guides, started a step study on Tuesdays, and got an accountability team. I did my best to follow their advice, knowing that they had been where I was and made it through without drinking or using.

Before long, I was due in court on the possession charges. While waiting for my turn, I listened to the people who stood before the judge. Most of them were there for DUIs. The judge was ruthless. I listened to her tell one after another that they were "going down." She was going to throw them in jail, put them on probation, and make their lives a living hell. Needless to say, when my name was called, I was terrified. As I stood before her, there was silence; a silence so loud it hurt my ears. She looked at my paperwork and looked up at me.

"A drug overdose. That must have really scared you," she said. I told her it had. As she began to talk, I wondered if I was standing before the same judge I had listened to all morning. "I'm impressed, Regina. You're not just looking for a free ride. You've shown a lot of responsibility. I see by your committed attendance at recovery meetings that you have developed a support system and that you are able to take care of yourself financially through your new job." She continued, "I don't know why you went wrong, but the minimum penalty I can give you is a diversion program and one year informal probation." She also dropped a felony charge against me. I feel very fortunate; I am told that it should have been much worse. I don't know why the judge looked at me and saw something different in me than she saw in the others, but I thank the Lord for being in the courtroom that morning.

I spent the next few months going to the diversion program, taking drug tests, and checking in with the judge. I continued going to Celebrate Recovery two days a week and working through the eight choices. It was during this time that I began to seek God more and ask for His direction. Since then I have been given the opportunity to give my testimony to a group of junior-high kids. I have found that speaking to youth is a passion of mine. I have continued to do that whenever the opportunity presents itself.

My youth pastors were right about reading my Bible more. They just didn't understand there was more to recovery. I had to take the first six choices and complete them to the best of my ability. It took choice 7 for me to be able to maintain the momentum of choosing daily how to avoid relapsing.

CHOICE 7

Maintaining MOMENTUM

Reserve a daily quiet time with God

for self-examination, Bible reading, and prayer
in order to know God and His will for my life
and to gain the power to follow His will.

In February of 2006, on my five-year sobriety birthday, I made a long-overdue amends to my mother. I apologized for who I was and the things I'd done to her through those years as a drug addict. Then I handed her my five-year sobriety chip, and for the first time I thanked her for saving my life. With tears running down her face, my mom looked me in the eye and told me I was her hero.

Over these last few years of serving at Celebrate Recovery, I have handed out bulletins at the door on Friday nights, co-led a step study, facilitated our Friday night newcomers group on a regular basis, and led our woman's chemically addicted group numerous times. Sharing my story of recovery and freedom through Christ has taken me all over Southern California and into multiple states. In the summer of 2004, I traveled throughout Malaysia and Singapore, speaking to churches and pastors about Celebrate Recovery. In March of 2006, I moved to San Salvador, El Salvador, where I spent six months teaching the Celebrate Recovery principles in a rehab center for drug addicts and gang members.

After years of not being able to get more than a few months of sobriety, in February of 2007, I celebrated six years of sobriety from drugs and alcohol, a feat that could have only been done through following the Lord's will. As I've walked through job changes, sick parents, deaths of friends, and new adventures in life, I have learned that

"I can do all things through Christ,
because he gives me strength."[18]

I no longer have to live in bondage to substances, negative feelings, or the words of others. I can wake up each morning and commit my day to the Lord, and get the strength I need for that day from Him. If I continually work choice 7, God will lead me where He wants me to be.

Steve's STORY

Hi, my name is Steve, and I am a believer who struggles with alcoholism and drug addiction. I grew up in Huntington Beach, California, with my mother, stepfather, and brother. As a family we enjoyed all the necessities of life. We always had food on the table, clothes on our backs, and a roof over our heads. My mother and I were very close, and I could always depend on her. My stepfather, on the other hand, came from the old school and ruled with an iron fist. He expected things to be done on command, and when they weren't, watch out! Obedience from my brother and me was expected. Early on, I learned how to walk on eggshells and to find acceptance through participating in high-school sports.

When I was fifteen, I found out that my stepfather and mother were getting a divorce. I now felt free from his control. But from that point forward, I began to rebel. I took a job at a local liquor store that summer as a stock boy. My duties included cleaning and stocking the beer cooler. It didn't take long before I figured a way to steal twelve packs of beer. I drank almost daily. From that summer on, any activity I did revolved around drugs and alcohol.

I started hanging out with the wrong crowd and looked forward to nothing but partying. Slowly but surely, school and sports became less of a priority. By the tenth grade, I was smoking pot and drinking on a daily basis. As my addiction progressed, I began getting in trouble with the law. By my eighteenth birthday I had been arrested four times, twice in Mexico for being drunk and belligerent, and twice in Huntington Beach for a DWI and for assault and battery. That same year, I was involved in an affair with a married woman, which caused a divorce. I ended up dropping out of high school my senior year to begin my career in construction.

I worked in construction and found that drugs and alcohol were an accepted way of life. That's when I started using methamphetamine. I found that with this drug, I could work longer hours and have more fun. For a few years this worked for me. I managed to hold a job regularly and stay out of jail. I would stay up for days without sleep.

I became obsessed with sex and pornography. They consumed my mind and body. I should have been arrested for the severity of my conduct. I was extremely abusive in my relationship with a girlfriend, who was also a speed addict. Because of the sinful lifestyle I was living, I was responsible for three abortions.

As my addiction progressed, I began to lose the jobs I had been able to hold earlier. My life was out of control. The emptiness I felt could not be filled with any amount of drugs or alcohol. To feed my addiction, I resorted to stealing and manipulation. I became a lying thief. My mother acquired an expensive stamp collection that my grandfather had assembled over his lifetime. I began to steal it from her piece by piece. I went so low as to steal her diamond rings and pawn them. I did this while living in her home. When my mom realized that I was stealing from her, as painful as it was, she was forced to kick me out of her home because she couldn't trust me any longer.

I was now homeless, jobless, and living on the streets. But this was still not my bottom. Over the next two years, I was arrested twice for possession of crystal meth and for being under the influence. I ended up receiving a sentence in 1992 for forty-five days in county jail. When I got out of jail, my mom graciously allowed me back into her home.

It was during this time that my mother began attending Saddleback Church. One weekend while at a Sunday service, my mother decided to fill out a visitor card with my name indicating that I wanted to know Christ. She did this without telling me.

Shortly after her "act of love," I received a phone call from Rob, who was in the new believer's ministry. He was responding to the visitor card that he thought I had written. I didn't know what to say, so I went along with him. Near the end of our talk, he asked if I would be willing to say the sinner's prayer, at which time I told him that I wasn't ready and that I was struggling with drugs and alcohol. I felt I would be a hypocrite. Only God could have given me that clarity!

He did, however, tell me about Celebrate Recovery. The next Friday, I found myself making my way up the hill for the very first time. That evening, I met some great guys, including my dear friend Bob. I accepted the Lord that night and the seed was planted. I was offered a job driving an eighteen-wheeler. As soon as I took the job, I got away from the church and my accountability partners, and I relapsed. I was off and running once again for another nine months. This was the most miserable and lonely time of my life. It came to an end when I was arrested for the last time. This time I was sentenced to six months in the county jail. While in jail, I was court ordered to attend an AIDS awareness class. I was given an HIV blood test. In the class the instructor told us that they would only inform those inmates who tested positive. In other words, no news is good news.

Two weeks after testing, the guards called my name. I was handed a medical slip that said in big bold red letters "Blood Test." I knew that could mean only one thing—I was HIV positive. I was terrified. I felt so alone. While sitting in the medical facility, with tears rolling down my face, I reflected over my whole life. I looked back at all the pain I had caused everyone, including myself, by the choices I had made. When I thought I was going to die from AIDS, I finally hit my bottom. This was my first step in completely surrendering my life to God. I admitted I was powerless over my addictions and compulsive behaviors and that my life had become unmanageable.

After an hour of sitting in the medical facility, I was finally called in and told that there had been a mistake. There had been a computer error; I was not HIV positive. Praise God! What a relief I felt, but the bottom I hit stayed with me. I realized that it could have been the other way. I knew I had to change everything in my life.

Upon being released from jail, the first thing I did was get back in Celebrate Recovery. I got a sponsor, a Bible, and the Celebrate Recovery Participant's Guides and started taking direction again. My first night back at Celebrate Recovery I was greeted by Big Al with one of his bear hugs. *The unconditional love I felt that night gave me the strength to come back. I found encouragement through my sponsor, the Tuesday night step study, and the awesome fellowship.*

For a year and a half I maintained sobriety. During this time I was asked by a number of men to be their sponsor, and on Friday nights it was common for men to approach me with affirmation. Although these things were good, I allowed them to feed my character defects of pride and ego. I began to take the credit for my sobriety. I thought I had all the answers. Because of this pride and arrogance, my time with God became less of a priority as well. I slipped back into denial and told myself I was not an alcoholic. I convinced myself that I was just a drug addict and decided it was okay for me to go into a bar. That night I relapsed again. By the grace of God I stopped at one beer, but this was the fatal blow to my ego. I now had to share with my accountability partners what I had done. This was the most humbling experience in my sobriety. I had thoroughly worked the first six choices, but failed to live out choices 7 and 8.

On October 31, 1996, I recommitted my will and my program to the Lord. I began an earnest search through Scripture to find out who God really is and what His will is for me and my life. I came to realize two things: first, I had not truly trusted God to restore me, and second, God was the most loving, compassionate, and forgiving Father that a man could ever hope for. He never lets me down, and He loves me unconditionally. I have found in the Gospel that Christ has walked this path before me. In the book of Hebrews, the fourth chapter (verse 15 NIV), it says, "We do not have a high priest who is unable to sympathize with our weaknesses, but we have one who has been tempted in every way, just as we are—yet was without sin." *He knows the pain of where I've been, the struggle of where I'm at today, and the hope of where I'm going.*

Today, I take specific steps to guard against relapse. First, I work choice 7 on a daily basis:

CHOICE 7

Maintaining MOMENTUM

Reserve a daily quiet time with God

for self-examination, Bible reading, and prayer
in order to know God and His will for my life
and to gain the power to follow His will.

Second, I attend my weekly meetings; third, I stay accountable to others; and fourth, I am committed to a consistent quiet time alone with God. During this time I evaluate myself, read God's Word, and pray. I know that temptation is a reality. Today I'm aware of my weaknesses and character defects. I heed the words of Christ where He tells His disciples to "watch and pray so that you will not fall into temptation. The spirit is willing, but the body is weak."[19]

Today I give credit where credit is due. I praise God for my sobriety. This past October 31 I celebrated five years of sobriety. God has replaced my despair with hope and my fear with joy. I live life one day at a time, trusting that He will make all things right if I surrender to His will. I am living my life with an attitude of gratitude. I am so grateful for all the gifts and victories that I have in the Lord. He has blessed me with the best friends in the world. These men have been a huge part in my recovery. God tells us in Proverbs 27:17 (NIV), "As iron sharpens iron so one man sharpens another."

God has restored the relationship with my mother. She and I are the best of friends, and I cherish our time together. God has also given me a beautiful godly woman, my wife, Gina, who is committed to the Lord Jesus Christ. I praise God for our friendship and our marriage.

Not only has He blessed me in my relationships, but He has also given me a purpose for living. Today I carry a message of hope to anyone who will listen. In Mark 16:15 (NIV) Jesus tells His disciples to "go into all the world and preach the good news to all creation." God is allowing me to serve other men in Celebrate Recovery. I have had the privilege of being a step study leader for a number of groups and have been given the responsibility of shepherding a Bible study in my home.

In closing, I am thankful to God for taking this broken sinner, who was addicted to drugs and alcohol for over twelve years, and restoring me to wholeness, and for making my life meaningful for His kingdom and His glory.

Regina and Steve had two very different childhoods. As they grew, they each learned that just praying and reading the Bible could not help them recover from their life's hurts, hang-ups, and habits. It wasn't until they applied all of the actions found in choices 1 through 7, including the self-examination, Bible reading, and prayer, that they were able to follow God's will for their lives and prevent relapse.

R
E
C
O
V
E
R
Y

"Happy are those who are persecuted because they do what God requires." [1]

Yield myself to God

to be *used* to bring this Good News to others,
both by my example and by my words.

Recycling
PAIN

The SHARING Choice

Your greatest contribution to this world—your greatest ministry—will not be found in your strength but in your weakness. The very thing you want least to talk about, the very thing you want to hide in the closet, is the very thing God wants you to share. One of the great things about God is that He never wastes a hurt. And He doesn't want to waste yours.

In this, the last chapter and the last choice, we'll see that the "Y" in R-E-C-O-V-E-R-Y stands for *yield*. It also stands for *you*. God wants *you* to yield to Him and allow Him to recycle the pain in your life for the benefit of others.

Most of us are under the misconception that God uses only the really gifted, extraordinarily talented people. That's not true. God uses ordinary people. In fact, He does His best work through weak people: *"'My gracious favor is all you need. My power works best in your weakness.' So now I am glad to boast about my weaknesses, so that the power of Christ may work through me."*[2]

People are not helped by our strengths; they're helped when we're honest about our weaknesses. When we share our strength, they say, "Big deal, I'll never have what he has." Or, "My faith is not as strong as hers." But when we share from our weaknesses, they say, "I can relate to that!"

I have the honor of giving my testimony several times a year. Every time I give it, people say, "Thank you for sharing your struggles and weaknesses with me. It is exciting to see the things God has done in your recovery." They do not thank me for my strengths. They thank me for being open and honest with my weaknesses. God gets the glory. They see that if God can restore a sinner like me, He can and will help them find freedom from their hurts, hang-ups, and habits.

When you understand that God uses your weaknesses and your pain, life takes on a whole new meaning and you experience genuine recovery. The proof that you are truly recovering is when you begin to focus outside yourself, when you stop being absorbed with *your* needs, *your* hurts, *your* problems. Recovery is evident when you begin to say, "How can I help others?"

In this final chapter, we'll answer two important questions: Why does God allow our pain? And, How can we use our pain to help others?

WHY DOES GOD ALLOW PAIN?

Why a good God allows pain and suffering is a universal question. There are several reasons, but here we'll share the big four.

1. GOD HAS GIVEN US A FREE WILL

God created us with the right to choose. In the Book of Beginnings, Genesis, we read, "*God created man in his own image.*"[3] One of the ways God's image is shown in you is in your freedom to choose. Simply considering the creation of the universe, we see that God made millions of choices. You, too, have the right to choose. You can choose good or bad, right or wrong, life or death. God says to us, "You can reject Me or accept Me. It's your choice."

God could have created you without a free will so that you always did right and never did wrong, but God didn't want a bunch of puppets. He wants you and me to love Him voluntarily. You can't really love someone unless you have the opportunity not to love that someone. You can't really choose good unless you have the option to choose bad.

Our free will is not only a blessing; it's also a burden. As you have read in the courageous stories in this book, poor choices cause painful consequences. We make choices that bring pain to ourselves and others. If we choose to experiment with drugs and get addicted, then it's our own fault. If we choose to be sexually promiscuous and get a sexually transmitted disease, we bear the consequences of our own bad choice. Do you see the dilemma? God will not overrule your will. God doesn't send anybody to hell. We choose to go there by rejecting His will for us. God loves you and wants you to be a part of His family, but if you thumb your nose at God and walk away from Him, you can't blame anyone but yourself. That is free will.

There's one more thing to consider about the free will God has given us. Not only does God give *you* free will, He gives it to everyone else, too. So this means that sometimes others choose to do wrong, and you may get hurt as an innocent victim. Many of you have been deeply hurt by a parent, spouse, teacher, friend, relative, or someone you didn't even know. God could have prevented that hurt by taking away that person's free will. But if He had done that, in order to be fair He would have had to take away your free will, too.

Pain is part of the free-will package.

> *The* PROOF *that you are truly recovering is when you begin to focus outside yourself.*

243

2. GOD USES PAIN TO GET OUR ATTENTION

Pain is not your problem. Your depression, your anxiety, and your fear are not even your problems. These are simply warning lights, telling you that something is wrong and you need to deal with it. Pain is God's wake-up call: *"Sometimes it takes a painful experience to make us change our ways."*[4]

Sometimes pain is severe, like the pain of a burn on our skin or the internal stab of a heart attack. Without these painful sensations, we might just go about our business, unaware of life-threatening dangers. But the "blessing" of pain is that it gets our attention and lets us know something is seriously wrong. Paul said this about the benefit of pain: *"I am glad . . . not because it hurt you but because the pain turned you to God."*[5]

Your problem may be low self-esteem, loss, abandonment, or abuse. Your pain is telling you that these issues need your attention! Nobody likes pain, but God uses pain to get your attention.

Do you remember the story of Jonah being swallowed by a great fish? Jonah was going one way, and God said, "I want you to go the other way." And at the bottom of the ocean, Jonah finally said, *"When I had lost all hope, I turned my thoughts once more to the* LORD."[6] Isn't that a great verse? God uses pain to get our attention.

3. GOD USES PAIN TO TEACH US TO DEPEND ON HIM

The apostle Paul was well acquainted with pain, and out of his experience, he tells us, *"We were really crushed and overwhelmed . . . [and] saw how powerless we were to help ourselves; but that was good, for then we put everything into the hands of God, who alone could save us."*[7] You will never know that God is all you need until God is all you've got. When it's all falling apart and you've lost it all, that's when you can see clearly the only One who is remaining beside you. Without problems, you'd never learn that God is the only real problem solver. God allows pain to teach you to depend on Him. *"The suffering you sent was good for me, for it taught me to pay attention to your principles."*[8]

The truth is, some things we only learn through pain. You've seen this demonstrated over and over in the stories of the courageous men and women at the end of each chapter, and you've seen how each of them learned to depend on God through pain, one of life's greatest teachers.

4. GOD ALLOWS PAIN TO GIVE US A MINISTRY TO OTHERS

Pain actually makes you humble, sympathetic, and sensitive to others' needs. It prepares you to serve. When we turn to God for healing from the source of our pain, He comforts us and gives us the help we need. *"Why does he [God] do this? So that when others are troubled, needing our sympathy and encouragement, we can pass on to them this same help and comfort God has given us."*[9] Being used by God for the benefit of others is what choice 8 is all about:

CHOICE 8

Recycling PAIN

Yield myself to God

to be used to bring this Good News to others, both by my example and by my words.

Everyone needs recovery of some type: mental, physical, spiritual, social, or relational. We all have hurts, hang-ups, and habits. Nobody's perfect. And when we're hurting, we want someone who understands, someone who's been through what we've been through—not someone whose life is all together.

Who better to help an alcoholic than someone who has struggled with alcoholism? Who better to help someone dealing with the pain of abuse than one who also suffered abuse? Who can better help the person who lost a job and went bankrupt than somebody who's experienced the same thing? Who can better help the parents of a teenager who's going off the deep end than a couple who had a child who did the same?

God wants to use and recycle the pain in your life to help others, but you've got to be open and honest about it. If you keep that hurt to yourself, you're wasting it. God wants to recycle your hurts, your hang-ups, and your habits to help others.

When you SHARE your story, it not only gives hope to others, it brings healing to you.

There's a beautiful story in the book of Genesis about Joseph. Family and others did terrible things to Joseph—and he was a good guy! He didn't deserve the pain in his life. One day his brothers decided to gang up against him and sell him into slavery. Then they went back home and lied to their dad and said that Joseph had been eaten by a lion. Now that's a dysfunctional family!

Joseph was sold into slavery and taken from Israel into Egypt. He faithfully did his job as a slave, minding his own business, when all of a sudden, his master's wife tried to seduce him. Joseph refused her advances, and she cried, "Rape!" Of course the husband sided with his wife, and Joseph was thrown into prison. This guy's whole life went downhill fast. He was at his bottom. But God had a plan and a purpose for Joseph.

Through a series of events, Joseph was promoted to second in command over Egypt. God used Joseph to save not only Egypt but other nations as well from destruction and famine. Later, during the famine, his brothers came to him to get food—only they didn't know they were standing before the very brother they had betrayed. When Joseph revealed himself, they expected to have their heads cut off, but Joseph surprised them: *"You meant to hurt me, but God turned your evil into good."*[10]

God is bigger than anyone who hurts you. No matter what other people have done to you, God can recycle it and use it for good. God never wastes a hurt. But you can waste it, if you don't learn from it and share it. Others will be blessed and encouraged if you share the problems and struggles you've gone through. God can and will use your pain to help others, if you let Him.

HOW CAN WE USE OUR PAIN TO HELP OTHERS?

The simple answer to the question, "How can I use my pain to help others?" is to *share your story.* That's it. It's that simple and that difficult—you share your experiences, your journey, your weaknesses, and how God has gotten you where you are today. As you share, you'll discover a blessing for yourself in addition to the one you pass on to others. When you share your story, it not only gives hope to others, it brings healing to you. Every time you share your story, you grow a little bit stronger, you experience another measure of healing.

At the end of this chapter you'll read the final two stories of the book—the stories of Tina and Bob who have allowed God to recycle their pain and use it for the benefit of others. God wants to recycle your pain, too, so He can use you to help others. The following scripture encourages you to share your story and even offers you some instruction as to how: *"Always be prepared to give an answer to everyone who asks you to give the reason for the hope that you have. But do this with gentleness and respect."*[11] You need to be prepared to give an answer to the questions,

"How did you make it? How did you keep from relapsing? How did you recover?"

ACCEPT YOUR MISSION

God has a mission for you. It's called the "Great Commission," and it's found in the Bible: "*Go and make disciples of all the nations, baptizing them in the name of the Father and the Son and the Holy Spirit.*"[12] The moment you step across the line and become a believer, you become a missionary. You become a part of God's great plan of reaching out to hurting, lost people.

Do you realize there are only two things you can't do in heaven? One is sin; the other is share the Good News with people who have never heard it. Which of those do you think is the reason God is leaving you on earth? Obvious, isn't it?

Sometimes in your mission of storytelling, God wants you to take the initiative. This is called intervention. "*If someone is caught in a sin, you who are spiritual should restore him gently. But watch yourself, or you also may be tempted. Carry each other's burdens, and in this way you will fulfill the law of Christ.*"[13] If you are a believer, it is your responsibility to share in the problems and troubles of other people.

This is where our beatitude for this chapter comes in: "*Happy are those who are persecuted because they do what God requires.*"[14] Reaching out to others with the Good News of how God has changed our lives is not always easy—or welcome. But we are blessed when we carry out the mission God has given us.

"*Life is worth nothing unless I use it for doing the work assigned me by the Lord Jesus.*"[15] What is that assignment? It is telling others the Good News of God's mighty love and kindness. There is no greater accomplishment in life than helping somebody find the assurance of heaven.

The world has far more people who are ready to receive the Good News than those willing and ready to share it. There are people who need to hear your story. You don't have to be a biblical genius. You can simply tell what happened to you. That's the most powerful kind of story. You can say, "I don't know where all the verses are, but this is what happened to me." Nobody can refute that—it's your personal experience.

God wants to use you. Share your story.

TELL YOUR STORY

In the "Write about It" action step, we'll get your story down on paper. Following are guidelines to consider as you prepare:

1. *Be humble.* We're all in the same boat; we're all fellow strugglers. When you share your story, when you witness, it's basically one beggar telling another beggar where to find bread. You're not saying, "I've got it all together," because you don't. You're getting it together. You're on the road to healing, but you're not there yet. Getting there is a lifelong journey.

2. *Be real.* Be honest about your hurts and faults. The men and women who have shared their stories in this book have modeled how to do this. They opened themselves up; they were transparent, vulnerable, and real. Can you imagine the courage it took for those people to have their struggles printed in black and white, for the world to see? Draw from their courage and open up your heart as well. You, too, can help other people by being honest about your hurts. When you are honest about your hurts, the honesty spreads and helps those who hear your story to open up too.

3. *Don't lecture.* Don't try to argue or force people into heaven. Just share your story. God wants you to be a witness, not a defense attorney. You may be the only Bible some people will ever read. Some people wouldn't be caught within a hundred yards of a church, so they would

probably never hear a sermon. But you have a story that can reach them, a story they can identify with. You can reach people a pastor never could. Just share what God has done for you, and they will want what you have!

CONSIDER YOUR BENEFICIARIES

Who could best benefit from hearing your story? The answer is people who are currently experiencing what you have already gone through, people who need to know Christ and the freedom found in Him and who need to know the eight choices found in this book. They might be your peers, your neighbors, or your family. Tell God you're available, then get ready. If you are prepared to share the Good News of how God has worked in your life, God will wear you out.

Can you imagine getting to heaven and someone saying to you, "I'm in heaven because of you, and I just want to thank you"? Do you think that sharing your story will have been worth it? It will far outlast anything you do in your career, anything you do in your hobby. We're talking *eternal* implications—getting people from darkness into light, from hell into heaven, from an eternity without God to an eternity with God. People will be thanking you the rest of eternity. There is nothing more significant in life.

MAKE THE *Choice*

ACTION 1: *Pray about It*

Ask God to lead you to somebody to share your story with, the Good News of how God made a difference in your life and how He can make the difference in theirs.

You can begin each day with a prayer something like this:

Dear God, help me be ready to share with someone today the victories You have given me. Help me find the right words and the right time to share my heart with someone who is hurting and doesn't know where to go or how to stop the pain. I pray that I can share the ways you freed me from my hurts, hang-ups, and habits. Let me do so with gentleness and respect. Thank You for letting me serve You today in this way. Amen.

ACTION 2: *Write about It*

If you prayed the prayer in the first action step, you need to prepare in advance to share your story. How do you get prepared to share your story? Review the three guidelines we presented earlier in the chapter under the heading "Tell Your Story." The following are some suggestions to help you get started:

+ Make a brief list of all the experiences that have significantly impacted your life to this day—positive and negative. Write down the ones you caused and the ones you didn't. Looking back at your moral inventory will help you remember these experiences.

+ Next, write out what you learned from each experience.

+ Write about how God helped you make it through the tough times.

+ Make a list of the people who need to hear your story.

+ Write your story out on paper.

Why is it so important to write out your story? Remember, thoughts disentangle themselves when they pass through the lips to the fingertips. Write it out.

ACTION 3: *Share about It*

After you have written out your story, your testimony, share it with your accountability partner. He or she can serve as a good sounding board. Your accountability partner has been with you from the start of your healing journey and knows you and your story. Your partner can help you review your story to ensure that you haven't left out any important events that would be helpful to others. Your accountability partner can also help you share your story in a way that is humble, real, and not lecturing.

Tina's STORY

My name is Tina. I'm a believer who struggles with sexual addiction. My admission of sexual addiction is the most difficult statement I have ever had to make, but for me, it is the most important. My battle with sexual addiction almost destroyed my life, until God intervened and transformed me for His purpose.

I was born into a Catholic Italian family. I have two sisters and a twin brother. My parents sacrificed to meet all our physical needs, provided a great house, and were very generous with gifts at holidays and birthdays. However, we were a love/hate family in constant chaos. The method of communication during conflict was yelling, name calling, and slamming doors. There was no resolution, no forgiveness. The central battleground for my parents' arguments was around the kitchen table at dinnertime. When they fought about their finances, I felt like a burden. When they fought about parenting, I felt worthless. When they fought about their sex life, I felt dirty. As my siblings and I witnessed their verbal attacks against each other, we, too, learned to fight with each other in much the same way.

My relationship with my mother when I was a little girl was special. She often called me her "little meatball." However, as I entered my preteens, something changed in our relationship. We began to constantly argue. I felt belittled while doing my many chores and criticized for the way I dressed and wore my hair. I felt betrayed, deceived, and outraged.

I idolized my older sister. She was so pretty and outgoing. However, she, too, was verbally abusive. She usually attacked me when I was practicing hobbies or before I went out with my friends. Her words affected me differently than my mother's; her words cut me like a knife. I felt deep pain as I believed every word she said. I would often look in the mirror and repeat over and over again, "I am ugly, I am ugly, and I'll never be good at anything."

My father was a wonderful, loving man. I would go to him for the nurturing love I longed for. He would let me snuggle on his lap and wrap his arms around me. But he was not a patient man. When he helped me with schoolwork or various new challenges, he would often call me a dummy.

One afternoon, after having an argument with my mom, I ran into our garage to be alone. While I was there, I found a box of pornographic magazines. Instantly, I became visually obsessed as I flipped through the pages. I went back as many times as I could, until one day the magazines were gone. To recapture the feeling, I sought out illicit books. The book that intrigued me the most was a book consisting of interviews with women about their sexuality, including bi-sexuality. This started me down a dark path, creating a thought life that took me in and out of reality.

The first time I drank was at my eighth-grade graduation party. I experienced a blackout but thought that happened to everyone who drank. As I entered high school, I was painfully shy but excelled in competitive dance. Academics, however, were a nightmare. I couldn't concentrate. My mind was consumed with sexual thoughts of my teachers and classmates. Outside of dance, the only fulfillment I had was going to high-school parties. When I would come home late, my mother would be waiting up for me. As I entered the house, she would knock me to the ground and call me a whore. I raged inside but wouldn't say a word or shed a tear. My father was willing to communicate with me, but my heart was too hard. In my rebellion, I made the choice to give away my virginity at fourteen. Based on what I had learned so far, I figured why wait until marriage.

I continued being sexually active with my steady boyfriends. I had a boyfriend of a different race and kept the relationship secret for two years. Eventually at seventeen, I became pregnant and aborted my child. My parents never knew. These were all choices I made using my free will.

One afternoon, my father came into the room where my mother was.

With fear in his voice, he told her there was blood in his urine. After he spent thirty days in severe pain, the doctors decided to perform surgery in order to remove a kidney stone. During surgery, the doctors found his kidney filled with cancer. Over the next six months, I watched my dad deteriorate. Throughout his illness I could hear him call out in pain, but I wouldn't go to him. I felt so overwhelmed with the thought of losing him; instead, I would run to my room to drown out his voice.

Two months later my family and I watched my father die in a hospital bed. I fed him morphine through a straw for fourteen hours to lessen his pain before he died. I tried to make up for the time I didn't take care of him while he was sick. I was so confused; I didn't know how to feel. I watched my younger sister as she sat down in the corner of the room and cried, but I didn't go to her. Emotionally I felt crippled.

A week later I went to a bar and drank tequila shooters with beer chasers. It felt so good to be numb. I remember saying to myself, "I am going to be all right, as long as I can just stay loaded." I became a lost soul, a hazard to myself. My life revolved around bars, men, and getting high. My steady relationships always ended up broken due to my constant unfaithfulness to the men who cared the most about me. I couldn't commit to anyone.

My drinking became more aggressive and the blackouts more frequent. One night on my way home, I was pulled over by an Orange County Sheriff and arrested for drunk driving. Four months later I was pulled over again and arrested for drunk driving. Deep into my denial, I started using cocaine. This became my pattern for the next five years.

In an effort to change, I took a job in "Corporate America" and changed the way I dressed and wore my hair. However, this new environment brought greater temptations. Over the next two years, I engaged in illicit relationships, mostly with men I knew: married coworkers, someone's boyfriend, a friend's husband. I was shameless. My roommate at the time asked me, "How do you do it?" I answered, "I just keep it separate." Had she asked me, "Why do you do it?" I would have answered, "I don't know."

That's when I realized I needed a savior, but it wasn't Jesus. I didn't even know who Jesus was. My messiah became the man I would marry. The first night I met my husband-to-be, I was convinced he could save me from myself. He was not an addict. I desperately wanted to change, but I just didn't know how! Shortly thereafter I became pregnant. Thinking I could not justify another abortion, I agreed to get married, and we were engaged. Now, after ten years of using, I found myself a dry drunk. Unexplained pain tormented me, reality and hopelessness reared its ugly head, and the grief of my father's death and enormous amounts of shame were more than I could bear. Three months later I had an abortion. Immediately following the procedure, I drank and told everyone, including my fiancé, that I had a miscarriage. I buried this lie deep inside me. My fiancé, not knowing the truth, still wanted to marry me.

I then started having nightmares about my dad. I would dream of him coming back from the dead, still sick so I could take care of him. In my dream, I believed this time he would not die. At the end of every dream, he would die anyway. That is when I decided to see a counselor. It did not take long for the counselor to see my alcoholism. I did not share about my inappropriate sexual conduct. A few weeks later I checked into an outpatient rehab center. For the first time in my life, I felt I could relate and connect with other people. However, I made my fiancé promise he would not tell anyone. I wanted to keep the option of drinking open. Everyone strongly advised us not to marry for another year, but we didn't listen. My secular recovery group became my higher power. Within two months I had relapsed. I left the program and started drinking again.

We got married, moved to another county, and bought a brand-new house. My surroundings changed, but I didn't. Together we made good money and could afford many nice things. But by the third year of marriage, I felt completely empty. Nothing I had satisfied me. I feared having children because, deep down, I knew something was wrong with me. So my husband and I became married singles.

I started going out drinking with friends. Too drunk to drive, I often had to call my husband to come pick me up. I began seeing less of him as the conflict in our home increased. During the course of my marriage, I allowed myself to have thoughts of other men. I thought it would be okay if I just kept it to myself and did not act out. But one day I crossed the line with a coworker. I justified it; I rationalized it. This act triggered my old behavior, but this time it was worse. As I lived this double life, I could no longer distinguish between right and wrong. After each affair, I swore to myself I would never do it again. Unable to focus, I was eventually fired from my job.

I then became involved with a man who claimed he was a Christian. This confused me, but I went along with it. One night he invited me to a crusade. The pastor spoke about Jesus and the woman at the well and all the men in her life: "For you have had five husbands, and you aren't even married to the man you're living with now."[16]

That got my attention. I began to sob as the pastor gave the invitation to accept Christ as Lord and Savior. The Holy Spirit began to pull on my heart. I fought it; no way could this Christ love me or want me! I was an adulterer. Instead of going down on the field, I ran out of the stadium. But something inside me changed.

Weeks later, I went alone to Saddleback Church. I don't remember a lot about the service. I was numb. But God's Spirit prompted me to pick up a visitor's card and check the box to make a commitment to Christ. An elder from the church responded by phone to my card. After a brief conversation, I prayed and asked Jesus to come into my life. He told me that my name was now written in the Book of Life.

The first thing I did was to get on my knees and beg this God I still did not know to take the obsession of alcohol away from me. I was convinced this was the reason for the sexual misconduct in my life. From that moment on, I never drank again.

God's power began to work in my life, little by little. My husband and I started to see a Christian counselor. During a visit alone with the counselor, I shared with her my secrets and my current affair. She told me I was a sex addict and wanted to send me to a secular sexual-addiction group. I told her, "No, I'm an alcoholic, and I will go to Alcoholics Anonymous." Angry, I never went back to her nor did I attend AA. Instead, I started studying the Word, going to church services, and attending Bible studies. As the days passed, God revealed the truth to me about my own life and the sinful cycle I was trapped in. I told my husband the truth about aborting our baby, and I told him about all the affairs, including the one with our neighbor, his best friend. He admitted he had been suspicious all along but never wanted to face the truth. As he walked out of the house, I felt paralyzed. I knew I was losing everything—my husband, my home, my car, my money, my furniture. I had no job and no friends.

I was completely broken. I wanted so badly to drink, but the Lord's Word spoke to my spirit. He said, "I am the true vine, and my Father is the gardener. He cuts off every branch in me that bears no fruit, while every branch that does bear fruit he prunes so that it will be even more fruitful."[17]

As time passed, my marriage ended. I became very involved at Saddleback, but I continued to hide my adultery. I couldn't understand why I habitually risked everything I had; I loved the Lord. But I was still acting on my free will. I finally realized, as in all my past relationships, I had been trying to keep the secrets in my life separate. This time I was trying to keep my secrets from the Creator of the Universe. A year later I was back down on my knees, this time in total surrender. I began to totally depend on God. That next Friday night, I went alone to my first Celebrate Recovery meeting.

For the first time in my life, I heard the words "I admit I am powerless." Pastor John was teaching on choice 1, "Realize I'm not God. I admit that I am powerless to control my tendency to do the wrong thing and that my life is unmanageable." Jesus said, "Then you will know the truth, and the truth will set you free."[18] I started to share my secrets with one safe person, Lori, a woman of great integrity and strong character. Within weeks of attending Celebrate Recovery, I stopped sexually acting out. My support system soon grew. A new friend, Brenda, wise beyond her years, walked me through some of the darkest and most shameful areas of my past. My special friend, Karrie, became the example of the kind of wife I wanted to be.

As I continued to work the biblical choices of this program, I began to feel whole again. Then I reached choice 6, "Evaluate all my relationships. Offer forgiveness to those who have hurt me, and make amends for harm I've done to others, except when to do so would harm them or others." I was stumped. How was I to work this choice? I could not make direct amends to the men in my past or to their wives or girlfriends. I could not make direct amends to my father. Then the Lord spoke to my spirit. He said, "Change, Tina; change," just as Jesus said to the woman caught in adultery, "Go now and leave your life of sin."[19] His power set me free.

I have experienced significant recovery by accepting God's forgiveness and by forgiving others. God's mercy and grace has freed me from isolation and has brought me tremendous joy. I no longer believe the lies told to me, and I have chosen to forgive.

Making my amends and offering forgiveness has reunited me with my dear mother, whom I have come to understand. My relationship has been restored with my siblings. I have male friends today! I consider this a gift. I feel connected in brotherly love to my friends Bob, Jay, Rick, Greg, and all those I serve alongside in the Celebrate Recovery ministry. These are rewards I never expected when committing myself to living God's choices.

I have been clean and sober since 1994, and pure since 1996. To God be the glory! Today I do not hide behind my addictions as an excuse for my past behavior. They were poor choices I made by my free will. I recognize my addictions as sin. "All of us also lived among them at one time, gratifying the cravings of our sinful nature and following its desires and thoughts."[20]

I've come to realize that female sexual addiction is not new; it's misunderstood. I wasn't looking for love; I was running from love, fearing commitment and true intimacy. I've learned that it was never about the sex, but about acting out deep wounds, my inadequacies, my rage, my self-hate, and the need to be in control. I have learned that my self-worth comes from my identity in Christ.

I have access to God's power every day and have made a spiritual decision for sobriety. I have given the Lord access to my mind through the power of prayer. I have memorized The Armor of God.[21] I know my triggers and the characteristics that fuel my addictions: lust, pride, jealousy, and revenge. I need to feed my spirit and starve my flesh on a daily basis to sustain me in times of temptation.

I love the eighth choice:

CHOICE 8

Recycling PAIN

Yield myself to God

to be used to bring this Good News to others,
   both by my example and by my words.

I love giving back. I love seeing how God can use all my mistakes, all my junk, and recycle it to help others. God has given me a vision for helping women struggling with sexual addiction. With Pastor John's support, I pioneered the Celebrate Recovery's women's group for sexual addiction. I never had a place to go before, but now I have a new extended family.

I know it's not easy to walk into a recovery meeting that addresses female sexual addiction. There were several weeks when I sat alone in my meeting room. I couldn't imagine that out of 15,000 people I was the only one suffering from this problem. I felt like giving up because no one was coming to my group. Slowly, God brought in one woman at a time. Now I get to spend my Friday evenings with the most courageous women in recovery. Together we are learning and accepting God's design for sexuality.

I had to completely depend on God's will before He would use my life. God has called me and uses my life for His purposes. As part of the

Celebrate Recovery ministry team, I have led step studies and have been asked to be the accountability partner with many brave women. God uses me to share my story with other Christian women who are struggling with a hurt, hang-up, or habit. After years of volunteering, I have the privilege of working full-time for Celebrate Recovery.

I don't share these things to boast, because without Christ, I am nothing. I share them to inspire. We have a powerful God who wants to transform our lives! For, "No eye has seen, no ear has heard, no mind has conceived what God has prepared for those who love him."[22]

The most amazing aspect of my life today is that God has given me a second chance in a new marriage. In November 1997, I married Kenny. For the first time in my life, I am not running away from love but facing my greatest fear, true intimacy. There are times when I feel completely inadequate as a wife, as I struggle to change my belief system. Kenny has illustrated a profound commitment to me and, above all, to Christ. I desire to experience all God intended for a husband and wife, including the hope and desire to someday be a mother.

I found Celebrate Recovery to be not only a safe place for the weak and broken, but also a place of changed lives, because,

"You were taught, with regard to your former way of life,
to put off your old self, which is being corrupted by its deceitful desires,
to be made new in the attitude of your minds;
and to put on the new self, created to be like God
in true righteousness and holiness."[23]

Bob's STORY

My name is Bob, and I am a believer who is in recovery for drug and alcohol addiction. Thanks to my Lord and Savior, Jesus Christ, I have recovered from a seemingly hopeless state of mind and body. I'd like to share how God has guided my life and led me in ways I never dreamed.

I grew up in Orange County, California. I came from a loving home, although my dad and I did not share much emotion or affection. My mom and I had a kind of kindred spirit. I did all the normal things kids do while I was growing up. All through elementary school, I was an A and B student and very involved in sports. I played soccer for almost twelve years. During these years everything seemed fine, until I got into junior high school. I began experimenting with drugs and alcohol. I really liked the effect they had on me, and at the time I thought it was cool. All my friends were doing it. I liked the effects so much that I began using on a regular basis. From the first time I tried drugs and alcohol, something in me clicked, and I felt right at home. This ultimately led to harder drugs and heavier drinking. I kept trying to control my using to find contentment, but the truth was, my addiction was controlling me. Drugs and alcohol became my solution for a problem based on low self-esteem; I did not see myself as a person created in God's image with value and purpose.

As my addiction progressed, and with my free will in full gear, I plunged down a road of destruction. I lived in a constant state of confusion because of the direction my chemical abuse was leading. My grades dropped throughout high school, and I was nearly expelled twice. When my parents found out I was using, they had no idea how bad it was. I ended up in an outpatient program for more than six months, where I did and said all the right things to get my parents off my back. In spite of numerous treatments in many rehab programs, which I agreed to only in order to satisfy my family, I continued to be in denial of my addiction. During one period when I was being drug tested, I discovered drugs that would not be detected. By this time, I would not let anything stand in the way of my using. At the last treatment center, they told my mom, "If he's not willing to get help, don't waste your time or money." She looked at me and asked, "Are you willing?" I said, "No." But what I was really saying was that drugs and alcohol were more important than her, my family, or me. I was like a tornado tearing a path through the lives of everyone around me.

I graduated high school by half of a percent; my mom was just proud that I graduated. She was the main reason I made it through. If it had not been for her, I would never have graduated. Shortly after high school, I moved out on my own so I could use more freely and hide it from my family, or so I thought. During those next three years, I started selling drugs. This served two purposes: first, it paid for my addiction, and second, it gave me a false sense of worth. I thought I was everybody's friend.

My addiction had gotten so bad that I lost my place to live and had to move back home. This was on the condition that I would admit my addiction and get sober. I thought I could quit on my own. Needless to say, I failed miserably and my life never changed. By this time, I had been using crystal meth for almost three years. I lost about forty pounds, and I wore baggy clothes to try and hide how thin I had become. I thought I was fooling everyone, but the only one I was fooling was myself.

Because I was living at home, my parents could see that I was now a threat to their safety and the safety of others in our family business. My family put their foot down by doing an intervention. They wrote a letter that said how much they loved me and cared about me, but they could no longer watch me destroy my life. They said that if I didn't get help, I would have to leave their house and our family business. My whole world started caving in on me, and the fear of being left with nothing gave me the willingness to get help. Finally, my pain was getting my full attention. This led me to my first AA meeting. After attending a few meetings, I began to understand how utterly powerless I was over my addiction. Admitting powerlessness was only the first part of choice 1; I also had to admit that my life had become unmanageable. This meant that my way did not work anymore, and I came to understand that it never really had.

In the meetings I attended, I met a Christian man who brought me to Celebrate Recovery. From my first meeting, I knew this was home. I have been coming every Friday night ever since. Coming to Celebrate Recovery helped me realize that just attending meetings was not enough. My recovery depended on a personal relationship with the only true Higher Power, Jesus Christ. It was then that I asked Him to be my Lord and Savior and director of my life. I came to fully believe that although I was powerless, Christ's power was more than I would ever need. These were the beginning steps on my road to recovery, but there was much work to be done.

Though God had lifted my denial, He required me to take action to mend the destruction of my past. God helped me do this as I worked through the remainder of the choices. My first fearless and thorough moral inventory, which I did shortly after I got sober, turned out to be anything but fearless and thorough. When Pastor John began teaching on choice 1 in January of 1995, I decided to get the Participant Guides and work through the choices again, including a new moral inventory. I really did not want to repeat this particular choice; however, I knew that I had to in order to progress in my recovery. So I connected with my accountability partner, and we set a date to start this rigorous housecleaning. Without accountability, I knew I would take every opportunity to avoid starting. This time I wanted to be thorough, so I asked God to search my heart and give me the strength to be fearless and thorough. At the heart of my moral inventory, I had to deal with my destructive habits, the pain and hurt I had caused my family and others, and the defects in my character that led me to make such bad choices. I had to pray often, because it was very painful at times. For the first time I was facing all the harm and hurt I had caused my family. I saw my selfishness and self-centeredness and how dishonest and inconsiderate I had been.

After finishing my fourth choice, I no longer felt the need to run from the wreckage of my past. With God's strength I could face life on life's terms, and as new issues came forward I faced them during my daily *evaluations, in choice 7. The Bible says, "If we confess our sins, he [God] is faithful and just and will forgive us our sins and purify us from all unrighteousness."*[24] *As I continued through the choices, I had to face my family and seek their forgiveness for the harm I had caused. I could no longer just say that I was sorry. Trust had been completely severed, and my amends had to be backed with action. I apologized for the person I had been and hoped they could see that my life was truly changing. I asked them to forgive me. It was on that day that trust began to be restored.*

When I reached the eighth choice, God gave me a sincere desire to serve Him by helping others who are struggling with a hurt, hang-up, or habit.

CHOICE 8

Recycling PAIN

Yield myself to God

to be used to bring this Good News to others,
both by my example and by my words.

God began leading me to make a real difference with my life through becoming an accountability partner and a group leader. I can now be of service to those who suffer with chemical dependency. I have a front-row seat in watching the power of God change lives in those around me.

Not only has He been faithful by guiding me in recovery, He has also blessed me with the wonderful relationships he has brought into my life. My wife, Karrie, and I were married by Pastor John in April of 1996, and I can truly say I love and cherish her more every day. He has also surrounded me with many Christian men, far more than I can list, who continually encourage and support me.

My mom, who never gave up on me and faithfully prayed for more than ten years, went to be with Jesus in 1997 after battling cancer. My mom was always there for me, every step of the way in sobriety, and God gave me the opportunity to be there for her during her final days—all the way until I saw her take her last breath on earth and go home to be with Jesus. Had I not been sober, I would have never been there for my mom and my family.

One of my greatest joys is to work the "bring this Good News to others" part of the eighth choice. This is especially true regarding my family. He has used me to bring other members of my family to a saving knowledge of Jesus Christ. My sister, who saw what happened in my life, began attending Saddleback Church and gave her life to Christ. She is now an active leader in Celebrate Recovery.

As if this was not enough, God gave me the courage to talk to my dad about Jesus. Pastor Rick developed a card describing how to establish a relationship with Christ. With this card, I had the privilege of leading my dad in a prayer to ask Jesus into his life. He joined my mom in heaven a year later. Praise God! "And we know that God causes everything to work together for the good of those who love God and are called according to his purpose for them."[25]

My life has been transformed in ways I never dreamed. God has given my life meaning and purpose. He has recycled the most meaningless parts of my life and used them to give my life the most meaning. God has not only restored my heart, soul, and body, but He has also restored my mind. He brought me from being a near high-school dropout to being accepted to a university, which prepared me for full-time ministry. As for low self-esteem, it disappeared when I was brought into the service of a loving God who will never leave me or forsake me. Today, I serve as the Pastor of Recovery at a large church in Las Vegas. Now on Friday nights, I have a front-row seat in watching the power of God change the lives of those around me.

God has done immeasurably more than I could ever ask or imagine. He has given me something I never thought I would have, the gift of sobriety. On April 22 of 1994, I celebrated my first day of continuous sobriety. During the years since then, I have been through many things:

I have seen life, when I was there the day my son was born.

I have seen death, the nights my mom and dad went home to the Lord.

I have faced the pain of my past.
I have hope for the future.
I have walked through the fear of living life sober.
I have had successes and failures.
I have learned to forgive, and I know what it is like to be forgiven.
Most of all, I have learned to love and to be loved.
I am convinced, just as the apostle Paul was,

"that nothing can ever separate us from his love.
Death can't, and life can't. The angels can't, and the demons can't.
Our fears for today, our worries about tomorrow,
and even the powers of hell can't keep God's love away."[26]

Tina's and Bob's stories are true examples of what the eighth choice is all about—recycling our pain. Each time they share what God has done in their lives, they help others. Each time they share what God has done in their lives, they receive further healing from their own hurts, hang-ups, and habits. The same can be true for you. Be ready to share with others what God has done in your life through completing the eight healing choices!

R
E
C
O
V
E
R
Y

Closing THOUGHTS

As we come to the end of the eight choices, I want to congratulate you on taking this healing journey with me. If you completed each choice to the best of your ability, you have already begun to see some amazing changes and healing in your life. And this is only the beginning of what God has planned for you.

I would like to share one more prayer with you. It is called the Prayer for Serenity:

> *God, grant me the serenity*
> *to accept the things I cannot change,*
> *the courage to change the things I can,*
> *and the wisdom to know the difference.*
>
> *Living one day at a time,*
> *enjoying one moment at a time,*
> *accepting hardship as a pathway to peace,*
> *taking, as Jesus did, this sinful world as it is,*
> *not as I would have it;*
> *trusting that You will make all things right*
> *if I surrender to Your will;*

so that I may be reasonably happy in this life
and supremely happy with You forever in the next. Amen.

—REINHOLD NIEBUHR

In this prayer, we are asking God that we *be reasonably happy in this life*. That's what we have been really striving for as we've worked through these eight choices—a reasonable, healthy way to live life in the reality of today. We are no longer looking for or expecting perfection in ourselves or others. Through your making the eight healing choices, it is my prayer that your definition of happiness has changed. I hope you have found that true happiness is having a personal relationship with Jesus Christ. Happiness is being free from your hurts, hang-ups, and habits. Happiness is having honest and open relationships with others.

The greatest loss would be for you to go all the way through this book, to read these great truths and the hope they bring, but take no action. Have you stepped across the line? Have you given your life to Christ? If you haven't done so, do so today. You can go back and reread chapter 3, and it will help you in making your commitment.

Just reading this book is not enough for recovery. It takes commitment, and it takes relationships. Commit yourself to a church family for support. If you do not already have a church family, find one that has a Celebrate Recovery program. That is a good indication that it is a healthy, safe, and caring church. (Go to www.celebraterecovery.com to find a church and program near you.) You will be able to continue your recovery journey there, and you will find people there to love and support you. If you already have a church family, start attending their Celebrate Recovery. If they do not have one yet, make an appointment with your pastor, share this book, and help start one! You have experienced firsthand the changes God has made in you. Now God wants to use you to help others change their lives! It's your choice!

For more information about Celebrate Recovery,
go to www.celebraterecovery.com

Notes

INTRODUCTION: *Finding* FREEDOM from Your *Hurts, Hang-ups, and Habits*

1. Romans 3:23 NIV
2. Isaiah 57:18–19 TEV
3. Matthew 5, portions of verses 3–10 TEV & NIV
4. Matthew 5:3 TEV
5. Matthew 5:4 TEV/NIV
6. Matthew 5:5 NIV/TEV
7. Matthew 5:8 TEV
8. Matthew 5:6 TEV
9. Matthew 5:7 TEV
10. Matthew 5:9 TEV
11. Matthew 5:10 TEV

CHOICE 1: *Admitting* NEED—The REALITY Choice

1. Matthew 5:3 TEV
2. Proverbs 14:12 NIV
3. Romans 7:15–17 NLT
4. See Genesis 3
5. Matthew 5:3 TEV
6. Genesis 3:10 NIV
7. Romans 7:21, 23 TLB
8. Psalm 32:3 TLB
9. Psalm 32:4–5 TLB
10. Proverbs 28:13 TEV
11. 2 Corinthians 12:10 MSG
12. Matthew 5:3 TEV
13. James 4:6 NIV
14. Psalm 70:1 MSG

15. Ecclesiastes 4:9–10, 12 NIV
16. 2 Corinthians 1:3–4 TLB

CHOICE 2: *Getting* HELP—The HOPE Choice

1. Matthew 5:4 TEV/NIV
2. Matthew 5:4 TEV/NIV
3. Isaiah 61:3 NLT
4. C. S. Lewis, *The Problem of Pain* (New York: MacMillan, 1944).
5. Hebrews 11:6 NIV
6. Romans 1:20 NIV
7. Psalm 31:7 TLB
8. Matthew 6:8 NIV
9. Psalm 34:18 NIV
10. Psalm 56:8 TEV
11. Job 13:27 NIV
12. Psalm 69:5 NLT
13. Psalm 103:13–14 NIV
14. Jeremiah 31:3 NIV
15. Romans 5:8 TLB
16. John 15:13 NIV
17. Ephesians 1:19–20 NLT
18. Luke 18:27 NIV
19. 2 Timothy 1:7 TEV
20. Philippians 2:13 Phillips
21. Isaiah 43:2 NLT
22. Isaiah 43:2 NLT
23. Proverbs 27:17 NCV
24. Romans 8:38–39 NIV
25. 2 Corinthians 5:15 NCV

CHOICE 3: *Letting* GO—The COMMITMENT Choice

1. Matthew 5:5 TEV/NIV

2. Matthew 11:28–30 Phillips

3. Proverbs 18:12 TEV

4. Proverbs 10:8 TLB

5. Psalm 40:12 TLB

6. Isaiah 44:22 NLT

7. Mark 5:6, 15 NLT

8. Mark 8:36–37 TLB

9. Matthew 17:20 NIV

10. Ephesians 1:13 NIV

11. Philippians 1:6 TLB

12. Acts 16:31 NIV

13. 2 Timothy 3:16 Phillips

14. Psalm 40:8 NCV

15. Philippians 4:13 TLB

16. Revelation 3:20 NLT

17. 1 Corinthians 15:2–4 NIV

18. Romans 3:22 NIV

19. Mark 1:16–18; Romans 12:2 NIV

20. Romans 10:9 NIV

21. Matthew 11:28–30 MSG

22. 2 Corinthians 5:17 NLT

23. Matthew 11:28–30 NIV

24. 2 Corinthians 5:17 NLT

25. Romans 10:9 NIV

26. Psalm 30:11 TLB

27. Romans 8:15–16 NIV

CHOICE 4: *Coming* CLEAN—The HOUSECLEANING Choice

1. Matthew 5:8 TEV

2. Psalm 32:1–2 TLB

3. Psalm 139:23–24 TLB

4. Proverbs 20:27 TEV

5. 1 John 1:8 NIV

6. 1 John 1:9 Phillips

7. Isaiah 1:18 TLB

8. James 5:16 TLB

9. Paraphrase, James 5:16

10. James 5:16 TLB

11. John 8:12 NIV

12. Romans 3:23–24 NCV

13. Hebrews 4:16 NCV

14. Romans 3:24 NCV

15. Romans 8:1 NIV

16. Lamentations 3:40 NIV

17. Isaiah 1:18 TLB

18. Galatians 3:3 NCV

19. 1 Peter 5:10 TLB

CHOICE 5: *Making* CHANGES—The TRANSFORMATION Choice

1. Matthew 5:6 TEV

2. Romans 12:1–2 TEV

3. John 8:44 NCV

4. John 8:32 NIV

5. Romans 12:2 NIV

6. Proverbs 17:24 TEV

7. Matthew 6:11 NIV

8. Matthew 6:34 TLB

9. Jeremiah 13:23 TLB

10. Philippians 4:13 NIV

11. Philippians 4:8 TLB

12. Mark 14:38 MSG

13. Galatians 5:16 JB

14. 1 Corinthians 15:33 NCV

15. Ecclesiastes 4:9–10, 12 NIV

16. Philippians 1:6 NLT
17. Proverbs 27:17 NIV
18. Psalms 46:10 NCV
19. Mark 8:34–37 MSG
20. Matthew 19:26 NIV

CHOICE 6: *Repairing* RELATIONSHIPS—The RELATIONSHIP Choice

1. Matthew 5:7 TEV
2. Matthew 5:9 TEV
3. Matthew 5:7, 9 TEV
4. Colossians 3:13 NLT
5. Ephesians 4:31–32 NIV
6. Job 5:2 TEV
7. Job 18:4 TEV
8. Job 21:23, 25 TEV
9. Matthew 5:7 TEV
10. Matthew 5:9 TEV
11. Mark 11:25 TLB
12. Matthew 6:12 KJV
13. Matthew 18:21–22 NLT
14. Romans 14:10–12 NIV
15. Colossians 3:15 NIV
16. Matthew 5:23–24 NLT
17. Hebrews 12:15 TLB
18. Romans 12:18 NIV
19. Luke 6:31 NIV
20. Ecclesiastes 8:6 TEV
21. Proverbs 12:18 MSG
22. Job 11:13, 15–16 TEV
23. Hebrews 10:24 NIV
24. Romans 8:1 NIV
25. Philippians 4:6 NLT

26. Romans 8:28 NLT
27. Philippians 1:6 NLT
28. Psalm 51:17 NLT

CHOICE 7: *Maintaining* MOMENTUM—The GROWTH Choice

1. Zechariah 4:6 NCV
2. Galatians 3:3 TEV
3. Galatians 5:7 TEV
4. Ecclesiastes 4:9–10 NCV
5. Hebrews 10:25 TEV
6. Proverbs 16:18 TLB
7. 1 Corinthians 10:12 NIV
8. James 4:10 NIV
9. Mark 14:38 NIV
10. 2 Corinthians 13:5 MSG
11. Lamentations 3:40 MSG
12. Galatians 6:4 NIV
13. Psalm 119:11 TLB
14. Psalm 1:2–3 TLB
15. Mark 14:38 NIV
16. Matthew 6:9–13 NIV
17. Romans 12:2 NCV
18. Philippians 4:13 NCV
19. Mark 14:38 NIV

CHOICE 8: *Recycling* PAIN—The SHARING Choice

1. Matthew 5:10 TEV
2. 2 Corinthians 12:9 NLT
3. Genesis 1:27 NIV
4. Proverbs 20:30 TEV
5. 2 Corinthians 7:9 TLB
6. Jonah 2:7 NLT

7. 2 Corinthians 1:8–9 TLB

8. Psalm 119:71 NLT

9. 2 Corinthians 1:4 TLB

10. Genesis 50:20 NCV

11. 1 Peter 3:15 NIV

12. Matthew 28:19 NLT

13. Galatians 6:1–2 NIV

14. Matthew 5:10 TEV

15. Acts 20:24 TLB

16. John 4:18 NLT

17. John 15:1–2 NIV

18. John 8:32 NIV

19. John 8:11 NIV

20. Ephesians 2:3 NIV

21. See Ephesians 6:10–18

22. 1 Corinthians 2:9 NIV

23. Ephesians 4:22–24 NIV

24. 1 John 1:9 NIV

25. Romans 8:28 NLT

26. Romans 8:38 NLT

GO DEEPER WITH THE GUIDED JOURNAL OR SMALL GROUP STUDY